WORLD
TRUCK
HANDBOOK

Nick Georgano

WORLD TRUCK HANDBOOK

NEW EDITION

JANE'S

Copyright © N. Georgano, 1983, 1986

First published in the United Kingdom in 1983
This edition published in 1986 by
Jane's Publishing Company Limited
238 City Road, London EC1V 2PU

Distributed in the Philippines and the USA
and its dependencies by
Jane's Publishing Inc, 115 5th Avenue, New York, NY 10003

ISBN 0 7106 0366 5

Computer typesetting by
Method Limited, Epping, Essex

Printed in the United Kingdom by
Biddles Limited, Guildford, Surrey

Cover illustrations
Contrasting aspects of European and North American trucking
are seen in pictures of a Scania R 142H and a Peterbilt 359.
(*Niels Jansen*)

CONTENTS

INTRODUCTION TO NEW EDITION

This new edition follows the same lines as its predecessor, and has been updated to autumn 1985. A number of truck makers have gone out of business since the last edition; among the saddest disappearances are those of the long-established Swiss firms, Saurer and F.B.W. whose factories are now devoted to making specialised vehicles of the Mercedes-Benz range. The Zimbabweian makes, A.V.M. and Panda, which were born during the years when economic sanctions against Rhodesia prevented imports of complete trucks, have now served their purpose and have been replaced by imported machines. On the other hand new makes continue to appear, and this book contains the products of 22 companies which did not appear in the first edition.

INTRODUCTION

Over the past ten years or so the truck has become much more newsworthy than ever before in its history. On the one hand it is seen in some quarters as a threat to the environment and to the way of life of those who live close to major trunk routes. At the same time, the growth of long-distance trucking and the beautifully-equipped machines of owner-operators has given the job of truck driver a glamour and romance far removed from the grimy and unloved image that persisted up to the 1950s. This has led to a greatly increased demand for information on the world's trucks, which are made in many more countries than passenger cars, though they are exported to a lesser extent.

The purpose of this book is to give a concise coverage of the world's trucks currently produced, so that the enthusiast travelling on business or pleasure can identify vehicles wherever he may be, while the stay-at-home may have his appetite whetted for new sights. The trucks are arranged according to axle layout, with special sections for off-road dump trucks and ultra-heavy road tractors. In order to give adequate coverage to trucks proper, some types which appear in a number of truck books are excluded. These are fire engines, which are not load carriers in the normal sense, light vehicles with a payload of under 2,000kg, and off-road vehicles such as aircraft handling equipment and yard spotters. Military trucks are also excluded as they are covered in other Jane's publications.

We have tried to give standard specifications for all the trucks, but in a few cases this has not been possible, either because the information was not forthcoming from the manufacturer or any other source, or because no standard specifications are offered. This is particularly true of premium American trucks such as Mack, Kenworth, Peterbilt and White, whose makers' proud boast is that they will provide any reasonable wheelbase that the customer requires. As the Kenworth L700 catalogue says, "You name it, we'll deliver it, in one-inch increments, from a super-short tractor for pulling extra long trailers, to maximum length straight trucks designed for any heavy load." Practically all heavy American trucks are offered with a choice of diesel engines by the 'big three', Caterpillar, Cummins or Detroit, the latter being a subsidiary of General Motors.

Some other points need to be made in connection with the specifications:

Gearbox: the number of speeds forward and reverse are indicated by '4F 1R'.

Axles: the front axle is only described when it is powered, as in a '4 × 4' or '6 × 6'.

Frame: the standard frame design of channel section steel with a number of cross members is described as 'channel section, ladder type'. Any deviations such as box section or tubular frame are mentioned as such.

Wheelbase: for two-axle trucks this presents no problem, being measured from the centre of the front axle to the centre of the rear axle. However, with three- and four-axle trucks there is some inconsistency in the way in which different manufacturers measure the wheelbase. Sometimes it is the distance between the front axle and a median point between the rear axles, or between the two interior axles in the case of 8-wheelers. In order to be consistent and to make for meaningful comparisons, we have chosen the distance between the leading and rearmost axles. Consequently our figures may differ from those quoted by some manufacturers.

For articulated vehicles the wheelbase and overall length quoted are for the tractor only. The only exception is for coal haulers whose trailers are an integral part of the unit.

Width: may vary slightly from the published figures according to the tyres used.

Height: is the figure quoted for the unladen truck. The laden figure would be up to 60mm less.

Payload: is the manufacturers' recommended limit, but this may vary according to operating conditions, and is therefore a guide rather than an absolute figure.

Maximum speed can vary greatly according to operating conditions and road surfaces, apart from inherent design factors such as axle ratios. When manufacturers have given a range of speeds dependent on axle ratios, these have been quoted.

Readers are reminded to make use of the index when seeking details of a particular model or when wishing to establish the range of models available from any manufacturer.

Any corrections or additions which readers may think desirable should be sent to the author via the publisher at: 238 City Road, London EC1V 2PU, England.

The majority of the photos in this book have been supplied by the
manufacturers, but among other sources are the following:

Automobile Technology (China) pages 36, 152, 244
Nick Baldwin, page 216
Oliver Barnham, pages 12, 21, 34, 35, 45, 47, 51, 73, 76, 123,
130, 156, 158, 160
CoVeDA International, pages 28, 44, 86, 88, 91, 95, 103, 106-9,
145, 197, 201, 228, 235, 271, 277, 291-2, 298
John H. Edwards, page 46
Nick Georgano, pages 52, 99, 166, 278
Erik van Ingen-Schenau, pages 83, 127
Niels Jansen, pages 13, 122, 177, 215, 239, 249, 259-60, 262-3
Elliott Kahn, pages 14, 266
Margus H. Kuuse, pages 29, 30, 84, 85, 92, 96, 161, 170, 171,
199, 213, 217-8, 248, 279-80, 300
Danny Ljubic, page 258
National Automotive History Collection, Detroit Public Library,
page 8
National Motor Museum, Beaulieu, Hants, pages 111, 175, 274
Hans-Otto Neubauer, pages 37, 318
Stephan Neubauer, page 87
Wallace S. Phinney, page 207
Marian Suman-Hreblay, page 168
Theo Wieringa, page 324

ACKNOWLEDGEMENTS

First of all, I must acknowledge the help of the Press and Publicity Offices of truck makers throughout the world, who contributed the bulk of the information and illustrations used in this book. Individual thanks are due to Margus Kuuse and Erik van Ingen-Schenau who respectively contributed the entries on Soviet and Chinese trucks, and to Geert de Kleijn and Louisa van Haaren of CoVeDA International, who wrote the entries on pages 28, 44, 86, 88, 91, 103, 106-9, 145, 197, 201, 228, 235, 271, 277, 291-2 and 298. I am also grateful for the help of George Avramidis, Nick Baldwin, Ferdy Hediger, Elliott Kahn, Hans-Otto Neubauer, Marian Suman-Hreblay and Tao Wang-Xiagji.

NICK GEORGANO, Guernsey

GLOSSARY

This is not intended as a complete glossary of truck design, but explains some terms frequently used in the book, which may not be familiar to all readers.

BBC Bumper to back-of-cab measurement, particularly used in connection with American trucks.

Double reduction a transmission system whereby the gear reduction between propeller shaft and wheels is made in two stages, a normal crown wheel and pinion in the centre of the rear axle, and a planetary system in the wheel hubs.

Glider or **Glider kit** a complete truck, less engine, transmission and rear axle, into which existing components can be fitted. These are sold by some American truck makers to operators who wish to rejuvenate their vehicles without going to the sometimes unnecessary expense of buying a complete new truck.

GVW Gross Vehicle Weight; the weight of the truck plus its load. Sometimes GCW (Gross Combination Weight) is used for articulated trucks.

Intercooling see Turbocharging.

LPG liquefied petroleum gas.

PTO power take off, a device attached to a truck's transmission to allow engine power to be used to operate a tipping body, compactor on refuse truck, transit concrete mixer, winch or any other auxiliary unit. On some trucks, but more especially agricultural tractors, the PTO can be used to drive equipment quite separate from the vehicle.

Splitter an auxiliary gear system attached to a gearbox which doubles the number of available ratios. Thus an 8-speed gearbox with 2-speed splitter gives 16 forward speeds.

Turbocharging a system whereby the exhaust gases from the engine are used to drive a centrifugal compressor which forces a greater mass of air into the cylinders. Sometimes this is used in conjunction with an *intercooler*, a radiator which cools the hot air from the turbo unit from about 150°C to 50°C. This is of great benefit to the engine as the smaller heat load and lower exhaust temperature increase reliability and lengthen the engine's life.

In the headings, the maker's nationality is indicated by the international registration letters of the country. These are as follows:

A	Austria	I	Italy
AUS	Australia	IND	India
B	Belgium	JAP	Japan
BR	Brazil	KO	South Korea
CDN	Canada	MEX	Mexico
CH	Switzerland	N	Norway
CHI	China	NL	Netherlands
CS	Czechoslovakia	PL	Poland
CY	Cyprus	R	Rumania
D	Germany	S	Sweden
	(Federal Republic)	SF	Finland
DDR	Germany	SU	Soviet Union
	(Democratic Republic)	TR	Turkey
DK	Denmark	USA	United States
E	Spain	YU	Yugoslavia
F	France	ZA	South Africa
GB	Great Britain	ZW	Zimbabwe
H	Hungary		

The first goods vehicles were based on contemporary passenger cars and appeared in the mid-1890s. They had very limited power, 6 or 8bhp at most, and short wheelbases, so their value was more for publicity for the shops which mainly operated them, than for serious load carrying. The first steps towards a practical purpose-built truck were taken by the German Daimler company who, in 1896, moved the driver forward so that he sat at the extreme front of the vehicle, with all the space behind him available for the load. The engine on these Daimlers was at the back anyway, so there was no problem, but when two years later Daimler moved the power unit to the front, the driver sat above it so that the load area remained reasonably large. This practice was soon adopted by other manufacturers, especially in America where the driver-over-the engine layout was widespread up to 1914. Cabs were rudimentary or non-existent on these early 'forward-control' trucks, and they also transmitted a great deal of vibration to the driver, which is perhaps why they were never so widely used in Europe, and disappeared in the USA before long, only to reappear on both sides of the Atlantic in the later 1920s and early 1930s. By then the driver and his mate sat on each side of the engine rather than on top of it, and cabs were enclosed and better equipped.

Purpose-built engines and chassis for trucks were developed during the years up to the First World War. By 1914 the typical truck engine was a 4-cylinder T-head or L-head unit of up to 8 litres capacity, developing about 40bhp at 1,000rpm. 6-cylinder engines were virtually unknown until the 1920s, except for a few fire engines. Few trucks were rated for more than 5 tons payload, though the American Hewitt company listed a 10-tonner which used the same engine and frame as their 5-tonner but with stronger springs and larger wheels.

Even by the 1930s the average 4-wheeler was not rated for more than a 6-ton load, and indeed overall weights were deliberately kept down so that higher speeds could be achieved. In Britain only trucks with an unladen weight of less than $2^1/_2$ tons (2,576kg) were permitted to travel at 30mph, heavier vehicles being restricted to 20mph. As power outputs increased so did truck sizes, and from the 1960s onwards the maximum weight for a two-axle chassis in Britain has been 16 tonnes, allowing about 10 tonnes payload. Today forward control is almost universal for the larger 4-wheelers in Europe, though in the USA, Latin America and Africa bonnetted trucks are still popular, both 4-wheelers and larger models. Some European manufacturers cater for this market with purpose-designed trucks such as Leyland's Landmaster and Landtrain ranges.

The 4-wheel-drive, or 4 × 4, truck appeared in the USA in

A typical example of the driver-over-engine truck popular in America in the first decade of the century is this Standard, made in Detroit in 1910.

1909 when the Duplex company of Charlotte, Michigan made a ³/₄-ton delivery wagon with internal gear drive to all four wheels. Within a few years they made a larger truck of 3¹/₂ tons capacity, and were joined by Jeffery and F.W.D., both of whose 4 × 4s were used in large numbers by the US Army in the First World War. Four-wheel-drive did not receive a great deal of attention between the wars, but the needs of the armed forces in the Second World War gave it a tremendous boost, and a wide variety of such vehicles was developed, from the ¹/₄-ton Jeep to 6-tonners by F.W.D., Mack and other makers.

Since 1945 the 4 × 4 truck has become widespread, its design often initiated for military needs and then adapted to the commercial market, as with the Bedford TM 4 × 4.

Some are adaptations of existing 4 × 2 trucks, such as the TM, Ebro 70 T.T., Saurer D.330B.N and many Soviet and Chinese designs, while others, usually at the lighter end of the scale, such as the Agricar, Brimont and Meili, are purpose-built cross-country vehicles. Payloads are inevitably lower than for the equivalent 4 × 2 trucks as they are designed for steep inclines and muddy conditions; seldom above 7 or 8 tonnes for a truck which may gross at up to 19 tonnes. Their main uses are on the more difficult building and road construction sites, for telephone and electricity pylon maintenance where there are no access roads, oilfield exploration and general carrying on dirt roads.

Maker: Avia n.p., Prague-Letnany

The Avia company derives its name from the fact that it originally built light aircraft, beginning in 1919. From 1946 to 1951 the factory built Skoda trucks and buses, and from 1961 to 1968, various models of Praga and Tatra. They then turned to the manufacture of light forward-control trucks under licence from Saviem in France. These are still made today, under the names Avia A21 and A31. They are both powered by a 3½-litre 4-cylinder engine which develops 61bhp. The A31 is made in several forms including platform truck with 3-seater cab or 7-seater crew cab, van or tanker as illustrated. The latter has an extra short wheelbase of 2,680mm, while the other A30s have wheelbases of 3,240 or 3,640mm.

Engine Avia 712.18 4-cylinder diesel 3,596cc 61bhp (45.5kW) **Transmission** Clutch: single dry plate; Gearbox: 5F 1R synchromesh; Rear Axle: single reduction spiral bevel **Frame** channel section ladder type **Brakes** dual circuit hydraulic **Dimensions** wheelbase: 2,680mm; overall length: 5,050mm; overall width: 2,030mm; height to top of cab: 2,270mm; gross weight: 5,950kg; load capacity: 3,130kg **Performance** maximum speed: 86km/hr

Maker: Vauxhall Motors Ltd, Luton, Bedfordshire

The Bedford TL series was introduced in 1980, covering many of the same models in the long-established TK series, but with a wider spread, from 5.7 to 16.3 tonnes GVW for rigid chassis and including two tractors for 16.3 and 19.3 tonnes GCW. This range is continued in 1985, and runs from the 5.7 tonne TL570 for non-HGV licence holders up to the 16.3-tonne TL1630. The range of tractors has been considerable extended (see page 209). Engine options in the TLs are the 4-cylinder 3.6/90TD, 6-cylinder 5.4/105TD and 5.4/135TD Red Series, and the 6-cylinder 8.2/130TD, 8.2/175TD and 8.2/210TD Blue Series. The first figure indicates the capacity in litres, the second the bhp, while TD stands for Turbocharged Diesel. Some non-HGV models use the 3½-litre nonturbocharged 3.5/80 petrol engine. Four- or five-speed gearboxes are offered, and a choice of Bedford or Eaton rear axles.

Engine Bedford Blue Series 8.2/175TD 6-cylinder turbocharged diesel 8198cc 175bhp (130.5kW) **Transmission** Clutch: single dry plate; Gearbox: Spicer T5C 4060 5F 1R synchromesh on four upper speeds; Rear Axle: Bedford single speed hypoid **Frame** channel section ladder type **Brakes** dual circuit fully air-operated **Dimensions** wheelbase: 3,760 to 6,030mm (6 options); overall length: 6,060 to 9,750mm (6 options); overall width: 2,410mm; height to top of cab: 2,520mm; gross weight: 16,260kg; load capacity: 11,500kg **Performance** maximum speed: 92 to 99km/hr

Maker: Vauxhall Motors Ltd, Luton, Bedfordshire

When Bedford introduced their TM range in 1975 they were entering a new field, that of the maximum GVW truck in rigid and articulated form which had previously been the preserve, in Britain, of manufacturers such as Leyland, Foden and E.R.F., though Ford entered the market at about the same time with their Transcontinental. The TM had a totally-new tilt cab and was at first offered only with a Detroit Diesel V6 engine, though later TMs have been available in lighter form with Bedford's 8.2-litre Blue Series straight six, or with larger Detroit Diesel V8 engines. For 1983 the new 10-litre Cummins LT10 was also offered in the TM series. Two cab designs are available, the regular, with small step at each side over the wheels, and the full width, as illustrated. The latter is available as a sleeper cab, though this is usually found on the articulated trucks rather than the rigids. The photograph shows a TM1700 with draw-bar trailer for operation at 32 tonnes gross train weight, operated by Wimpy International Ltd.

Engine Bedford 8.2/210TD Blue Series turbocharged 6-cylinder diesel 8,198cc 211hp (155.5kW) **Transmission** Clutch: twin dry plate; Gearbox: ZF 6F 1R all-synchromesh; Rear Axle: Bedford single reduction hypoid **Frame** channel section ladder type **Brakes** dual circuit fully air-operated **Dimensions** wheelbase: 4,902mm; overall length: 7,875mm; overall width: 2,480mm; height to top of cab: 2,925mm; gross weight: 16,260kg; load capacity: 11,146kg **Performance** maximum speed: 98km/hr

Maker: Beijing No. 2 Motor Vehicle Factory, Beijing (Peking)

One of the basic Chinese motor vehicles, the Beijing BJ 130 had its origins in 1966 when it was decided that a diesel truck repair shop in Peking should start manufacture of a simple design by teachers and students of the Industrial Art Institute. The 2½-litre engine is a copy of the Russian GAZ M-21, and is also used in the Beijing BJ 212 jeep-type vehicle. Two wheelbases are available on the BJ 130 on which various bodyworks mount a variety of bodies including tippers, tankers, refuse collectors and minibuses. The Peking automobile factories now belong to the 'Jingjinji' group, consisting of automobile makers of Beijing city (Peking), Tianjin city and Hebei province. They are united to rationalize production. The 130-type of 2-ton trucks are very popular in China, especially the crew-cab versions. The photograph shows the standard BJ 130, with short wheelbase and single row of seats.

Engine BJ 492Q 4-cylinder petrol 2,445cc 75bhp (56kW) **Transmission** Clutch: single dry plate; Gearbox: 4F 1R; Rear Axle: single reduction spiral bevel **Frame** channel section, ladder type **Brakes** hydraulic **Dimensions** wheelbase: 2,800 or 4,000mm; overall length: 4,710 or 5,910mm; overall width: 1,850mm; height to top of cab: 2,100mm; gross weight: 4,075kg; load capacity: 2,195kg **Performance** maximum speed: 85km/hr

Maker: BMC Sanayi ve Ticaret AS, Izmir

Austin began exporting trucks to Turkey in 1947, and an assembly plant was set up in 1965 in an agreement between the British Motor Corporation and Turkish business interests. Although the former became British Leyland in 1968 the Turkish company has retained the name BMC in its title. As well as Land Rovers, light trucks and agricultural tractors, the company makes normal and forward-control trucks. The latter use the old Redline Bathgate cab familiar in Britain, but the normal-control TM 100 and TM 140 have a bonnet and cab of local design. They use Turkish-built diesel engines of Leyland design, and are similar in appearance. The main difference is that the TM 140 is rated for a slightly heavier GVW, and has a 5-speed gearbox in place of the 4-speed unit on the TM 100.

Engine Leyland 6/98 NV 6-cylinder diesel 5,700cc 120bhp (89.5kW) **Transmission** Clutch: single dry plate; Gearbox: 5F 1R, synchromesh on four upper ratios; Rear Axle: single reduction spiral bevel **Frame** channel section, ladder type **Brakes** hydraulic **Dimensions** wheelbase: 4,597mm; overall length: 7,647mm; overall width: 2,490mm; height to top of cab: 2,250mm; gross weight: 11,786kg; load capacity: 8,086kg **Performance** maximum speed: 90km/hr

Maker: Crane Carrier Company, Tulsa, Oklahoma

As its name implies the Crane Carrier Company originally specialised in the manufacture of chassis for mobile cranes, which they still make today. However they have expanded into other fields including chassis designed for concrete mixer and refuse collection applications. The latter are known as the Centurion range, and come with standard cab or with low entry cab as illustrated. On this model the floor is only 18 inches (457mm) from the ground. The LE cab is equipped with a complete set of dual controls, so that the truck can be driven from either side. 4 × 2 and 6 × 4 chassis are available with the LE cab. The standard engine is a Cummins NTC 230-S, but options include the Detroit Diesel 6-71 or Caterpillar 3208. Allison automatic transmissions are standard.

Engine Cummins NTC 230-S 6-cylinder turbocharged diesel 14,000cc 230bhp (171.6kW) **Transmission** Clutch: torque convertor; Gearbox: Allison MT-653 automatic; Rear Axle Rockwell single reduction hypoid **Frame** channel section ladder type **Brakes** dual circuit fully air operated **Dimensions** wheelbase: 3,404mm; overall length: 7,874mm; overall width: 2,400mm; height to top of cab: 2,438mm; gross weight: 20,865kg; load capacity: 14,740kg

Maker: Chevrolet Motor Division, General Motors Corporation, Warren, Mich.

The largest producer of passenger cars in the world, Chevrolet has also held first or second place, (alternating with Ford) in the truck field for many years. Most models are also available with different trim under the GMC label, and the heavier cab-over Chevrolets were discontinued after October 1980, being only made as GMCs. The conventional truck illustrated is typical of the medium-duty line, and comes in three basic models, from 8,510 to 15,272kg GVW. As with most American trucks, a wide variety of engine and transmission options are available, engines including a six and three V-8 petrol units, and eight diesels, by Detroit or Caterpillar. Transmissions include manual and automatic, the largest of the former being a Fuller 13-speed unit available on the 70 Series. Six-wheelers with the 6×2 or 6×4 drive are made, and there are two distinct cab/bonnet designs, the conventional illustrated and the higher Kodiak which rides about 7 inches higher for a better view of the road. All these options mean that there are 4,800 possible combinations in the Medium Duty range alone.

Engine General Motors V-8 petrol 5,700cc 161bhp (120kW) overhead valves **Transmission** Clutch: single dry plate; Gearbox: General Motors 4F 1R all-synchromesh; Rear Axle: Rockwell single reduction hypoid **Frame** channel section, ladder type **Brakes** Delco dual-power vacuum/hydraulic **Dimensions** wheelbase: 3,784mm; overall length: 5,816mm; overall width: 2,360mm; height to top of cab: 2,350mm; gross weight: 8,510kg; load capacity: 4,500kg **Performance** maximum speed: 120km/hr *(typical available specification for the truck illustrated)*

Maker: Intreprinderea de Autocamione Brasov, Brasov

This conventional 5-ton truck has been one of the staples of the Rumanian industry since its introduction in 1954. Originally known as the S.R. (Steagul Rosu = Red Star), the name was changed to Bucegi in 1962, and to its present title of DAC in the mid-1970s, when the old V-8 petrol engine was replaced by an in-line diesel six, made under Saviem licence. Apart from the engine, and slight alterations to the grille, the truck has changed little since 1962. The 4 × 2 model is made in four wheelbases, the shortest for tipper bodywork (6.135RK), and there is also a tractor version (6.135RS) and two 4 × 4 chassis (6.135RA-362 and 6.135RAN).

Engine 797-05 6-cylinder diesel 5,488cc 135bhp (99kW) **Transmission** Clutch: single dry plate; Gearbox: ZF 5F 1R; Rear Axle: two-speed spiral bevel **Frame** channel section, ladder type **Brakes** air-assisted hydraulic **Dimensions** wheelbase: 3,620, 4,000, 4,400 or 4,800mm; overall length: 5,580, 6,915, 7,433 or 8,207mm; overall width: 2,350mm; height to top of cab: 2,350mm; gross weight: 9,450kg; load capacity: 6,000kg **Performance** maximum speed: 95km/hr

Maker: DAF Nederland Bedrijfswagen BV, Eindhoven

The van Doorne brothers, Hub and Wim, built trailers in the 1930s and some experimental trucks during World War 2. They began to build trucks commercially in 1950, and have since become one of Europe's most important makers of medium- and heavy-duty trucks, as well as buses. The 1100 is one of the smaller of the 2-axle trucks, which run from the 7.8 tonne FA900 to the 19 tonne FA3305. It is powered by a 6.1-litre turbocharged engine, while the larger models have engines of 8.2 or 11.6 litres, the latter intercooled as well as turbocharged.

Engine DAF DT615 6-cylinder turbocharged diesel 6170cc 151bhp (111kW) **Transmission** Clutch: single dry plate; Gearbox 5F 1R synchromesh; Rear Axle: single reduction hypoid **Frame** channel section ladder type **Brakes** air-assisted hydraulic **Dimensions** wheelbase 3850 or 5850mm; overall length: 7260 or 9260mm; overall width: 2140mm; height to top of cab: 2480mm; gross weight: 9700kg; load capacity: 6460kg **Performance** maximum speed: 105km/hr

Maker: Hestair Dennis Ltd, Guildford, Surrey

Dennis had been one of Britain's leading independent truck makers for many years, but manufacture of commercial trucks was suspended in the mid-1970s in favour of refuse vehicles, fire engines and buses. However, in 1979 the company returned to the regular truck field with the Delta 1600, built for the 16-ton maximum weight four-wheeler market. The standard engine is the Perkins 6.354 six-cylinder, but the Perkins V8 540 or Gardner GLX13 are available as options. Five wheelbases are offered, two for tipper chassis and three for general haulage. The all-steel tilt cab is also used on the Dennis Phoenix municipal chassis, and this can be supplied with a crew cab for five persons.

Engine Perkins 6.354 6-cylinder diesel 5,800cc 155bhp (116kW) **Transmission** Clutch: single dry plate; Gearbox: 6F 1R all-synchromesh; Rear Axle: single speed spiral bevel (two-speed optional) **Frame** channel section, ladder type **Brakes** fully air-operated **Dimensions** wheelbase: 5,700mm; overall length: 9,292mm; overall width: 2,402mm; height to top of cab: 2,675mm; gross weight: 16,260kg; load capacity: 9,000kg **Performance** maximum speed: 101km/hr (with overdrive)

Maker: Diesel Nacional SA, Monterrey

The Government-owned Diesel Nacional company is the largest producer of trucks and buses in Mexico, and has been in business since 1957. The trucks are based on International designs, though Perkins diesel engines are used in the smaller models as Diesel Nacional controls the Mexican Perkins plant. As well as the Model 351 illustrated, Dina make a larger two-axle chassis, the V-8 powered 631, and also 3-axle chassis for rigid and articulated work.

Engine Cummins V-6 diesel 6,200cc 155bhp (115kW) **Transmission** Clutch: single dry plate; Gearbox: 5F 1R all-synchromesh; Rear Axle: two-speed fully floating **Frame** channel section, ladder type **Brakes** fully air-operated **Dimensions** wheelbase: 4,978mm; overall length: 8,019mm; overall width: 2,490mm; height to top of cab: 2,050mm; gross weight: 11,794kg; load capacity: 7,945kg **Performance** maximum speed: 95km/hr

Maker: Renault Truck Industries Ltd, Dunstable, Bedfordshire

The Dodge Commando first appeared in 1973 under the name Commer Commando, but the Commer name was phased out in 1976 and replaced by that of Dodge to aid the international marketing strategy of the parent company, Chrysler UK. This concern was sold two years later to Peugeot-Citroën who named it the Talbot Motor Company. In 1983 Renault Vehicles Industrial acquired a 90% holding in Talbot, and the company name was changed to Renault Truck Industries, though the vehicles continue to carry the Dodge name. The re-styled Commando 2 appeared in 1981 in ten models, eight rigid chassis and two tractors, covering the range from 7.38 tons GVW up to 26 tons GCW for the largest articulated unit. Four engine options are available, two naturally aspirated sixes and one turbocharged six, and a naturally aspired V-8, all made by Perkins. Variations in gearboxes, axle ratios and wheelbases mean that there are over 5,000 permutations available for the Commando 2, but if an operator cannot find what he needs, then Special Equipment Operations can often provide the particular requirement.

Engine Perkins D6.3544 6-cylinder diesel 5,800cc 98.2bhp (73.3kW) **Transmission** Clutch: single dry plate; Gearbox: 4F 1R synchromesh on upper three ratios; Rear Axle: single reduction spiral bevel **Frame** channel section, ladder type **Brakes** dual servo air-hydraulic **Dimensions** wheelbase: 3,454 or 4,039mm; overall length: 6,385 or 7,300mm; overall width: 2,281mm; height to top of cab: 2,280mm; gross weight: 7,500kg; load capacity: 4,415kg **Performance** maximum speed: 98km/hr *(specifications for Model G75 C illustrated)*

Maker: No. 2 Motor vehicle Factory, Shiyan municipality, Hubei province

The Dongfeng (East Wind) EQ 140 (export name Aeolus) is a conventional 5-ton truck. Only a petrol version is made in large quantities at the moment. Shiyan, where the Dongfeng is made, is a new city of 300,000 inhabitants, nearly all of whom are employed in the No. 2 Motor Vehicle Factory or one of the 27 branch factories. The No. 2 Factory is the base of the Dongfeng Automobile Industry Complex, an organization that coordinates 40 car factories all over the country. These factories produce different forms of the Dongfeng truck: buses, tractor trucks, dumpers, parts and accessories. A special test batch with Renault diesel engine was made under the name Dongfeng EQD 142. These vehicles (500 units) were exported to Cameroon in Africa.

Engine Dongfeng Q6100 6-cylinder petrol 5,417cc 135bhp (100.7kW) **Transmission** Clutch: single dry plate; Gearbox: 5F 1R; Rear Axle: single reduction spiral bevel **Frame** channel section, ladder type **Brakes** fully air-operated **Dimensions** wheelbase: 3,950mm; overall length: 6,910mm; overall width: 2,470mm; height to top of cab: 2,455mm; gross weight: 9,290kg; load capacity: 5,210kg **Performance** maximum speed: 90km/hr

Maker: Motor Iberica SA, Barcelona

Motor Iberica had its origins in the Spanish Ford company (Ford Motor Iberica) which had made Fords in Spain since 1920. In 1954 the company became Spanish owned and the name was changed, though trucks still bore a close resemblance to the British Ford Thames range. The name Ebro was chosen after the Spanish river, just as the Thames was named after the English river, and when Ebros came to be sold in Syria they were named Frat after the river Euphrates. The current Ebro range still resembles the Ford D series in its cab, and is made in ten models from 3,500 to 12,500kg GVW. Perkins 4- and 6-cylinder engines are used. Standard bodies include dropside trucks, integral vans and the unconventional BC series illustrated, which has a single backbone chassis member for low loading of beer and soft drinks.

Engine Perkins 6.354 6-cylinder diesel 5,800cc 129bhp (95kW) **Transmission** Clutch: single dry plate; Gearbox: Clark 5F 1R synchromesh on upper four ratios; Rear Axle: single reduction spiral bevel **Frame** single rectangular backbone type, with normal side members at front **Brakes** dual circuit vacuum-assisted hydraulic **Dimensions** wheelbase: 4,500 or 5,100mm; overall length: 7,915 or 8,815mm; overall width: 2,198mm; height to top of cab: 2,435mm; gross weight: 10,000 or 12,500kg*; load capacity: 6,360 or 8,630kg; **Performance** maximum speed: 90km/hr

*M-125 model with lower gear ratios

Maker: E.R.F. Ltd., Sandbach, Cheshire

The E.R.F. company was started in 1933 by Edwin Richard Foden who left his family business to set up on his own in the same town of Sandbach. Apart from fire engines, nearly all E.R.F.s have been diesel powered, the majority using Gardner engines, though Perkins and Cummins power units are also employed. The current SP steel safety framed fibreglass cab was introduced in 1974, and was used in lowered form on the M range from 1978. The M Series represents the lighter end of the E.R.F. range and is aimed at the maximum GVW market in two-axle (16 tons) and three-axle (26 tons) models. The standard engine is a Perkins T6-3544, but a Gardner 6LXCT is also available. Five wheelbases are offered on the two-axle M Series, with two wheelbases available in three-axle form.

Engine Gardner 6LXCT 6-cylinder turbocharged diesel 10450cc 223bhp (166.7kW) **Transmission** Clutch: twin dry plate; Gearbox: Spicer 10F 1R, Rear Axle: Rockwell R144 single reduction hypoid **Frame** channel section ladder type **Brakes** fully air-operated dual system **Dimensions** wheelbase: 5,537mm; overall length: 9,399mm; overall width: 2,494mm; height to top of cab: 2,810mm; gross weight: 16,260kg; load capacity: 10,000kg **Performance** maximum speed: 110km/hr

Maker: FAP Famos, Priboj

The FAP concern (Fabrika Automobila Priboj) began building trucks in 1953 with medium-capacity vehicles based on Austrian Saurer designs. Various engines were used in subsequent models, including Leyland and Perkins, but the main supplier of engines is the Famos factory which belongs to FAP. In 1972 began an agreement with Mercedes-Benz which led to the adoption of Mercedes-Benz cabs on the heavier truck models of FAP. The current range runs from the 1516/80 which uses FAP's own design of cab through the 1616 and 1620 maximum load four-wheelers to six-wheelers and articulated trucks with two- and three-axle tractors. The 1620 BD illustrated is fitted with a sleeper cab, and can be operated with a drawbar trailer up to a combined load of 32 tons.

Engine Famos 2F 114B 6-cylinder diesel 11,040cc 200bhp (147kW) **Transmission** Clutch: twin dry plate; Gearbox: 6F 1R; Rear Axle: single reduction **Frame** channel section ladder type **Brakes** fully air-operated dual system **Dimensions** wheelbase: 4,800mm; overall length: 8,400mm; overall width: 2,460mm; height to top of cab: 2,975mm; gross weight: 16,000kg; load capacity: 8,700kg **Performance** maximum speed: 90km/hr

Maker: Ford Motor Co Ltd, Langley, Bucks.

Introduced in 1981, the Ford Cargo series was a replacement for the highly successful D series, of which more than 540,000 had been made since 1965. The new range replaced all models covered by the previous one, and also added extra wheelbases, higher powered options at lighter gross weights and smaller tipper chassis (minimum 7.5 tonnes compared with 12.5 tonnes on the D series). The Cargo cab is all-new, and gives exceptionally good all-round visibility together with plenty of space for signwriting. Four Ford-built engines are offered, one of them turbocharged, together with Cummins 504, Deutz V6 and Perkins V8.540 or 640 on the larger models. The Ford engines wer uprated in the new Dover series early in 1982. The Cargo range consists of 27 basic 4 × 2 models, from 6 to 16.25 tonnes of GVW, as well as 6-wheelers and artics up to 32 tonnes. Cargo models are identified by a four-digit designation. The first two denote the approximate GVW, the second two the approximate horsepower divided by ten. So 0913 = 9 tonnes 130bhp. The cargo range is also made by Ford's German plant at Cologne.

Engine Ford 6-cylinder diesel 6,224cc 130bhp (97kW) **Transmission** Clutch: single dry plate; Gearbox: Ford 4-310 4F 1R synchromesh; Rear Axle: single reduction hypoid **Frame** channel section ladder type **Brakes** dual circuit air/hydraulic **Dimensions** wheelbase: 3,075 to 5,450mm; overall length: 5,685 to 7,240mm; overall width: 2,280mm; height to top of cab: 2,495mm; gross weight: 9,000kg; load capacity: 5,532kg **Performance** maximum speed: 100km/hr

Maker: Ford Motor Co, Dearborn, Michigan

One of the most familiar trucks on American highways, the Ford C-Series has been made continuously since 1956. Now nearly thirty years old, it has easily outlived its ancestor the Ford Model T which is so often quoted as having the longest production record. It was the first forward control Ford to feature a tilt cab which has been an important feature of the design ever since. Appearance has hardly changed over the years, but current C-types include up to date Ford features such as split-power hydraulic brakes with discs on the front wheels. Petrol, diesel or LPG engines are available, three sizes made by Ford as well as the Caterpillar 3208 from 175 to 225bhp for the heavier duty C-types. These include 6 × 4 chassis for GVWs up to 25,400kg, and tractors for GCWs up to 34,000kg. As well as regular hauling duties, the C-type has been a popular choice as a fire engine chassis, carrying equipment by many of the leading specialists such as Luverne, Maxim, Pierce and Ward La France. For 1986 the C-600 will be replaced by a Brazilian-built version of the Cargo.

Engine Ford 2V V8 petrol 6, 100cc **Transmission** Clutch: single dry plate; Gearbox: New Process 435 4F 1R all synchromesh; rear Axle: single reduction; **Frame** channel section ladder type **Brakes** split power Hydraulic (single vacuum hydraulic optional) **Dimensions** wheelbase 3429mm; overall length: 6,375mm; overall width: 2,420mm; height to top of cab: 2337mm; gross weight 10,886kg; load capacity: 5,000kg **Performance** maximum speed: 100km/hr
(Typical available specification for the truck illustrated)

Maker: Ford Motor Co, Dearborn, Michigan

With Chevrolet, Ford are the leading suppliers of light and medium trucks to the US market, and in the medium to heavy field they have held the top position for the past 26 years. Their truck products range from light passenger-car-based pick-ups to maximum-weight highway tractors. The F Series represents the medium-duty category which has a very wide variety of applications. As with most American trucks, there are many options within the series, including four petrol and five diesel engines, nine wheelbases, fourteen transmissions including two automatics, eleven axles, and GVW ratings up to 14,062kg. There are also 4 × 4 and 6 × 4 trucks in the F Series. Cab trims come in standard, custom, and custom hi-level, and options include air conditioning, radio and stereo tape systems.

Engine Ford 2V V-8 petrol 6,100cc 174bhp (130kW) **Transmission** Clutch: single dry plate; Gearbox: New Process 435 4F 1R all-synchromesh; Rear Axle: single reduction **Frame** channel section ladder type **Brakes** split Power Hydraulic (single vacuum-hydraulic optional) **Dimensions** wheelbase: 3,580mm; overall length: 5,616mm; overall width: 2,200mm; height to top of cab: 2,140mm; gross weight: 11,113kg; load capacity: 5,100kg **Performance** maximum speed: 110km/hr

Maker: Officine Franchin SpA, Treviso

Founded in 1960, Officine Franchin SpA. belongs to one of Italy's main producers of trailers and semi-trailers, although they manufacture containers, vehicle bodies and special vehicles too. Nowadays 400 people are employed at four different plants, all located within a maximum radius of 20 kilometres of Treviso. The Delivery 115 is one of Franchin's special vehicles. It has been designed to satisfy the demands for rapid and easy distribution and collection of goods over medium and short distances. Its design exhibits various applications which increase the safety of the truck, as well the safety of the driver and other people in traffic. The cabin-floor is only 290mm from the ground, making entry and exit effortless. The door on the driver's side is single and wide-opening, but the right door is double and opens automatically. A third door, made up of four folding doors, is situated at the back of the cabin and allows easy access to the loading area. The cabin height enables a person to stand in an erect position. The Delivery 115 is powered by a Fiat 8060.04 engine, located between the axles. The photo shows the Delivery 115 bodied with a Alukit light alloy van, also made by Officine Franchin SpA.

Engine Fiat 8060.04 6-cylinder diesel 5,500cc 130bhp (95.6kW) **Transmission** Clutch: torque converter; Gearbox: Allison AT540, 4F 1R; Rear Axle: single reduction **Frame** channel section ladder type **Brakes** dual circuit fully air-operated **Dimensions** wheelbase: 3,850mm; overall length: 7,570mm; overall width: 2,500mm; gross weight: 11,500kg; load capacity: 7,450kg **Performance** maximum speed: 83km/hr

The Gorky Auto Works are the oldest in the Soviet Union, having been set up in 1932 to manufacture Ford cars and trucks under licence from the USA. The GAZ-53A has been made since 1965, and is the staple 4-tonner in Russia, fitted with a wide variety of bodies including tippers (53-02), vans and tankers (53-11), and buses (53-40). An LPG-burning model is designated the 53-07. Then there is available a 4½-tonner GAZ-53-12 since 1983, fitted with the same mechanics and having the same body dimensions. The same all-aluminium wet-liner V-8 engine has been used throughout the model's life, but the output has been recently increased by 5bhp. Unexpectedly factory specifications show maximum speed decreased by 5km/hr. Of similar appearance is the smaller 2½-tonner GAZ-52, powered by a 3,480cc 6-cylinder engine whose ancestry dates back to before World War 2.

Engine ZMZ-53 V-8 petrol 4,250cc 120bhp (88kW) **Transmission** Clutch: single dry plate; Gearbox: 4F 1R, synchronised on 3rd and 4th; Rear Axle: single reduction hypoid **Frame** channel section ladder type **Brakes** hydraulic with hydrovac servo **Dimensions** wheelbase: 3,700mm; overall length: 6,395mm; overall height: 2,220mm; gross weight: 7,400kg; load capacity: 4,000kg **Performance** maximum speed: 80km/hr

Maker: Gorky Avto Zavod, Gorky

GAZ, like ZIL, has recently become interested in diesel power and the first truck so fitted is a 4-tonner agricultural vehicle, destined for a work with a 4.6-tonne drawbar trailer (the combination (train) is called GAZ-6008). Along with KAZ-4540, Ural-5557 and KamAZ-55102 it is one of four tractors, specially designed for agricultural purposes and because today 70 percent of trucks in Soviet agriculture bear the GAZ badge, its importance to rural development in the late 1980s and early 1990s cannot be underestimated. Perhaps the most interesting part of the truck is its engine, the first air-cooled unit installed in a Russian-made truck. Perhaps the experience with Tatra and Magirus tippers, both imported in good quantities, has led to the conclusion that this kind of powerplant can work in Russian cold and heat, too.

Engine GAZ-542 6-cylinder air-cooled diesel 6230cc 125bhp (92kW) **Transmission** Clutch: single dry plate; Gearbox: 5F 1R, all-synchromesh; Rear Axle: single reduction hypoid **Frame** channel section ladder type **Brakes** hydraulic **Dimensions** wheelbase: 3,850mm; overall length: N/A; overall width: 2,500mm; overall height: 3,120mm; gross weight: N/A; load capacity: 4,000kg **Performance** maximum speed: 85km/hr

Maker: GMC Truck & Coach Division, General Motors Corporation, Pontiac, Michigan

Introduced in the spring of 1984, the GMC Forward is built for General Motors by Isuzu in Japan, and corresponds to the Isuzu FTR 11. It is powered by a 5785cc 6-cylinder turbocharged diesel engine, and is available in ratings for 12,500 or 13,500kg GVW. A 5-speed manual transmission is standard. Unlike most American trucks there are no variations on these standard specifications but four wheelbases are available, and the Forward can be used for a wide variety of applications, from city delivery to long-distance hauling. It is sold and serviced at more than 130 GMC dealerships in the United States.

Engine Isuzu 6BD1 6-cylinder turbocharged diesel 5785cc 165bhp (123kW) **Transmission** Clutch: single dry plate; Gearbox: 5F 1R synchromesh on upper four ratios; Rear Axle: single reduction hypoid **Frame** channel section ladder type **Brakes** air assisted hydraulic **Dimensions** wheelbase 3,600 to 5,000mm; overall length: 6,360 to 8,460mm; overall width: 2,370mm; height to top of cab: 2,475mm; gross weight: 12,500 to 13,500kg; load capacity: 9,105 to 9,905kg **Performance** maximum speed: 115km/hr

Maker: GMC Truck & Coach Division, General Motors Corporation, Pontiac, Michigan

The GMC 5000, 6000 and 7000 Series trucks are similar to the Chevrolet Medium Duty range apart from badging, and are made in in the same factory. This short wheelbase tipper has the higher level cab known as the Top Kick, equivalent to the Chevrolet Kodiak. It rides about 7 inches higher for a better view of the road, yet has a shorter BBC measurement (2,344mm compared with 2,457mm for the standard cab). The same engine, transmission and axle options are available as on the Chevrolets, as are cab trims, air conditioning and radio/cassette stereo systems.

Engine General Motors 7.0L V-8 petrol 6,991cc 210bhp (156.7kW) **Transmission** Clutch: single dry plate; Gearbox: 5F 1R all synchromesh; Rear Axle: single reduction hypoid **Frame** channel section ladder type **Brakes** Delco dual power vacuum/hydraulic
 Dimensions wheelbase: 3,175mm; overall length: 4,902mm; overall width: 2,342mm; height to top of cab: 2,540mm; gross weight: 11,040kg; load capacity: 6,000kg **Performance** maximum speed: 105km/hr
(typical available specification for the truck illustrated)

Maker: Hino Motors Ltd, Tokyo

Hino trucks were first made in 1947, and from the start they employed diesel engines. They made Japan's first heavy articulated truck in 1947, and amongst other products in a wide range they have made 4 × 4 and 6 × 6 trucks, twin-steer 'Chinese six' models and half-cab dump trucks. They are now the second largest manufacturer of heavy trucks (over 7 tonnes GVW) in the world, with an annual production of over 80,000 units. (Mercedes-Benz is the largest, with 120,000). The present Hino range includes forward control 4 × 2 trucks from 8 to 19 tonnnes GVW, 6 × 2 and 6 × 4s from 26 to 35 tonnes, 4 × 2 and 6 × 4 tractors for GCWs up to 79 tonnes, dump trucks and buses. The 4 × 2 range starts with the 7 to 9-tonne FB and FC models, followed by the 9.9-tonne FD, the 11.5 to 13-tonne FE and FF, and the 15 to 17½-tonne FH. The FF illustrated is available in four wheelbases.

Engine Hino EH700 6-cylinder diesel 6,443cc 165bhp (121kW) **Transmission** Clutch: single dry plate; Gearbox: 5F 1R or 6F 1R synchromesh on all but bottom gear; Rear Axle: single or double reduction spiral bevel, electric-vacuum two speed control **Frame** channel selection ladder type **Brakes** vacuum-assisted hydraulic **Dimensions** wheelbase 3,780 to 5,530mm; overall length: 6,435 to 9,450mm; overall width: 2,385mm; height to top of cab: 2,565mm; gross weight: 13,000kg; load capacity: 6500kg; **Performance** maximum speed: 96 to 105km/hr according to axle ratios

Maker: Dandong Automobile Factory, Liaoning province

The Dandong Automobile Factory is a refit factory producing specialist vehicles on Jiefang, Dongfeng and Huanghe base. At present this factory produces a range of long-distance buses, Jiefang and Dongfeng conversions, such as tippers, tanker trucks and machinery repair engineering vehicles, and an 8-ton torpedo front truck introduced in 1980. This truck was originally named Yalujiang (Yalu river, the border river between China and Korea), but the present name is Huanghai (Yellow Sea). Several versions are designed: the basic 8-ton truck (DD 151), a dumper (DD 352), a 12-ton long wheelbase 4 × 2 version (DD 160) and a 15-ton long wheelbase 6 × 4 version. Annual production is low. The Dandong factory belongs to the Jiefang Corporation.

Engine Hangzhou 6 120Q-1 6-cylinder diesel 9500cc 160bhp (119.4kW) **Transmission** clutch: twin dry plate; Gearbox: 5F 1R; Rear axle double reduction **Frame** channel section ladder type **Brakes** fully air-operated **Dimensions** wheelbase 4,000mm; load capacity: 8,000kg

Maker: Jinan Motor Vehicle Factory, Shandong province

The Huanghe (Yellow River) prototype introduced in 1960 was an exact copy of the Skoda 706RT, but it was not successful, and a new, improved 8-ton truck was put into production in 1964. It has remained little changed up to the present day apart from having a simplified grille. Two different diesel engines are used, one made in Shanghai (truck model JN 150), and the other in Hangzhou (truck model JN 151). As with many Chinese trucks, the basic chassis is fitted with special bodywork by various factories; these include tippers, tankers, crane trucks, cement trucks and well-boring trucks. Other factories making copies of the JN chassis are in Hunan, Anhui and Heilongjiang provinces.

Engine Shanghai 6 135Q 6-cylinder diesel 12,000cc 160bhp (119.4kW) *or* Hangzhou 6 120Q-1 6-cylinder diesel 9,500cc 160bhp (119.4kW) **Transmission** Clutch: twin dry plate; Gearbox: 5F 1R; Rear Axle: double reduction **Frame** channel section ladder type **Brakes** fully air-operated
Dimensions wheelbase: 4,000mm; overall length: 7,600mm; overall width: 2,400mm; height to top of cab: 2,600mm; gross weight: 15,060kg (JN 150) or 14,860kg (JN 151); load capacity: 8,260kg
Performance maximum speed: 71km/hr (JN 150), 67km/hr (JN 151)

Maker: Jinan Automobile Factory, Shandong province

Since 1980 three types of trucks from Romania have been assembled in the Jinan factory. The Chinese introduced their own variant in 1982. In 1985 a first batch of 300 items was made. The Jinan factory is part of a heavy-truck consortium, with other factories in Chongqing, Dazu, Qijiang, Hangzhou, Shaanxi, Hefei, Qingdao and Zuzhou. Besides the new Huanghe JN 162, there is already a local dumper variant produced in Qingdao, named Huanghe QD 362. (This vehicle is illustrated here).

Engine 6 130 6-cylinder diesel 11,950cc 200hp **Transmission** Clutch: single dry plate; Gearbox: 6F 1R synchromesh; Rear axle: double reduction **Frame** channel section ladder type **Brakes** dual circuit air-assisted hydraulic **Dimensions** wheelbase: c.4,500mm; overall length: c.8,000mm; overall width: c.2,500mm; height to top of cab: c.2,900mm; gross weight: c.16,000kg; load capacity: 10,000kg **Performance** maximum speed: N/A

Maker: VEB IFA Automobilwerke, Ludwigsfelde

This is the standard heavy truck of East Germany, and has been in production in various forms since 1965. The 4-cylinder engine is made under licence from MAN in West Germany. Variants on the standard open truck illustrated include a tipper made in 4 × 2 or 4 × 4 models, and tractors for drawbar trailers and for semi trailers. The latter have the same wheelbase as the tipper, giving an unusually long gap between the rear of the cab and the front of the trailer. During the 1970s annual production of the W 50 ran at over 20,000, and they were widely exported to other Comecon countries and also to China.

Engine Typ 4 VD 4-cylinder diesel 6,560cc 125bhp (93.25kW) **Transmission** Clutch: single dry plate; Gearbox: SR 50-60 K 5F 1R synchromesh on upper four ratios; Rear Axle: single reduction spiral bevel **Frame** channel section ladder type **Brakes** dual circuit air-assisted hydraulic **Dimensions** wheelbase: 3,700mm; overall length: 7,250mm; overall width: 2,500mm; height to top of cab: 2,600mm; gross weight: 9,900kg; load capacity: 5,000kg **Performance** maximum speed: 90km/hr

Maker: International Harvester Co, Chicago ,Illinois (factory at, Springfield, Ohio)

The International Harvester Co, world famous for their agricultural equipment, built their first truck in 1907, and have made an increasingly wide series of commercial vehicles since then. In 1984 the farm equipment business was sold, and International are now truck makers only. The medium-duty S Series (named after the Springfield, Ohio plant where they are made) are the smallest trucks made today, and compete directly with similar-sized vehicles from Ford and General Motors. They are offered in a wide range of models with diesel engines, and transmission choices from four- to thirteen-speed manual gearboxes and four- or five-speed automatics. Two and three-axle models are made, as well as tractors and 4 × 4 or 6 × 6 chassis. In 1981 International introduced glider kits based on the Heavy Duty S Series, consisting of complete trucks less engine, transmission and rear axle, into which existing components can be introduced.

Engine International V-8 diesel 9,000cc 165bhp (123kW) **Transmission** Clutch: single dry plate; Gearbox: 5F 1R; Rear Axle: single reduction **Frame** channel section ladder type **Brakes** Hy-power dual split system with electric pump backup **Dimensions** wheelbase: variable; overall length: variable; overall width: 2,210mm; height to top of cab: 2,490mm; gross weight: 9,200kg; load capacity: 6,100kg **Performance** maximum speed: 108km/hr
(typical available specification for the truck illustrated)

Maker: International Harvester Co, Chicago, Illinois (factory at Chatham, Ontario)

The Cargostar is International's offering in the medium-duty cab-over market. Although introduced under this name in 1975, the Cargostar is descended from a long line of International cab-overs dating back to 1936. Designed for maximum manoeuvrability in confined city streets, the Cargostar is especially suited to local delivery work, heating oil delivery and refuse collection. Two- and three-axle models are available, also a tractor, and engine options include a choice of three International mid-range diesels. Transmissions include four manuals from four to thirteen speeds, and four- or five-speed automatics. Wheelbases run from 2,565 to 4,876mm, and with the shortest, the turning circle is only 5.4m. Cargostars are produced at Internationals' Canadian plant at Chatham, Ontario, but all cabs are made at the Springfield, Ohio, body plant.

Engine International V-8 diesel 9,000cc 165bhp (123kW) **Transmission** Clutch: single dry plate; Gearbox: 5F 1R; Rear Axle: single reduction **Frame** channel section ladder type **Brakes** Hy-Power dual split system with electric pump backup **Dimensions** wheelbase: variable; overall length: variable; overall width: 2,350mm; height to top of cab: 2,310mm; gross weight: 9,525kg; load capacity: 6,100kg **Performance** maximum speed: 95km/hr
(typical available specification for the truck illustrated)

Maker: International Harvester Australia Ltd, Dandenong, Victoria

International's Australian branch began truck building after the Second World War, and introduced their first locally designed models in 1959. These were military trucks, and were followed by civilian counterparts two years later. These are now made in a wide variety of two-, three- and four-axle rigids, artics and 4 × 4 models. Among the most popular are the ACCO range of two- and three-axle cab-overs covering GVWs from 9.84 to 20.87 tonnes. Engine options include a diesel six and two petrol V-8s by International, and Perkins six or Cummins V-8 diesels.Transmissions are by New Process, Eaton or Fuller, and rear axles by Rockwell, International or Eaton. There is also a 4 × 4 version of the ACCO 1800. The same basic cab design is used on the larger 6- and 8-wheeled T Series.

Engine International V-392 V-8 petrol 6400cc 185bhp (138kW) **Transmission** Clutch: single dry plate; Gearbox: Eaton 5F 1R all-synchromesh; Rear Axle: Eaton 2-speed single reduction spiral bevel **Frame** channel section ladder type **Dimensions** wheelbase: 4,040mm; overall length: 7,000mm; overall width: 2,438mm; height to top of cab: 2,700mm; gross weight: 13,900kg; load capacity: 8,000kg; maximum speed: 100km/hr
(typical available specification for the truck illustrated)

Maker: Isuzu Motors Ltd, Tokyo

Isuzu is Japan's oldest commercial vehicle maker, the company having built their first trucks, based on British Wolseleys, in 1918. The Isuzu name was adopted in 1934, and in 1971 the company became part-owned by General Motors, who now look after world-wide marketing. The Chevrolet LUV and Bedford KB pick-ups are both Isuzu built. The current range is very wide, from light pick-ups to heavy 6 × 6 trucks. The FSR11 illustrated is one of the smaller models in the intermediate F range, which runs from the 9000kg FSR to the 15,000kg FVR11T. All these models use Isuzu's 6BT 5,785cc 6-cylinder diesel engine, turbocharged for the larger models. Power output varies from 135 to 180bhp. A wide variety of bodies can be fitted, including concrete mixers, cranes, tankers and refuse collecters. Crew cabs for up to seven passengers are also available.

Engine Isuzu GBD1 6-cylinder diesel 5,785cc 150bhp (110kW) **Transmission** Clutch: single dry plate; Gearbox: 5F 1R synchromesh on all but first gear, 6F 1R optional; Rear Axle: single reduction hypoid **Frame** channel section ladder type **Brakes** vacuum-assisted hydraulic or air-over hydraulic **Dimensions** wheelbase: 3,700mm; overall length: 6,510mm; overall width: 2,170mm; height to top of cab: 2,400mm; gross weight: 9,000kg; load capacity: 5,000kg **Performance** maximum speed: 92 to 126km/hr according to gearbox and rear axle ratios

Maker: Isuzu Motors Ltd, Tokyo

This 16,000kg tipper is part of Isuzu's normal control range whose ancestry dates back to the 1950s. They are now made in two- and three-axle form with 4 × 2, and 6 × 4 drive. A choice of three engines is offered, including one with turbocharger. All are Isuzu-built 6-cylinder diesels of 11, 12 or 13.7 litres capacity, and there is a full range of direct and overdrive transmissions in five- or six-speed versions. Sizes run from 16,000 to 24,000kg GVW, the latter being the 6 × 4 long-wheelbase TMK78Z model. Among the many uses of the Normal Control series are tippers, tankers, bulk carriers, concrete mixers and crane carriers.

Engine Isuzu 6QA1 6-cylinder diesel 11,044cc 204bhp (152kW) **Transmission** Clutch: single plate; Gearbox: Isuzu MLF5A 5F 1R all-synchromesh; Rear Axle: single or two-speed single reduction spiral bevel or hypoid **Frame** channel section triple plate ladder type **Brakes** vacuum-assisted hydraulic **Dimensions** wheelbase: 4,200mm; overall length: 7,240mm; overall width: 2,450mm; height to top of cab: 2,540mm; gross weight: 16,000kg; load capacity: 10,540kg **Performance** maximum speed: 80km/hr

Maker: Fiat SpA, Turin

In 1975 a new European commercial vehicle consortium called IVECO (Industrial Vehicles Corporation) was formed. Fiat contributed their heavy vehicle interests which included Lancia, OM and Unic, and Klockner-Humboldt-Deutz contributed their Magirus-Deutz truck firm. Since then there has been increasing rationalisation and the trucks have recently carried the IVECO name more prominently than their own brand names. Those sold on the UK market have been badged solely as IVECO in recent years. The 159.17 illustrated is one of two rigid axle models in the 16 tonnes class. It shares the same cab and chassis with its companion the 160.16, but has a Fiat-built naturally aspirated water cooled engine whereas the 160.16 has a Deutz-built turbocharged air cooled engine. Two other models in the IVECO two axle range are the 165.24 rigid chassis for use with a draw bar trailer for 32 tonnes GCW, and the 165.24 4 × 2 tractor 24, 28, 32.5 or 35 tonnes. These models are powered by a 9,572cc IVECO diesel engine. All the models described are equipped with a single bunk sleeper cab.

Engine Fiat-IVECO 8360.05 6-cylinder diesel 8102cc 158bhp (117.6kW) **Transmission** Clutch: Fichtel & Sachs single dry plate; Gearbox: ZF S6.36 6F 1R synchromesh (12F 2R with splitter); Rear Axle: single reduction spiral bevel **Frame** channel section ladder type **Brakes** dual circuit fully air-operated **Dimensions** wheelbase 3,800 5,550, or 5,900mm; overall length: 6,210, 8,890 or 9,420mm; overall width: 2,348mm; height to top of cab: 2,876mm; gross weight 16,000kg; load capacity: 10,965kg **Performance** maximum speed: (without splitter) 96.6km/hr (with splitter) 103.8km/hr

Maker: Jelczanskie Zaklady Samochodowe, Jelcz k/Olawy

During the period 1960-1968 Jelczanskie Zaklady Samochodowe produced 8 ton trucks using ZUBR brand name. The activities of the factory were reorganized in 1968 and this resulted in the production of trucks and truck tractors using the name of the town, Jelcz. Various of the techniques used today are acquired from foreign truck and equipment producers. The SW680 6-cylinder 243bhp engine is a Leyland licence, the B4A turbocharger used is from Westinghouse. ZF licences are the gearbox and power steering. Both 4 × 2 and 6 × 2 trucks and truck tractors are offered, all using the Raba 018.79 rear driving axle and a new modern-style standard or sleeper cab which was introduced two years ago.

Engine Wola-Leyland SW680 6-cylinder turbocharged diesel 11,100cc 243bhp (181.3kW) **Transmission** Clutch: single dry plate; Gearbox: S6-90 6F 1R; Rear Axle: Raba 018.79 single reduction spiral bevel **Frame** channel section ladder type **Brakes** dual circuit fully air-operated **Dimensions** wheelbase: 4,900mm; overall length: 8,675mm; overall width: 2,500mm; height to top of cab: 2,830mm; gross weight: 15,700kg; load capacity: 8,000kg **Performance** maximum speed: 90km/hr

Maker: Jianghuai Motor Vehicle Factory, Hefei City, Ankhui province

This 3-ton open truck is a typical example of a local Chinese product. Nearly all the production is sold in Anhui province. In production since 1969, the HF 140 is not made in very large numbers, 1976 figures being 3,000 while in 1980 only 1,927 trucks were made. The Jianghuai factory belongs to the Nanjing Joint Corporation. A crew-cab model and diesel types of the HF 140 are under development.

Engine Jianghuai HF 440 6-cylinder petrol 4,387cc 120bhp (89.5kW) **Transmission** Clutch: single dry plate; Gearbox: 4F 1R; Rear Axle: single reduction spiral bevel **Frame** channel section ladder type **Brakes** vacuum-assisted hydraulic **Dimensions** wheelbase: 2,900mm; overall length: 5,450mm; overall width: 2,260mm; height to top of cab: 2,360mm; gross weight: 6,150kg; load capacity: 3,120kg **Performance** maximum speed: 85km/hr

Maker: No.1 Motor Vehicle Factory, Changchung municipality, Jilin province

The Jiefang (Liberation) CA 10 is the longest-lived Chinese truck and the most important in terms of production figures. First produced in 1956, it was a copy of the Russian ZIS-150, which in turn was based on the American International K series, of which a large number were supplied to Russia during World War 2. By 1958 production was running at more than 10,000 per annum, but this dropped to zero ten years later because of the Cultural Revolution. Since then it has picked up, and in 1980 the figure was 62,586. The one millionth Jiefang came off the assembly lines on 26 February 1983. The standard engine was a 95bhp side valve unit, but the present CA 15 version has a 115bhp side valve unit. The new Jiefang, the CA 141 with ohv engine, will replace the CA 15 soon. It is a modern styled 5-ton truck. The Jiefang factory is the base of the Jiefang Corporation, which controls vehicle production in China's North Eastern provinces and in Shandong, Qinghai and Sichuan. The CA 10/15 has been assembled all over China; some factories make their own versions, such as the Qinghai factory who make the Qinghaihu QH 140 truck for high altitude operation, in both petrol and diesel forms.

Engine Jiefang CA 15 6-cylinder petrol 5,550cc 115bhp (86kW) **Transmission** Clutch: twin dry plate; Gearbox: 5F 1R; Rear axle: double reduction **Frame** channel section ladder type **Brakes** air-operated **Dimensions** wheelbase: 4,175mm; overall length: 6,855mm; height to top of cab: 2,330mm; gross weight: 9,135kg; load capacity: 5,210kg **Performance** maximum speed: 80km/hr

Maker: Shenyang Automobile Factory, Liaoning province

The Shenyang Automobile Factory is very succesful with the production of small trucks and vans. This Jinbei (Gold Cup) pick-up truck—also sold under Shenyang and Liaoning brand—is in fact based upon the Beijing BJ 130, described earlier in this book. In 1980, 3,001 units were made. The different variants are designated as follows; SY 132: standard model, SY 132A: long wheelbase version, SY 132B: tilt cab version, SY 132C: double row version, SY 132D: double row/long wheelbase version, SY 132E: diesel version, SY 450: refrigerator van. The Shenyang factory belongs to the Jiefang Corporation; it also assembles the Jiefang CA 15 as Liaoning LN 140 5-ton truck.

Engine SY 492 QA 4-cylinder petrol 2,445cc 75bhp (56kW) **Transmission** Clutch: single dry plate; Gearbox: 4F 1R; Rear axle: single reduction hypoid bevel gear **Frame** channel section ladder type **Brakes** hydraulic **Dimensions** wheelbase: 2,800mm; overall length: 4,891mm; overall width: 1,930mm; height to top of cab: 2,085mm; gross weight: 3,850kg; load capacity: 2,000kg **Performance** c.85km/hr

Maker: Leyland Vehicles Ltd, Bathgate, Scotland

The Landmaster is part of Leyland's ambitious range of bonnetted trucks aimed specifically at overseas markets such as Africa, the Middle East, the Far East and Latin America. Larger models for the same markets are the rigid and articulated Landtrains. The Landmaster is made in five models, from 9 to 17 tonnes GVW. The same 5.7-litre 6-cylinder engine is used in the three smaller models but in the 12.15 it is turbocharged to give 145bhp compared with 115bhp in the normally-aspirated version. The 15- and 17-tonners use the Perkins 8.8-litre V-8 540 engine. A choice of four wheelbases is available, and the Landmaster is made in a choice of chassis-cab or chassis-front end for fitment of local specialist bodywork. It is widely used for local and general haulage, as well as tanker and tipper operations. As well as the Bathgate factory, the Landmaster is made at Ibadan, Nigeria.

Engine Leyland 6.98 NV6 6-cylinder diesel 5,700cc 115bhp (86kW) **Transmission** Clutch: single dry plate; Gearbox: Eaton 5F 1R synchromesh on upper four ratios; Rear Axle: Bathgate single-speed fully floating **Frame** channel section ladder type **Brakes** vacuum-hydraulic single line system **Dimensions** wheelbase: 5,500mm; overall length: 8,041mm; overall width: 2,304mm; height to top of cab: 2,496mm; gross weight: 12,000kg; load capacity: 8,020kg **Performance** maximum speed: 74 or 87km/hr, dependent on rear axle ratio

Maker: Leyland Vehicles Ltd, Leyland, Lancashire

Leyland is Britain's largest truck-builder wholly owned by British capital, having been nationalised in 1975. Commercial vehicles are made by Leyland Vehicles Ltd, a division of British Leyland plc. Their history dates back to 1896 when a 2-ton steam wagon was built by the Lancashire Steam Motor Company. The Roadrunner is a new range of trucks in the light/medium category introduced in 1984 to replace the long-lived Terrier range. It has a distinctive cab with safety window on the nearside to give a view of the kerb, very large windscreen and front panel made of non-corroding SMC. The Roadrunner is made in five models, from 6.2 to 10 tonnes GVW, four of them being in the 7½ tonnes or under class so that they can be driven with an ordinary car licence. Four wheelbases are available, from 3,250mm to 4,400mm, with a choice of the Leyland 6.98DV (97bhp) or 6.98NV (115bhp) engines.

Engine Leyland 6.98DV or NV 6-cylinder diesel 5,655cc, 97 or 115bhp (72.4 or 86kW)
Transmission Clutch: single dry plate; Gearbox: Turner T5-250 5F 1R all synchromesh; Rear Axle: single reduction spiral bevel **Frame** channel section ladder type **Brakes** dual circuit air/hydraulic
Dimensions wheelbase: 3,250 to 4,400mm; overall length: 5,650 to 7,960mm; overall width: 1,760mm; height to top of cab: 2,402mm; gross weight: 6,500 to 9,000kg; load capacity: 3,589kg to 7,156kg **Performance** maximum speed: 83 to 98km/hr according to axle ratio.

Maker: Liberecke Automobilove Zavody, Jablonec nad Nisov

Liaz was founded in 1951 and built the former Skoda 706 trucks, although these generally went under their old name until the 1970s. The first trucks to bear the Liaz name exclusively, with no Skoda connections, were the 100.05 4 × 2 rigid chassis and 100.45 tractors which were introduced in late 1974. They are powered by a 6-cylinder turbocharged diesel engine of 11.94 litres mounted at an angle of 45°. This is available in two versions, giving 270 and 304bhp respectively. The 100.05 has a GVW of 16 tonnes as a solo truck, but this can be increased to a maximum of 38,000kg with drawbar trailer. A sleeper cab is fitted as standard to the 100.05 and 100.45 models. The range has recently been supplemented by the 110 series, with a greater variety of engines, 210 to 320 bhp, though still of the same size, 11.94 litres. There is also a short wheelbase 4 × 4 version, the 111.124D, one of which was well placed in the 1985 Paris-Dakar Rally.

Engine MS 637 6-cylinder turbocharged diesel 11,940cc 270bhp (200kW) *or* MS 638 6-cylinder turbocharged diesel 11,940cc 304bhp (222.1kW) **Transmission** Clutch: twin dry plate; Gearbox: Praga 10 P 80 10F 2R synchromesh; Rear Axle: double reduction **Frame** channel section ladder type **Brakes** dual circuit fully air-operated **Dimensions** wheelbase: 5,000mm; overall length: 8,500mm; overall width: 2,500mm; height to top of cab: 2,715mm; gross weight: 16,000kg; load capacity: 11,300kg **Performance** maximum speed: 92km/hr

Maker: Lingyuan Automobile Industrial Company, Liaoning province

Designated as a production unit by the First Ministry of Machine Building Industry, this corporation has an annual output of 10,000 motor vehicles. Its Linghe brand (formerly known as Liaoning) LN 142 5-ton diesel truck is one of the products listed in the State Plan. This diesel truck has 125 horsepower and a speed of 75 kilometers per hour. Its fuel consumption is 17.5 litres per 100 kilometres. The original LN 140 used the CA 10 petrol engine, later a 4-ton diesel truck was developed, named LN 140B. The Lingyuan factory belongs to the Jiefang Corporation.

Engine 6102Q 6-cylinder diesel 5,550cc 125bhp (xxkW) **Transmission** Clutch: twin dry plate; Gearbox: 5F 1R; Rear Axle: double reduction **Frame** channel section ladder type **Brakes** air-operated **Dimensions** wheelbase: 4,000mm; overall length: 6,660mm; overall width: 2,460mm; height to top of cab: 2,200mm; gross weight: c.9,000kg; load capacity: 5,000kg **Performance** maximum speed: 75km/hr

Maker: Mack Trucks Inc, Allentown, Pennsylvania

In 1979 Renault acquired a 20% stake in Mack Trucks, and one of the first visible fruits of this was the appearance of the Midliner range of medium-sized trucks which are in fact the Renault G models badged for the US market. Two engines are available, both turbocharged and after-cooled 6-cylinder units of 175 (175200P) or 215bhp (175300P). Standard wheelbase is 3,505mm, but there are five optional longer wheelbases and shorter ones of 2845 or 3048mm for tractor work (MS300T). Two five-speed synchromesh transmissions are offered, on the MS200P, and a choice of Renault five, six or ten speed synchromesh boxes, or four speed Allison automatics, on the MS300P and MS300T.

Engine Renault MIDR 06.02.12 6-cylinder turbocharged diesel 5,496cc 175bhp (131kW) **Transmission** Clutch: single dry plate; Gearbox: Spicer 5052A 5F 1R all-synchromesh; Rear Axle: Renault single reduction hypoid **Brakes** dual circuit fully air-operated **Dimensions** wheelbase: 3,505mm; overall length: 5,910mm; overall width: 2,500mm; height to top of cab: 2,765mm; gross weight: 11,500kg; load capacity: 6,000kg **Performance** maximum speed: 95km/hr

Maker: Maschinenfabrik Augsburg-Nürnberg AG, Munich (factory at Salzgitter)

Introduced in 1979, the M.A.N.-VW range of medium-duty trucks from 6 to 9 tonnes GVW resulted from collaboration between the heavy truck builders, M.A.N., and Volkswagen who had hitherto made nothing larger than their 2.5 tonne LT series. The two options of 4-cylinder diesel engine are made by M.A.N., while the synchromesh 5-speed gearbox is made by Volkswagen, as is the cab which is a modified version of the LT cab. Three wheelbases are made and the trucks are available from the factory in dropside truck or tipper forms. A wide variety of special bodies have been used with the M.A.N.-VW, including delivery vans, mobile exhibitions and car recovery trucks. The 4 × 2 chassis is available as a tractor for semi-trailer work, and 4 × 4 chassis are also made.

Engine M.A.N. 6-cylinder diesel 5,687cc 136bhp (100kW) **Transmission** Clutch: single dry plate; Gearbox: 5F 1R all synchromesh Rear Axle: single reduction spiral bevel **Frame** channel section ladder type **Dimensions** wheelbase: 3,600mm; overall length: 6,546mm; overall width: 2,366mm; height to top of cab: 2,385mm; gross weight: 8,760kg; load capacity: 4,060kg **Performance** maximum speed: 94km/hr

Maker: Maschinenfabrik Augsburg-Nürnburg AG, Munich

M.A.N. Is one of the most important manu-facturers of heavy vehicles in Germany, and was a pioneer of diesel engined trucks in the mid-1920s. In 1967 they began co-operation with the French Saviem company, which led to some of the lighter Saviems appearing in Germany under the M.A.N. name, and the heavy bonnetted M.A.N. range being sold in France with Saviem badges. In 1971 M.A.N. took over another old-established German company, Bussing, and the Bussing lion has appeared on all M.A.N. trucks since then. The 15-tonne GVW milk truck illustrated is part of a wide range of bonnetted 4 × 2 and 4 × 4 models, and is powered by a 5-cylinder M.A.N. diesel engine. It is made in two wheelbase lengths, 4,600 and 5,200mm, and a choice of three rear axle ratios is offered. The 4 × 4 chassis, known as the 15.168 HA, is made only on the shorter wheelbase.

Engine M.A.N. D2555M 5-cylinder diesel 9,204cc 185bhp (136kW) **Transmission** Clutch: single dry plate; Gearbox: ZF AK6-70/3 6F 1R constant mesh; available with splitter box giving 12F; Rear Axle: double reduction **Frame** channel section, ladder type **Brakes** vacuum-assisted hydraulic front; fully air-operated rear **Dimensions** wheelbase: 4,600 or 5,200mm; overall length: 7,715 or 8,715mm; overall width: 2,490mm; height to top of cab: 2,580mm; gross weight: 15,000kg; load capacity: 9,870kg **Performance** maximum speed: 74 to 96km/hr, according to axle ratio

Maker: Minsk Avto Zavod, Minsk

This is the base model of the MAZ 5000 series family which was introduced in 1978. The range also includes a tipper (5549), and tractors (5429, 5430). The standard engine develops 180bhp and is used in conjunction with a 5-speed gearbox, but some models like the 53352 offer a V-8 diesel of 14,860cc developing 265bhp and an 8-speed gearbox. Double reduction final drive is used on all models. Externally, the 5000 series differs from the preceding 500 series by the wider radiator grille and headlamps mounted in the bumpers. Soon these may be replaced by the 6000 series.

Engine YaMZ-236 V-6 diesel 11,150cc 180bhp (132kW) **Transmission** Clutch: twin dry plate; Gearbox: 5F 1R, synchromesh on four upper ratios; Rear Axle: double reduction **Frame** channel section, ladder type **Brakes** fully air-operated dual circuit **Dimensions** wheelbase: 3,950mm; overall length: 7,250mm; overall width: 2,500mm; height to top of cab: 2,720mm; gross weight: 14,950kg; load capacity: 8,000kg **Performance** maximum speed: 85km/hr

Maker: Toyo Kogyo Co Ltd, Hiroshima

Well known for their passenger cars and light commercials, Mazda began to build trucks in the 2/3-ton range in 1964. The T Series is their largest current production, and covers 55 variations including four different engines, three overall lengths and three overall widths. The wide cab is also made in a six passenger four door crew cab model. The engines, all diesels, are of 2522, 2977, 3485 and 4100cc. The 3485cc SL engine has direct injection. On the 4100cc model a Back Monitoring device is featured, which alerts the driver when a person or obstacle is at the rear of the vehicle. Three wheelbases are available, and the T series is made as a tipper in addition to dropside and low-deck models.

Engine Mazda SL 6-cylinder diesel 3455cc 105bhp (78.33kW) **Transmission** Clutch: single dry plate; Gearbox: 5F 1R all synchromesh; Rear Axle: single reduction spiral bevel **Frame** box section, ladder type **Brakes** dual circuit vacuum-assisted hydraulic **Dimensions** wheelbase: 2,505mm; overall length 4,690mm; overall width: 1,690mm; height to top of cab: 1,980mm; gross weight: 4,340kg; load capacity 2,000kg **Performance** maximum speed: 95km/hr

Maker: Daimler-Benz AG, Stuttgart

Daimler-Benz is the largest manufacturer of heavy trucks (over 7 tonnes GVW) in the world, but they also make lighter vehicles, from 3.49 tonnes upwards. The 809, 814 and 1114 models replaced the LP series in 1984, and are part of the range collectively known as the LN2 series. Made at Worth on the Rhine, the LN2s are available in 418 basic models, excluding wheelbase variations, and the options programme contains 1800 items. GVWs run from 6½ to 13 tonnes for rigid trucks, and up to 24 tonnes for artics. Major variations include four engines from 90 to 201bhp, gearboxes from 5 to 12 speeds (and automatics) day or sleeper cabs, conventional or air suspension. The 814 is a 7½-tonner so can be driven without an HGV licence. The LN2 was the winner of *Truck* magazine's Truck of the Year award for 1985.

Engine Mercedes-Benz OM366 6-cylinder diesel 5,960cc 134bhp (100kW) **Transmission** Clutch: single dry plate; Gearbox: Mercedes-Benz G3/60 5F 1R all synchromesh; Rear Axle: single reduction hypoid **Frame** channel section ladder type **Brakes** dual circuit fully air-operated **Dimensions** wheelbase: 3,150mm to 4,900mm; overall length: 6,040 to 8,940mm; overall width: 2,300mm; height to top of cab: 2,455mm; gross weight: 7,500kg; load capacity: 4,270 to 4,425kg **Performance** maximum speed: 108km/hr

Maker: Daimler-Benz AG, Stuttgart

This short-wheelbase tipper is part of a wide range of four-wheeled Mercedes-Benz trucks. The tippers alone include 29 different models, from the 5,000kg GVW model LK 508D on a chassis mainly used for delivery vans, up to the 16,000kg 1936K illustrated, and its companion the four-wheel-drive 1936AK. These are powered by the 216bhp Mercedes-Benz V–8 engine. Smaller 6-cylinder engines in the 130 to 170bhp range are also used in 4 × 2 and 4 × 4 tippers. Four gearboxes are offered, with 5, 6, 7 or 8 speeds. Mercedes-Benz make more than fifteen models of two axle medium-heavy construction site trucks.

Engine Mercedes-Benz OM 421 V–8 diesel 10,600cc 216bhp (159kW) **Transmission** Clutch single dry plate; Gearbox: ZF 8F 1R all-synchromesh; Rear Axle: single reduction spiral bevel **Frame** channel section ladder type **Brakes** dual circuit fully air-operated **Dimensions** wheelbase: 3,800mm; overall length: 6,510mm; overall width: 2,500mm height to top of cab: 2,790mm; gross weight: 16,000kg; load capacity: 9,155kg **Performance** maximum speed: 95km/hr

Maker: Mitsubishi Motors Corporation, Tokyo

Mitsubishi is one of the leading Japanese combines in the fields of shipbuilding and heavy engineering. They built their first bus in 1930, and introduced Japan's first diesel engined trucks and buses in 1936. For many years the heavier vehicles have gone by the name Fuso. The FM series illustrated is part of a medium-duty range covering GVWs from 9,400 to 14,030kgs, and there is also the NP series of normal-control trucks from 15,400 to 16,800kg. The FM is powered by a 6½-litre diesel engine, but the smaller FK has the option of this or a 5.4-litre engine. Among many possible applications for these trucks are cement mixers, mobile workshops, refuse collectors, gulley emptiers and fire engines.

Engine Mitsubishi 6D14-1A 6-cylinder diesel 6,557cc 154bhp (113kW) **Transmission** Clutch: single dry plate; Gearbox: 5F 1R, 6F 1R *or* 10F 2R synchromesh on all but 1st and reverse ratios; Rear Axle: single reduction spiral bevel **Frame** channel section ladder type **Brakes** vacuum-assisted hydraulic **Dimensions** wheelbase: 4,460mm; overall length: 7,865mm; overall width: 2,300mm; height to top of cab: 2,560mm; gross weight: 14,030kg; load capacity: 8,500kg **Performance** maximum speed: 86 to 119km/hr, according to axle ratio

Maker: Nissan Diesel Motor Co Ltd, Tokyo

Nissan Diesel is part of the Nissan company which makes Datsun passenger cars and light commercials. The heavy vehicles used to be known as Minsei after the company with which Nissan became associated in 1955, while the name UD is used in some export markets including Australia. Today Nissan offers a wide range of trucks from 2 to 45 tons capacity as well as off-road dump trucks, crane carriers and buses. The CK forward-control series was introduced in 1972 and now covers the range 15,400 to 17,500 GVW. The CKA21 and CKB21 models come in four wheelbases, the shortest of which (3,750mm) is available as a dump truck as well as for regular on-road haulage. Two engines are available, the 10.8 litre 185bhp PDG and the 11.7 litre 234bhp PEG.

Engine Nissan PD6 6-cylinder diesel 10,308cc 185bhp (139kW) **Transmission** Clutch: single dry plate; Gearbox: 5F 1R or GF 1R synchromesh or constant mesh; Rear Axle: single reduction spiral bevel or hypoid **Frame** channel section ladder type **Brakes** full vacuum with dual air-line system **Dimensions** wheelbase: 3,750mm; overall length: 6,650mm; overall width: 2,475mm; height to top of cab: 2,840mm; gross weight: 16,500kg; load capacity: 11,195kg **Performance** maximum speed: 95km/hr

Maker: Comercial Pegaso SA, Madrid

The Pegaso marque was first made in 1949 by the state-owned Empresa Nacional de Autocamiones SA (Enasa) in the former Hispano-Suiza works at Barcelona. Leyland became a major shareholder in 1960 and many Leyland components were used in Pegaso trucks and buses at that time. In 1980 International Harvester gained a controlling interest (relinquished in 1982) in the company which is now the leading heavy vehicle maker in Spain, with a production capacity of 70 vehicles per day. Five models of 4 × 2 are made, with GVWs of 14.2 to 20 tonnes, of which the 1217 illustrated is one of the largest. A 170bhp normally aspirated engine is standard in the 1217, while the similar sized 1223 has a 225bhp turbocharged engine. Day or sleeper cabs are available, and all Pegasos use the characteristic ribbed metal tilt cab which was introduced in 1972. On the new Tecno range, introduced in 1985, this cab has been greatly improved, with greater space and comfort.

Engine Pegaso 9100/55 6-cylinder diesel 10,170cc 170bhp (127kW) **Transmission** Clutch: single dry plate; Gearbox: ZF S6-90 all synchromesh 6F 1R; Rear Axle: double reduction **Frame** channel section ladder type **Brakes** dual circuit fully air-operated **Dimensions** wheelbase: 4,000 to 6,350mm; overall length: 7,135 to 11,120mm; overall width: 2,450mm; height to top of cab: 3,022mm; gross weight: 20,000kg; load capacity: 14,000kg **Performance** maximum speed: 85 to 107km/hr, according to axle ratio

Maker: Puma Industria de Veiculos S/A, São Paulo

Puma is the only Brazilian truck company making vehicles of local design, having entered the truck market in 1978 after several years of manufacturing sports cars based on Volkswagen or Chevrolet running gear. The Puma truck is a straightforward design made in 4- and 6-tonne versions; there are three engine options, diesels by M.W.M. or Perkins, and a General Motors unit designed to run on alcohol/gasol which is a widely used fuel in Brazil. The latter is available only on the 6 tonner. Three wheelbases are available for each model, and there is a special bus chassis in the 6 ton range. Fibreglass tilt cabs are featured on all truck models.

Engine M.W.M. 229-4 4-cylinder diesel 3,922cc 83bhp (62kW) *or* Perkins 4.236 4-cylinder diesel 3,860cc 82bhp (61kW) **Transmission** Clutch: single dry plate; Gearbox: Clark 4F 1R; Rear Axle: Rockwell single reduction spiral bevel **Frame** channel section ladder type **Brakes** vacuum-assisted hydraulic **Dimensions** wheelbase: 3,400mm (2,900 and 3,900mm optional); overall length: 6,100mm; overall width: 2,111mm; height to top of cab: 2,285mm; gross weight: 6,000kg; load capacity: 4,000kg **Performance** maximum speed: 92km/hr

Maker: Renault Vehicules Industriels, Suresnes, Seine

Renault are now the dominant producers of medium and heavy trucks in France, as the ranges of Saviem and Berliet were rationalised from 1978, and sold mostly under the Renault name from 1980. The G Range is a very wide one, covering trucks and tractors from 7.8 to 38 tonnes, and featuring four engines of 133, 149, 171 and 280bhp, the higher output units being turbocharged. Like the smaller J Range the G models use the 'Club of Four' cab which Saviem acquired as part of their brief association with Volvo, Daf and Magirus Deutz. As a result of Renault's acquisition of a 20% stake in Mack Trucks, some of the G Range is sold in America under the name Mack Midliner, with 5.5- and 8.8-litre engines and an enlarged version of the 'Club' cab. The G170 illustrated is available with five wheelbases from 3,000 to 5,200mm.

Engine Renault 171DR 06.02.12 6-cylinder turbocharged and intercooled diesel 5490cc 169bhp (125kW) **Transmission** Clutch: single dry plate; Gearbox: 5F 1R all synchromesh; Rear Axle: double reduction **Frame** channel section ladder type **Brakes** dual circuit fully air-operated **Dimensions** wheelbase: 3,000 to 5,200mm; overall length: 6,372 to 9,920mm; overall width: 2,330mm; height to top of cab: 2,647mm; gross weight: 16,000kg; load capacity: 9,850kg **Performance** maximum speed: 95km/hr

Maker: VEB Robur Werke, Zittau

The Robur 2500 was introduced in 1961 as a replacement for the bonnetted Robur Garant. This was descended from the Phänomen Granit whose ancestry dated back to pre-war days when Phänomen was an independent company, and not part of the State-owned VEB (Volkseigenen Betrieben-People's Own Works). The current Robur 3000 is of similar design to the 2500, and is unusual in employing an air-cooled engine. It is available in two wheelbase lengths, and a wide variety of bodywork is fitted, including mobile shops, vans, linesman's maintenance trucks and fire engines. A 4 × 4 version was also made, mainly for military use.

Engine Robur LO 4/2 4-cylinder petrol 3,345cc 75bhp (56kW) *or* Robur LO 4-cylinder diesel 3,927cc 68bhp (50kW) **Transmission** Clutch: single dry plate; Gearbox: 5F 1R synchromesh on upper four ratios; Rear Axle: single reduction spiral bevel **Frame** channel section ladder type **Brakes** dual circuit servo-assisted hydraulic **Dimensions** wheelbase: 3,025mm; overall length: 6,075mm; overall width: 2,405mm; height to top of cab: 2,490mm; gross weight: 5,750kg; load capacity: 3,100kg **Performance** maximum speed: 85km/hr

Maker: Intreprinderea de Autocamione Brasov, Brasov

Built in the same factory responsible for the DAC normal-control trucks, the Romans are based on M.A.N./Saviem designs, and use a locally pressed and assembled version of the older Saviem cab. Engines are of M.A.N. design, but made at Brasov. Several models of four-wheeler are made, the smaller 8.135s powered by the 5.5-litre 6-cylinder engine also used in the DAC 6.135R and the larger 10.215s by the 10.3-litre engine. The basic chassis can be fitted with a variety of bodies such as tippers (10.215FK), refrigerated vans (10.FFP 1), tankers (10.ALP 1) and refuse collectors (10.G 1).

Engine D.2156HMN-8 6-cylinder diesel 10,344cc 215bhp (158kW) **Transmission** Clutch: single dry plate; Gearbox: ZF 6F 1R synchromesh; Rear Axle: double reduction **Frame** channel section ladder type **Brakes** dual circuit air-assisted hydraulic **Dimensions** wheelbase: 4,500mm; overall length: 8,000mm; overall width: 2,490mm; height to top of cab: 2,920mm; gross weight: 16,000kg; load capacity: 10,280kg **Performance** maximum speed: 95km/hr

Maker: Saab-Scania AB, Sodertalje

Scania is one of Sweden's two major truck manufacturers, and can trace its ancestry back to two pioneer firms, Scania who began production in 1903, and Vabis who date from 1902. These firms merged in 1911, and for many years their products were known as Scania-Vabis, but when they joined forces with the Saab car making company in 1969 the original name of Scania was revived. Currently both bonnetted and forward-control trucks are made; the bonnetted range is made in three groups whose designations indicate engine size, 82, 112 and 142 (8, 11 and 14 litres respectively). The suffixes M H and E indicate chassis class where M is used for medium duty, H heavy duty and E extra heavy duty. The M class is primarily intended for distribution and general work, the H class for general work and light to heavy construction site jobs, and the E class for very heavy construction operations. Two day cabs and three sleeper cabs are available, and chassis come in rigid 4, rigid 6 and articulated versions. The T 82 H illustrated is made in five wheelbase sizes and with nine different rear axle ratios.

Engine Scania DN801 6-cylinder diesel 7,786cc 163bhp (120kW) *or* Scania DS805 6-cylinder turbocharged diesel 7,786cc 211 bhp (155kW) **Transmission** Clutch: single dry plate; Gearbox: 5F 1R *or* 10F 1R; Rear Axle: single reduction spiral bevel *or* hypoid **Frame** channel section ladder type **Brakes** dual circuit fully air-operated **Dimensions** wheelbase: 4,200mm; overall length: 6,840mm; overall width: 2,490mm; height to top of cab: 2,845mm; gross weight: 16,000kg; load capacity: 11,800kg **Performance** maximum speed: 81 to 115km/hr depending on axle ratio

Maker: Saab-Scania AB, Sodertalje

The forward control Scania range is divided into three groups according to cab design, the G low-profile cab for urban distribution work, the P cab for general domestic haulage, and the R cab for long distance international work. Like the bonnetted range, the trucks carry a final letter designation indicating the type of work, M for medium duty, H for heavy duty and E for extra heavy duty. The G82M illustrated uses the DS8 05 7786cc turbocharged engine as standard, with the options of less powerful normally aspirated engines or a more powerful one with turbocharger and intercooler. It has the low profile G cab, and is operated by the Swedish Post Office. The box van is by Sala Kaross.

Engine Scania DS8 05 V–8 turbocharged diesel 7786cc 211bhp (155kW) *or* DS18 01 turbocharged and intercooled 231bhp (170kW) *or* DN8 01 normally aspirated 163bhp (120kW) **Transmission** Clutch: single dry plate; Gearbox: Scania G770 5F 1R *or* GS771 10F 1R synchromesh on 4 (8) higher speeds; Rear Axle: single reduction hypoid; **Frame** channel section ladder type **Brakes** dual circuit fully air-operated **Dimensions** wheelbase: 4,200 to 5,800mm (5 options); overall length: 7,375 to 9,810mm; overall width: 2,480mm; height to top of cab: 2,675mm; gross weight: 17,000kg; load capacity: 11,000kg **Performance** maximum speed: 67 to 106km/hr, according to axle ratio

Maker: Seddon Atkinson Vehicles Ltd, Oldham, Lancashire

In 1970 Seddon acquired another well-known Lancashire truck maker, Atkinson, and in 1974 the new combine was bought by International Harvester Corporation. The following year the ranges were rationalised and in 1976 came the 200 Series four-wheeler for the 16 tonnes market, powered by International's 6-cylinder diesel engine. This had a Motor Panels cab of similar design to that fitted to the larger Seddon Atkinsons, but with a lower profile for ease of entrance. For 1983 it was replaced by the generally similar 201, which uses the same grille as the larger 401 series. Four wheelbase lengths are available, three for general haulage and the shortest for tipper applications. Two engines are available, the International D-358 or the more powerful turbocharged and aftercooled Perkins TG.3544, which is fitted to the tipper illustrated.

Engine Perkins TG.3544 6-cylinder turbocharged diesel 5800cc 148bhp (110.82kW) *or* International D-358 6-cylinder diesel 5,870cc 134bhp (100kW) **Transmission** Clutch: single dry plate; Gearbox: Eaton 542 SMJ 5F 1R synchromesh; Rear Axle: Eaton two speed spiral bevel or Seddon Atkinson single speed spiral bevel **Frame** channel section ladder type **Brakes** triple line fully air-operated **Dimensions** wheelbase: 3,810, 4,470, 5,105 or 5,640mm; overall length: 6,085, 7,790, 8,420 or 9,080mm; overall width: 2,480mm; height to top of cab: 2,640mm; gross weight: 16,260kg; load capacity: 11,000kg **Performance** maximum speed: 88 to 112km/hr, according to axle ratio

Maker: Shelvoke Dempster Ltd, Letchworth, Hertfordshire

For the greater part of their 64 year history, this company was known as Shelvoke & Drewry, the name being changed to Shelvoke Dempster in 1983 as a result of a merger with Dempster Systems. They have always specialised in municipal vehicles, starting with the curious but very practical Freighters with 20inch tyres and tram-style controls. For a while they built fire engines and all-wheel-drive cross country vehicles, but are now concentrating on refuse trucks on 4 × 2 and 6 × 4 chassis. Four engine options are available, by Leyland or Perkins, and there is a choice of manual or automatic transmissions. Two loading systems are offered on each Shelvoke chassis, the RouteChief intermittent operation and the Revopak continuous operation system. There is a choice of single cab for driver and two crew, or crew cab (illustrated) for driver and five crew.

Engine Leyland 410T 6-cylinder turbocharged diesel 5,660cc 155bhp (115.6kW) **Transmission** Clutch: single dry plate; Gearbox: Leyland GB 283/1 5F 1R constant mesh; Rear Axle: Eaton spiral bevel **Frame** channel section ladder type **Brakes** Girling fully air-operated **Dimensions** wheelbase: 3,962 or 4,343mm; overall length: 8,026 or 8,407mm; overall width: 2,489mm; height to top of cab: 3,200mm; gross weight: 16,260kg; load capacity: 7,300kg

Maker: Oy Sisu Auto AB, Helsinki (factory at Karjaa)

Sisu began making trucks in 1931 and are now Finland's most important vehicle manufacturer, building 4-, 6-, and 8-wheeled trucks, terminal tractors, crane carriers and buses. Scania has a 8.4% stake in the company, most of the balance being held by the Finnish State. For many years Sisus used Rolls-Royce or Leyland engines, but now standardise on Cummins and Valmet. Three basic ranges of truck are made, the medium-sized SK series, heavy forward-control SM series and bonnetted SL and SR series. There is also the 4 × 4 SA series which is chiefly made for military use. The SK series was introduced in 1980 and is aimed at the 16-ton 4-wheeler market. The engine is a 6-cylinder Valmet 611, and the truck is offered in eight wheelbases, from 3,400 to 5,800mm. The cab is an all-new steel design, in contrast to the rather dated, squared-off cab used on the larger M series.

Engine Valmet 611 CSBA 6-cylinder turbocharged diesel 6,510cc 210bhp (157kW) **Transmission** Clutch: Sisu single dry plate; Gearbox: ZF 5S-92 GP 9F 1R synchromesh *or* Allison MT-650 automatic; Rear Axle: Sisu BEL single reduction hypoid **Frame** channel section ladder type **Brakes** dual circuit fully air-operated **Dimensions** wheelbase: 3,800mm; overall length: 6,280mm; overall width: 2,470mm; height to top of cab: 2,760mm; gross weight: 16,000kg; load capacity: 10,680kg **Performance** maximum speed: 103km/hr

Maker: S.I.T.A. (Société Industrielle de Transports Automobiles), Paris

The S.I.T.A. 18-36 is one of the few battery electric vehicles with a load capacity of over 2 tonnes made today. It is designed specifically for refuse collection, and carries a hydraulically-operated compaction system which S.I.T.A. also make for mounting on other chassis. The hydraulic pump is powered by a separate 2.5kW (4hp) electric motor. There are also two other supplementary motors, one of 1.2kW (about 1.6hp) for the power steering, and one of 1.5kW (about 2hp) for the air-operated brakes. The batteries for propulsion have a rated capacity of between 750 and 1,050 amp/hours depending on the range required, while the service batteries for lighting and auxiliary systems have a capacity of 45 amp/hours. Voltages are 96 and 24 respectively. With the maximum battery capacity, the range is 160km constant travelling, or 60–70km for average collection. The ST 18-36 is based on a Renault chassis, and uses a Saviem 'Club of Four' cab.

Engine Leroy Somer electric motor 40bhp (29kW) **Transmission** Clutch: none; Gearbox: none; Rear Axle: Glaenzer single reduction spiral bevel **Frame** channel section ladder type **Brakes** dual circuit fully air-operated **Dimensions** wheelbase: 3,600mm; overall length: 7,665mm; overall width: 2,450mm; height to top of cab: 3,300mm; gross weight: 18,000kg; load capacity: 7,500kg **Performance** maximum speed: 35km/hr

Maker: Fabryka Samochodow Ciezarowych, Starhovice

Star trucks are named after the first part of the city where they are made. Production began in 1948, and they are now one of two state-owned Polish truck makers, the other being Jelcz which makes larger capacity trucks for highway use, while Stars have better cross-country ability, being made in 4 × 4 and 6 × 6 form as well as 4 × 2. The 200 is a 6-ton truck which can be operated with drawbar trailer, increasing its payload to 11 tons. It is also made in 4 × 4 form as the 244, and as a tractor for semi-trailers under the designation C200. An agricultural version of the 244 is the 244S which has gearing enabling it to keep pace with slow-moving farm tractors for harvesting and other work. Some Star models are sold under the Jelcz name, such as the Jelcz 005 which is a 4 × 4 fire engine on the Star 244 chassis.

Engine Star S-359 6-cylinder diesel 6,842cc 150bhp (112kW) **Transmission** Clutch: single dry plate; Gearbox: ZF S6-45 5F 1R synchromesh on four upper ratios; Rear Axle: Gleason single reduction spiral bevel **Frame** channel section ladder type **Brakes** dual circuit air/hydraulic **Dimensions** wheelbase: 3,400mm; overall length: 6,430mm; overall width: 2,380mm; height to top of cab: 2,330mm; gross weight: 10,000kg; load capacity: 6,000kg **Performance** maximum speed: 95km/hr

Maker: Sungri Motor Vehicle Combine, Pyongyang

In 1958 the Soviet Union helped the Democratic People's Republic of Korea (North Korea) to set up the Sungri (Victory) factory in Pyongyang to manufacture trucks. The Sungri 58 2½-ton open truck was an exact copy of the GAZ 51, and the present version is a development of this with a restyled front end. It is exported in large numbers to North East China, and this example was photographed in Shenyang, Liaoning province. The same factory assembles the Russian KrAZ-222 10-ton 6 × 4 dumper. A 4 × 4 version named Sungri 61NA (2-ton, the same cab) is also in production. The fourth vehicle this factory produces is the Konsor 25-ton dumper.

Engine 6-cylinder petrol 3,480cc 70bhp (51.5kW) **Transmission** Clutch: single dry plate; Gearbox: 4F 1R; Rear Axle: single reduction spiral bevel **Frame** channel section ladder type **Brakes** hydraulic **Dimensions** wheelbase: 3,300mm; overall length: 5,715mm; overall width: 2,270mm; height to top of cab: 2,080mm; gross weight: 5,350kg; load capacity: 2,640kg **Performance** maximum speed: 70km/hr

Maker: Tovarna Automobilov in Motorjev, Maribor

The first TAM trucks appeared in 1947, and were licence-built Pragas. These were made for some fifteen years, but in 1957 TAM signed an agreement with Klockner-Humboldt-Deutz to manufacture Magirus-Deutz vehicles in Yugoslavia, and these soon supplanted the Praga designs. In 1960 the factory began to build Deutz air-cooled engines, and all the larger TAM trucks and buses made since then have been Deutz-powered. Some models resemble Magirus trucks while others have cabs of local design. The 130 T 11 is made as an open truck as illustrated, and there is also a 4 × 2 tractor for 21,000kg GCW, powered by a 9½-litre 175bhp engine. TAM also makes 4 × 4 and 6 × 6 trucks for military and commercial use. TAM vehicles are exported to a number of countries, one of their best markets being South Africa.

Engine F4L 413 FR 4-cylinder diesel 6,381cc 128bhp (94kW) **Transmission** Clutch: single dry plate; Gearbox: TAM Z5-35S 5F 1R synchromesh; Rear Axle: TAM single reduction spiral bevel **Frame** channel section ladder type **Brakes** dual circuit air/hydraulic **Dimensions** wheelbase: 3,800mm; overall length: 7,038mm; overall width: 2,325mm; height to top of cab: 2,545mm; gross weight: 11,000kg; load capacity: 7,000kg **Performance** maximum speed: 92.7km/hr

Maker: Terberg Benschop BV, Benschop

Like Ginaf and the now defunct RAM, Terberg began by selling reconditioned ex-US Army trucks, and as the supply of original components dried up they incorporated an increasing proportion of modern parts of European origin, and became truck manufacturers in their own right. Most current Terbergs use Volvo engines and sheet metal, including the TSR 1000 municipal truck, although Mercedes-Benz units can be specified. It is designed for refuse collection in narrow streets, and is only 2,000mm wide although having a GVW of 16.5 tonnes. The low-entry crew cab can have left or right-hand steering, and accommodates three men. The very low first gear gives a collection speed of 3.34km/hour, so that in some areas the truck does not need to stop at all between collections. A 4 × 4 version is also available.

Engine Volvo TD60B 6-cylinder turbocharged diesel 5,480cc 174bhp (128kW) **Transmission** Clutch: single dry plate; Gearbox: ZF S6-65 6F 1R synchromesh; Rear Axle: Terberg TB100 single reduction hypoid **Frame** channel section ladder type **Brakes** dual circuit fully air-operated **Dimensions** wheelbase: 3,150mm; overall length: 5,380mm; overall width: 2,000mm; height to top of cab: 2,630mm; gross weight: 16,500kg; load capacity: 8,000kg **Performance** maximum speed: 70km/hr

Maker: Tianjin Motor Vehicle Factory, Tianjin

During the second half of the 1970s China has imported a large number of small Japanese pick-up trucks, and under the influence of these vehicles many local factories developed their own modern-looking trucks of around 2 tons capacity. The most important are the factories in Tianjin city and Liaoning province, who between them made 5,747 of these trucks in 1980. Other factories making basically similar vehicles are in Guangdong, Hebei, Heilongjiang, Hubei, Jiangsu, Shanxi, Sichuan, Yunnan and Zhjiang. There are several variants including a crew-cab model, long wheelbase version and diesel-powered models. The Tianjin factory has produced since 1980 their Tianjin TJ 130, also sold as Yanpai TJ 130, with single and double row seat cab. This vehicle is mass produced on the old TJ 210 (jeep) assembly line.

Engine 492Q 4-cylinder petrol 2,445cc 75bhp (55.95kW) **Transmission** Clutch: single dry plate; Gearbox: 4F 1R synchromesh; Rear Axle: single reduction spiral bevel **Frame** channel section ladder type **Brakes** hydraulic **Dimensions** wheelbase: c.2,800mm; overall length: c.4,710mm; overall width: c.1,850mm; height to top of cab: c.2,080mm; gross weight: c.4,000kg; load capacity: c.2,000kg **Performance** maximum speed: c.85km/hr
(provisional specifications)

Maker: Toyota Motor Corporation, Tokyo

Toyota is the biggest vehicle manufacturer in the world to sell all its products under one name, their production being exceeded only by General Motors who have five brand names for cars and two for trucks in the United States, as well as several overseas affiliates. Toyota's annual production of trucks alone is around 1 million. The Toyota Loom Works, as it was then, built its first truck in 1935, and the company has concentrated on light to medium vehicles ever since. The current range embraces pick ups and vans from 1 ton payloads upwards and two lines of truck, the forward control Dynas with GVW from 4300 to 7000kgs, and the bonnetted DA with GVW of 11,500kg. The latter is a conventional truck available in only one wheelbase length with one engine, a 6½-litre 6-cylinder diesel. However a wide variety of bodies can be fitted to the DA, including tankers, refuse collectors and fire engines. The DA is popular in many Third World countries where its simple design and rugged construction are appreciated.

Engine Toyota 2D 6-cylinder diesel 6,494cc 148bhp (110.4kW) **Transmission** Clutch: single dry plate; Gearbox: 5F 1R synchromesh; Rear Axle: single or two speed hypoid **Frame** channel section ladder type **Brakes** vacuum-assisted hydraulic **Dimensions** wheelbase: 4,100mm; overall length: 6,835 to 7,620mm according to bodywork; overall width: 2,385mm; height to top of cab: 2,520mm; gross weight: 11,500kg; load capacity: 7,100kg **Performance** maximum speed: 110km/hr

Maker: Volkswagenwerk AG, Wolfsburg

The first commercial version of the Volkswagen was made in 1950, but the company did not turn out anything larger than the 1,000kg Transporter until the appearance of the LT series in 1975. These have front-mounted water-cooled 6-cylinder engines, all of 2,383cc. Two are diesels, one normally aspirated (75bhp), and the other turbocharged (102bhp), and the third is a 90bhp petrol unit. Three wheel-bases are offered, 2,500mm, 2,950mm, and 3,650mm with GVWs from 2.8 to 5 tonnes in seven models. Factory-supplied bodies include vans, dropside trucks and crew-cab dropside trucks, but many specialist builders have supplied bodies on the LT. These include mobile shops, tippers, refuse vehicles and armoured bullion vans. One of the latter, converted by Sulzer, is a six wheeler. Sulzer also make 4× 4 conversions for the LT Series.

Engine Volkswagen 6-cylinder petrol 2,383cc 90bhp (66kW) *or* Volkswagen 6-cylinder diesel 2,383cc 75bhp (55kW) *or* Volkswagen 6-cylinder turbocharged diesel 2,383cc 102bhp (75kW) **Transmission** Clutch: single dry plate; Gearbox: 4F 1R or 5F 1R all-synchromesh; Rear Axle: rigid single reduction hypoid **Frame** welded box section **Brakes** dual circuit hydraulic, discs at front, drums at rear **Dimensions** wheelbase: 2,950mm; overall length: 5,625mm; overall width: 2,140mm; height to top of cab: 2,145mm; gross weight: 4,600kg; load capacity: 2,350 to 2.420kg, according to engine **Performance** maximum speed: 102 to 120km/hr, according to model

Maker: Volkswagen do Brasil SA, São Bernardo do Campo

Volkswagen cars of local design have been made in Brazil since 1969, but truck activities only began with the acquisition by VW of a majority holding in Chrysler do Brasil in 1979. Four truck models are currently made, the 6-80, 6-90, 11-130 and 13-130, of 6.3, 11 and 13 tonnes GVW respectively. They have tilt cabs derived from that of the LT series, and 4- or 6-cylinder diesel engines made by the Brazilian branch of MWM (Motoren-Werke Mannheim). Most components such as axles, springs, steering, brakes, gearbox and clutch are made in Brazil, as are the bodies. Many of the dropside bodies are made of local hardwood. Three wheelbases are available, 3,670, 4,127 and 4,686mm. In addition trailing axle six-wheeler versions are made, with GVWs of 19 or 21 tonnes.

Engine MWM D.229.6 6-cylinder diesel 5,883cc 130bhp (96kW) **Transmission** Clutch: single dry plate; Gearbox: Clark 5F 1R all-synchromesh; Rear Axle: Braseixos HL-145 rigid single reduction spiral bevel **Frame** channel section ladder type **Brakes** dual circuit fully air-operated **Dimensions** wheelbase: 4,127mm; overall length: 7,580mm; overall width: 2,244mm; height to top of cab: 2,517mm; gross weight: 13,000kg; load capacity: 8,930kg **Performance** maximum speed: 95km/hr

Maker: Volvo Truck Corporation, Goteborg

Volvo began production of passenger cars in 1927, and trucks appeared a year later. Since then they have built up a commanding position in the medium and heavy vehicle world, and are now Europe's third largest manufacturer of heavy vehicles. The FL6 is part of a new range introduced by Volvo in September 1985 which includes two-axle trucks from 12 to 16.26 tonnes, or as drawbar or articulated combinations up to 28 tonnes. The 6-litre TD61 engine is available in two versions, the 180bhp turbocharged TD61G and the 207bhp turbocharged and intercooled TD61F. Transmission options include five-, six or eight-speed Volvo synchromesh gearboxes or a six-speed Allison automatic. Seven wheelbases are available in the FL6 range. The new FL models, which include 6 × 2, 6 × 4, 8 × 2 and 8 × 4 trucks and tractors, are made at plants in Gothenberg, Ghent and Irvine (Scotland). *Picture:* Volvo FL612 turbo (right), FL612 intercooler (left).

Engine Volvo TD61GS 6-cylinder turbocharged diesel 5,480cc 180bhp (132kW) **Transmission** Clutch: single dry plate; Gearbox: 5, 6 or 8F 1R synchromesh *or* Allison 6F 1R automatic; Rear Axle: single reduction hypoid **Frame** channel section ladder type **Brakes** dual circuit fully air-operated **Dimensions** wheelbase: 3,400 to 6,500mm; overall length: 6,120 to 11,000mm; overall width: 2,368mm; height to top of cab: 2,590mm; gross weight: 12,000kg; load capacity: 7,783kg **Performance** maximum speed: 94 or 102km/h according to axle ratio

Maker: Volvo Truck Corporation, Goteborg

Unlike many heavy truck manufacturers, Volvo have built a line of normal-control trucks consistently alongside their forward-control models, and these are of equal importance in their production programme. The current N series are made in three basic sizes, N7, N10 and N12, for GVWs of up to 23.5 tonnes, 33.5, or 38 tonnes as a tractive unit. The N7 is ideal for medium heavy construction site work, the N10 for similar work and also bulk and tanker haulage, and the N12 for really heavy construction site work, long-distance haulage of weight-intensive materials such as gravel and rock, or as a heavyweight highway tractor, in which form it is popular in America. Four engines are available in the N series, from 213 to 330bhp. Three of these engines are especially designed for cold weather conditions, and have an exhaust pressure governor which increases back pressure so that the engine remains clean running during cold starting, and an electric starting heater which warms up the induction air for reliable cold starting.

Engine Volvo TD70G 6-cylinder turbocharged diesel 6,700cc 213bhp (157kW) **Transmission** Clutch: single dry plate; Gearbox: 8F 1R all-synchromesh (with splitter, 16F 1R) *or* 5F 1R automatic; Rear Axle: single reduction hypoid **Frame** channel section ladder type **Brakes** dual circuit fully air-operated **Dimensions** wheelbase: 3,800 to 5,800mm; overall length: 6,160 to 8,630mm; overall width: 2,448mm; height to top of cab: 2,707mm; gross weight: 19,500kg; load capacity: 13,775 to 13,900kg **Performance** maximum speed: 100km/hr

Maker: W & E Vehicles Ltd, Shrewsbury

Founded in 1945 as Wales & Edwards Ltd,
W & E are one of the leading British makers
of electric vehicles, and are familiar throughout the country for their 3- and 4-wheeled
milk floats. The 6/80 is their largest model,
and is the only British electric vehicle with a
payload as high as 4 tonnes. It was developed
in conjunction with the Unigate Dairy Group
who are the leading operators of W & E
vehicles, and is used for wholesale dairy
work, although other bodies can be fitted,
and some dairies use enclosed van bodies
rather than the open float type. The 6/80 is
fitted with Chloride High Energy Density
batteries with the Autofil topping up system.
The front axle is designed to take Leyland
Terrier components such as king pins,
swivel axle and hub, brakes and drums. The
traction battery is of 132 volts, and there is a
separate 12 volt battery for auxiliary services
such as lighting.

Engine EDC 132V 17bhp electric motor **Transmission** Clutch: none; Gearbox: none; Rear Axle:
single reduction spiral bevel **Frame** channel section ladder type **Brakes** air/hydraulic **Dimensions**
wheelbase: 3,276mm; overall length: 4,800mm; overall width: 1,854mm; gross weight: 7,500kg;
load capacity: 4,000kg **Performance** maximum speed: 33km/hr

Maker: Nanjing Motor Vehicle Factory, Nanjing (Nanking)

The Nanking factory started truck production in 1958 with a copy of the Russian GAZ-51 which was also made in North Korea as the Sungri-58. Though the Yuejin is still in production for over 25 years, the factory is now rapidly developing new types, like the NJ 131 3-ton cab-over-engine truck, the NJ 121 1¾-ton cab-over-engine truck and the NJ 221 4 × 4 1-ton van. Diesel-engined versions are available for most of the types. The present standard type is the NJ 134 3-ton truck. The Nanjing Corporations unites 24 factories, most of them in Jiangsu province, but also in Anhui, Fujian, Jiangxi, Hubei, Jilan, Zhejiang, Guandong and Sichuan province.

Engine Yuejin NJ 70F 6-cylinder petrol 3,480cc 80bhp (59kW) **Transmission** Clutch: single dry plate; Gearbox: 4F 1R; Rear Axle: single reduction spiral bevel **Frame** channel section ladder type **Brakes** hydraulic **Dimensions** wheelbase: 3,300mm; overall length: 5,838mm; height to top of cab: 2,117mm; gross weight: 5,640kg; load capacity: 3,094kg **Performance** maximum speed: 80km/hr

Maker: Zavod Imieni Likhachev, Moscow

Introduced in 1964, the ZIL-130 is one of the commonest trucks in the USSR. The updated 80 version is made in a number of different models. These include the 130S-80 for cold climates (400kg heavier), the long-wheelbase (4500mm) 130G-80 and a model 138, designed to run on LPG, though it can also use 76 octane petrol for short journeys. Interestingly, despite its long life (and early experiments by ZIL, in those days ZIS, with diesel engines before 1940) the 130 has never acquired a diesel engine. For off-road work rear axles of many Soviet trucks, including the 130-80 shown, can be fitted with sizeable low-pressure tyres instead of ordinary double wheels.

Engine ZIL-130 V-8 petrol 5,966cc 150bhp (110kW) **Transmission** Clutch: single dry plate; Gearbox: 5F 1R, not synchronized on low; Rear Axle: hypoid bevel *or* double reduction **Frame** channel section ladder type **Brakes** dual circuit air-operated **Dimensions** wheelbase: 3,800mm; overall length: 6,675mm; overall width: 2,500mm; overall height: 2,400mm; gross weight: 10,525kg; load capacity: 6,000kg **Performance** maximum speed: 90km/hr

Maker: Zavod Imieni Likhachev, Moscow

For years one has wondered why ZIL's 5-6 tonners (in the case of the 133G2 even a ten-tonner) have not received a diesel engine. ZIL's early experiments with diesel date from 1939, but nothing resulted from this experience. By 1977 the works prepared early prototypes of the diesel powerplant to be installed in a new generation of trucks—it was called ZIL-645. It is said to be 30 to 40% more economical than current petrol units and huge savings in national crude oil resources can be foreseen after hundreds of thousands of 4331s come into use. A turbocharged ZIL-645 will give around 215bhp and for carrying light loads a 6-cylinder diesel will be sufficient. Also, for some applications, a small number of petrol engines will be installed, but using a comparatively economical pre-chamber design. Along with this base model a new family of ZILs includes a tractor (4421), two tippers (4506, 4507) and chassis with a standard, shortened (3,800mm) and lengthened (5,600mm) wheelbase.

Engine ZIL-645 V-8 diesel 8,740cc 185bhp (136kW) **Transmission** Clutch: single dry plate; Gearbox: 8F 1R; **Frame** channel section ladder type **Brakes** air-operated **Dimensions** wheelbase: 4,500mm; load capacity: 6,000kg **Performance** maximum speed: 85km/hr

Maker: Garage Martinet SA, Chavornay

All-wheel drive trucks are a necessity for transporting goods in the mountainous areas of Switzerland. Some of the Swiss truck producers who originally supplied this kind of truck have disappeared from the market. Saurer stopped production of their range of vehicles in 1982, and F.B.W. completed their last truck on 3 September 1984. Both companies already announced their disappearance in the early eighties. At that time, Simon Martinet decided to construct a 4 × 4 truck to take the place on the truck market formerly belonging to the 4 × 4 bonneted Saurer and F.B.W. trucks. Martinet uses a 4 × 2 Daf FAV2505 DHS chassis for his truck, as Garage Martinet SA. in Chavornay has been a dealer for this Dutch brand for years now. The chassis is converted to a 4 × 4 truck by using a Steyr front axle and transfer case, and is renamed from DAF into A.F.D.

Engine DAF 825DHS, 6-cylinder turbocharged intercooled diesel 8,283cc 250bhp (184kW) **Transmission** Clutch: single dry plate; Gearbox: ZF S6-90, 6F 1R synchromesh *or* ZF Ecosplit 16S112, 16F 1R; Transfer Box: Steyr two speed: Front Axle: single reduction planetary; Rear Axle: single reduction planetary **Frame** channel section ladder type **Brakes** dual circuit fully air-operated **Dimensions** wheelbase: 3,650mm; overall length: 6,750mm; overall width: 2,300mm; height to top of cab: 2,970mm; gross weight: 16,000kg; load capacity: 9,500kg **Performance** maximum speed: 102km/hr

Maker: Maschinenfabrik Buckau R Wolf, Grebenbroich

This unusual vehicle is designed to load and unload seagoing vessels in locations where there are no port facilities. It can also be used to transport goods to off-shore islands, or as an emergency supply vehicle in flooded areas. Jointly developed by Buckau-Wolf and the truck makers, Kaelble, it is powered by a rear-mounted 408bhp V-12 turbocharged engine, and has fully hydrostatic four-wheel-drive. Water propulsion is by a propeller situated below the cab; this is steerable through 360° giving excellent manoeuvrability. In water the truck normally moves in the opposite direction from its land movement, hence the propeller is at the rear for water travel, while an elevated section above the cab gives the driver a good view over the load area. The road wheels have four wheel steering, and the vehicle can travel sideways. Maximum gradient on full load is 25%.

Engine Deutz V-12 turbocharged diesel 408bhp (300kW) **Transmission** Clutch: none; Gearbox: none (hydrostatic drive by four variable displacement axial-plunger pumps); Transfer Box: none; Front Axle: planetary hub final drive; Rear Axle: planetary hub final drive **Frame** all steel monocoque **Brakes** dual circuit fully air-operated **Dimensions** wheelbase: 8,300mm; overall length: 12,700mm; overall width: 3,500mm; height to top of cab: 4,000mm; gross weight: 43,000kg; load capacity: 20,000kg **Performance** maximum speed: (land) 40km/hr (water) 10km/hr

Maker: ARDCO Industries Inc, Houston, Texas

ARDCO, Applied Research & Development Company Inc was founded in 1954 as a rental company of off-road vehicles for the geophysical exploration industry. Thirty years later, the firm sells and leases its vehicles and equipment as well providing contract drill crews, geophysical supplies and air gun equipment. Presently, 4×4, 6×6 and 10×10 vehicles with articulated frames are produced with a choice of normal-control or forward-control cabs. The 10×10 version is a combination of a tractor with trailer, both powered. The price of this combination, the twin-engined K 10 × 10 is around $195,500.00. The price of the smaller K 6×6 is $106,000.00 and the K 4 × 4 costs $82,450.00. Plants are located in Houston (Texas), Lafayette (Louisiana), Laurel (Missisippi) and Edmonton, Alberta (Canada).

Engine Detroit Diesel 4-53, 4-cylinder diesel 130bhp (97kW) **Transmission** Clutch: single dry plate; Gearbox: New Process 5F 1R synchromesh; Transfer Box: ARDCO one-speed; Front Axle: Rockwell 204 single reduction planetary; Rear Axle: Rockwell 204 single reduction planetary **Frame** box section, articulated **Brakes** mechanical **Dimensions** wheelbase: 3,810mm; overall length: 7,300mm; overall width: 3,430mm; height to top of cab: 2,900mm; gross weight: 10,500kg; load capacity: 5,000kg **Performance** maximum speed: 35km/hr

Maker: Vauxhall Motors Ltd, Luton, Bedfordshire

This is the only four-wheel-drive Bedford truck, and was derived from the TM series as a military vehicle, in which form the British Army placed a contract for 2,000, to be supplied from 1980 to 1982. The civilian version became available in 1981, and is offered by the factory with dropside, tipper or high-sided body with Atlas self-loading crane, or as a chassis with mid-mounted winch. Other bodies such as tankers have also been provided by outside bodybuilders. The tanker shown is by Buckingham and was delivered to the Severn Trent Water Authority. The TM 4 × 4 has a tilt stability of 43° unladen, and 28° with full load of 8 tons. The turning circle of 18.5 metres is exceptionally good for a vehicle with driven front axle.

Engine Bedford 8.2/205D turbocharged Blue Series diesel 8,198cc 202bhp (152.7kW) **Transmission** Clutch: twin dry plate; Gearbox: Turner 6F 1R all synchromesh; Transfer Box: Rockwell; Front Axle: Kirkstall single reduction spiral bevel; Rear Axle: Kirkstall single reduction spiral bevel **Frame** channel section ladder type **Brakes** fully air-operated **Dimensions** wheelbase: 3,883mm or 4,325mm; overall length: 6,181mm or 6,623mm; overall width: 2,476mm; height to top of cab: 2,997mm; gross weight: 16,300kg; load capacity: 8,000kg **Performance** maximum speed: 92km/hr

Maker: Bennes Brimont SA, Rheims

Brimont are an agricultural equipment, trailer manufacturing and bodybuilding company who acquired the rights to the Latil forestry tractor in 1974. They also make a load-carrying version of this known as the ETR series. It has four-wheel-drive and steering, and the chassis is pivoted behind the cab to allow the front and rear halves to twist independently, keeping all four wheels in equal contact with the ground on rough terrain. Power comes from a Renault 6-cylinder diesel engine, in normally-aspirated or turbocharged form. A variety of different transmission combinations is available, from a six-speed gearbox with single ratio transfer box (model 106) to a twelve speed gearbox with double ratio transfer box and hydromechanical reduction (model 412) giving 48 forward speeds from 0.1 to 85km/hour, and eight reverse speeds! The Brimont has many military and civilian applications; among the latter are as a fire engine, pole layer, concrete mixer, snow plough, mobile crane and personnel carrier, all with excellent cross-country mobility. The ETR is also made in the United States under the name Commando, when it is fitted with a Mack MIDR 6-cylinder engine.

ETR benne

brimont s.a.

Engine Renault 797 6-cylinder diesel 5,500cc 133bhp (99.2kW) normally-aspirated or 155bhp (115.6kW) turbocharged or 175bhp (130.55kW) turbocharged and intercooled **Transmission** Clutch: single dry plate; Gearbox: ZF 6F 1R with double ratio transfer = 12F 1R: Transfer Box: Brimont hydro-mechanical double ratio; Front Axle: arch type single reduction hypoid; Rear Axle: arch type single reduction hypoid **Frame** channel section articulated at centre **Brakes** dual circuit hydro pneumatic discs **Dimensions** wheelbase: 2,995mm; overall length: 4,965mm; overall width: 2,270mm; height to top of cab: 2,660mm; gross weight: 11,000kg; load capacity: 5,000kg **Performance** maximum speed: 85km/hr

Maker: Eisenwerke Kaiserslautern Goppner GmbH, Kaiserslauten

Several NATO countries have used the E.W.K. amphibious bridging and ferrying vehicles in their armed forces for years now. Based upon this military experience, E.W.K. Eisenwerke Kaiserslautern Göppner GmbH. decided to start using their methods on vehicles for civilian purposes The Bison, their 5-7 ton amphibious mulit-purpose lorry was presented in 1980. This all round multi-purpose vehicle has several civilian uses, like transport vehicle, ambulance/rescue vehicle, fire-extinguishing vehicle, as well as military applications. E.W.K. produces several amphibious vehicles as well as the Bison; the bridging and ferrying vehicles M2B and the armoured ambulance/rescue vehicles named Samarita.

Engine K.H.D. BF8L413F V-8 turbocharged diesel 320bhp (235kW) **Transmission** Clutch: none Gearbox: ZF 6HP500 6F 1R automatic (hydrostatic drive by two Schottel steering propellers, switchable auxiliary drive for hydraulic pump) Transfer Box: A 600 3 D, 1 speed; Front Axle: single reduction planetary; Rear Axle: single reduction planetary **Frame** box section **Brakes** dual circuit fully air-operated **Dimensions** wheelbase: 5,100mm; overall length: 9,340mm; overall width: 2,500mm on land, 4,460 in water; height to top of cab: 2,960mm; gross weight: 11,000kg; load capacity: 7,000kg **Performance** maximum speed: 80km/hr on land, 12km/hr in water

Maker: Ginaf Automobielbedrijven BV, Ederveen

This is a single cab-over design from Gorky, in production since 1964. Its two-seater cab can be fitted as a sleeper for driver only and all metal bodies sport bench type seats. No drop-side bodies are produced, the chassis is supplied by the factory for mounting anything from van bodies to drilling equipment. Quite a number of model 66s are fitted with a front-mounted winch. A number of parts from the engine downwards are similar to those mounted on the GAZ-53A. Air pressure in 12.00-18 size tyres can be varied at speed and positioned behind the cab, the spare has a lifting device. Instead of GAZ-53A's single tank of 90 litres, this model has got two, 105 litres each.

Engine ZMZ-66 V-8 4,250cc 115bhp (84.6kW) **Transmission** Clutch: single dry plate, hydraulic actuator; Gearbox: four speed, synchronized on 3rd and 4th; Transfer Box: two-speed; Axles: single reduction hypoid **Frame** channel section ladder type **Brakes** hydraulic, with hydrovac servo **Dimensions** wheelbase: 3,300mm; overall length: 5,805mm; overall width: 2,322mm; overall height: 2,440mm; gross weight: 5,800kg; load capacity: 2,000kg **Performance** maximum speed: 95 km/hr

Maker: Ginaf Automobielbedrijven BV, Veenendaal

The Ginaf company began as re-conditioners of ex-US Army trucks for the civilian market, and in 1967 they introduced their first trucks sold under their own name. These still used American chassis, but cabs, engines and other components were increasingly of local manufacture. Their current range of 4 × 4, 6 × 6, 8 × 8 and 10 × 8 trucks uses Daf engines and cabs, ZF gearboxes and Ginaf or Daf axles. They are mostly used for construction site work or hauling sand and gravel, but there is a long-wheelbase 6 × 4 model for general road haulage. Other Dutch truck makers who began in the same way as Ginaf are R.A.M. and Terberg.

Engine DAF DKX 1160 6-cylinder turbocharged and intercooled diesel 11,630cc 330bhp (243kW) **Transmission** Clutch: Fichtel & Sachs single dry plate; Gearbox: ZF 16S-130 8F 1R with dual ratio transfer = 16F 2R; Transfer Box: M.A.N. VG 2000 3W 2 speed; Front Axle: Ginaf APG20 double reduction; Rear Axle: Daf 2699T double reduction **Frame** channel section ladder type **Brakes** dual circuit fully air-operated **Dimensions** wheelbase: 3,650mm; overall length: 6,400mm; overall width: 2,480mm; height to top of cab: 3,100mm; gross weight: 23,700kg; load capacity: 15,925kg **Performance** maximum speed: 85km/hr

Maker: Hino Motors Ltd, Tokyo

Hino's 4 × 2 trucks are all of forward control layout, and the only bonnetted four wheeler is the 4 × 4 NZ. Aimed at the on/off-road construction site market, the NZ is a tough, high-built truck with a ground clearance of 260mm in standard form, and 350mm when the larger 14.00 × 20 tyres are used. These tyres are singles all round, whereas the normal 10.00 × 20 tyres are twinned at the rear, as in the illustration. The NZ chassis can also be used for mounting special equipment such as seismographs, and as a snow plough.

Engine Hino EM 100 6-cylinder diesel 9,419cc 215bhp (158kW) **Transmission** Clutch: single dry plate; Gearbox: 6F 1R synchromesh on upper four ratios; Transfer box: 2 speed; Front Axle: single reduction spiral bevel: Rear Axle: single reduction hypoid **Frame** channel section ladder type **Brakes** dual circuit fully air-operated **Dimensions** wheelbase: 4,350mm or 5,000mm; overall length: 7,265mm or 8,765mm; overall width: 2,490mm; height to top of cab: 2,820mm; gross weight: 14,300 to 16,000kg; load capacity: 9,500kg **Performance** maximum speed: 80km/hr

Maker: MAFSA, Lugo

I.P.V. is the brand name featuring on four-wheel drive trucks made by the Spanish MAFSA factory. Since the end of the last decade, MAFSA has delivered large numbers of all-wheel drive trucks to national customers, and nowadays, they have undoubtedly the leading position on this specific part of the Spanish truck market. Their program contains the 85TT, 110TT and 4T-115. The first two feature a rather simple cab, which is deliverable roof-less too. The 4T-115 uses a cab strongly resembling the cabs used on the 65, 75 and 90PC series 4×4 trucks made by Fiat, OM and Unic. The 85TT can carry 4 tons, the other trucks, 5 tons. All models are powered by a Perkins 6.354.3 diesel engine. Recently, MAFSA added a terminal tractor to their existing program.

Engine Perkins 6.354.3 6-cylinder diesel 5,800cc 115bhp (87kW) **Transmission** Clutch: single dry plate; Gearbox: ZF 5F 1R synchromesh; Transfer Box: two speed; Front Axle: single reduction, disengagable drive; Rear Axle: single reduction **Frame** channel section ladder type **Brakes** dual circuit fully air-operated **Dimensions** wheelbase: 2,910mm; overall length: 4,945mm; overall width: 1,865mm; height to top of cab: 2,530mm; gross weight: 11,500kg; load capacity: 5,000kg **Performance** maximum speed: 95km/hr

Maker: Kutaisi Avto Zavod, Kutaisi, Georgia

For anticipated developments in the USSR's agriculture, trucks, tractors, semi-trailers and drawbar trailers specially prepared and fitted for rural conditions were designed. Forward control is preferred in Kutaisi, making a comparatively long cargo body possible on a comparatively short wheelbase. Both tractor and trailer have identical 7m³ bodies (with side extensions up to 14m³) which can be tipped to three and two sides, respectively. The six-cylinder engine is a derivative of a famous KamAZ unit, less two cylinders. A turbocharged version may be introduced, developing 205bhp (150kW). Gearbox with one-speed transfer box is fixed to the frame separately, which helps for distribution of masses between the two axles and makes for lower bodywork. Rear and central differentials can be blocked by driver. Special low profile radial tyres were designed for this truck and those 14.75/80-20s, along with appropriate gearing and 300mm ground clearance allow exemplary mud-going qualities. KAZ, like the new air-cooled GAZ can crawl along with a harvester combine at 2 to 3km/hr for long periods without overheating. The KAZ-4540 is expected to be in full production in late 1986.

Engine YaMZ-642 V-6 diesel 8,138cc 160bhp (118kW) **Transmission** Clutch: dry plate; Gearbox: 8F 1R all synchromesh; Transfer box: one-speed; Axles: single reduction hypoid, wheel reductors **Frame** channel section ladder type **Dimensions** wheelbase: 3,600mm; overall length: 6,575mm; overall width: 2,500mm; overall height: 2,830mm; load capacity: 5,500kg **Performance** maximum speed: 80km/hr

Maker: Nissan Diesel Motor Co Ltd, Tokyo

This truck is part of Nissan's range of bonnetted heavy duty trucks for on/off highway work which includes 4 × 4 and 6 × 6 chassis. Even heavier dump truck work is catered for by the WD series. The TFA21 is powered by Nissan's PD6 185hp engine, and is available in two wheelbase lengths, 4,280mm on the tipper illustrated, and 4,900mm for a dropside truck, tanker and mobile workshop, where cross-country mobility is needed as well as reasonable performance on the road. The five-speed gearbox is linked with a two-speed transfer box, giving ten forward ratios, and two reverse. Final reduction is by single-speed hypoid gears on front and rear axles.

Engine Nissan PD6 6-cylinder diesel 10,308cc 185bhp (138kW) **Transmission** Clutch: single dry plate; Gearbox: Nissan Diesel TMH412 5F 1R constant mesh *or* 5F 1R synchromesh; Transfer Box: Nissan Diesel dual ratio; Front Axle: single reduction hypoid; Rear Axle: single reduction hypoid **Frame** channel section ladder type **Brakes** dual circuit fully air-operated **Dimensions** wheelbase: 4,280 or 4,900mm; overall length: 7,220 or 8,595mm; overall width: 2,480mm; height to top of cab: 2,815mm; gross weight: 15,400kg; load capacity: 9,655 or 9,505kg **Performance** maximum speed: 80km/hr

Maker: Oshkosh Truck Corporation, Oshkosh, Wisconsin

Oshkosh is one of America's leading special-ist truck makers, and builds several distinct series of trucks for such varied applications as snow ploughs, concrete mixers, oilfield and general haulage, as well as fire engines for cities and airports, and military vehicles. The P Series are designed for snow plough work, though they can be used for road gritting and other highway maintenance duties in the summer. Oshkosh have been active in this field since the early 1920s, and the world's oldest active snowplough, a 1929 Oshkosh, is still in use in Crivitz, Wisconsin. The P Series is made in three 4 × 4 models, and one 6 × 6, powered by various models of Caterpillar, Cummins or Detroit Diesel engine, from 210 to 350bhp. Transmissions are either Fuller manual or Allison automatics. GVWs range from 20,800 to 30,400kg.

Engine Cummins PT-270 6-cylinder diesel 14,000cc 270bhp (201.4kW) **Transmission** Clutch: twin dry plate; Gearbox: Fuller T-11605C 1R constant mesh; Transfer Box: Oshkosh 13300 single speed; Front Axle: Oshkosh 25K single reduction; Rear Axle: Rockwell R-170 single reduction **Frame** channel section ladder type **Brakes** dual circuit fully air-operated **Dimensions** wheelbase: 4,013mm; overall length: 6,293mm; overall width: 1,438mm; height to top of cab: 2,870mm; gross weight: 21,773kg; **Performance** maximum speed: 70km/hr
(typical available specification for the truck illustrated)

Maker: Reynolds-Boughton Chassis Ltd, Winkleigh, Devon

T.T. Boughton of Amersham, Bucks, have made forestry and agricultural winches since the 19th century, and they teamed up with Reynolds, who specialised in off-road conversions to trucks, to manufacture fire engines, particularly airfield crash tenders. In 1978 they added to their range the RB44, a general purpose truck using some components from the Ford A Series, including the cab. The standard engine is a Bedford 3½-litre petrol unit, but a Perkins 4.236 diesel can also be fitted. Manual or automatic gearboxes are listed, while the transfer box and axles are of Reynolds-Boughton manufacture. The RB44 chassis is the basis for a number of fire engines, when it is known as the Apollo, and has been suplied in considerable numbers to Electricity Boards who use it with Simon elevating platforms.

Engine Bedford 214 6-cylinder petrol 3,519cc 100bhp (74.6kW) *or* Perkins 4.236 4-cylinder diesel 3,860cc 76bhp (56.6kW) *or* Rover 3500 V-8 petrol 3,528cc 91bhp (67kW) **Transmission** Clutch: single dry plate; Gearbox: Ford 4F 1R all synchromesh *or* Allison AT475 automatic; Transfer Box: Boughton 2 speed; Front Axle: Boughton single reduction hypoid; Rear Axle: Boughton single reduction hypoid **Frame** channel section ladder type **Brakes** dual circuit hydraulic **Dimensions** wheelbase: 3,680mm; overall length: 5,650mm; overall width: 2,118mm; height to top of cab: 2,347mm; gross weight: 5,500kg; load capacity: 3,350kg **Performance** maximum speed: 96km/hr *(typical available specification for the truck illustrated)*

Maker: RFW Truck Manufacturing Co, Chester Hill, New South Wales

Founded by Robert F. Whitehead, this company began to make trucks in 1969, using a Scania engine and Bedford cab to start with. Current models have purpose-built cabs and are powered by American engines made by Caterpillar, Cummins or Detroit Diesel. Various models have been made, including buses, but today R.F.W. concentrates on all-wheel-drive trucks made in 4 × 4, 6 × 6 and 8 × 8 versions. These are used for carrying tipper bodies, oilfield exploration and drilling equipment and also as airfield crash tenders. The 4 × 4 is made in two forms, Standard and Heavy Duty, the latter having more powerful engine options, heavier capacity rear axles and larger radiator. An unusual application of the 4 × 4 chassis was a 26 passenger bus designed for outback tours. The Standard offers a choice of Cummins 200bhp, Detroit Diesel 170bhp or Caterpillar 3208 175bhp. The truck illustrated is an explosives carrier operated by ICI Australia Pty Ltd.

Engine Detroit Diesel 4-53T 4-cylinder turbocharged diesel 3,471cc 170bhp (127kW)
Transmission Clutch: torque converter; Gearbox: Allison MT-653DT 5F 1R automatic; Transfer Box: R.F.W.; Front Axle: R.F.W. single reduction; Rear Axle: Rockwell Q155 single reduction hypoid
Frame channel section ladder type **Brakes** dual circuit fully air-operated **Dimensions** N/A; gross weight: 13,181kg **Performance** maximum speed: 90km/hr
(typical available specification for the truck illustrated)

Maker: Oy Sisu Auto AB, Helsinki (factory at Karjaa)

Sisu's SL/SR range of bonnetted trucks is a wide one, including 4 × 2, 4 × 4, 6 × 2, 6 × 4, 8 × 2, and 8 × 4 chassis. All share the same cab, which is one of the very few tilting bonnetted cabs in the world. The 4 × 4 SL150 and 170VK are available in three wheelbases, all using the Finnish-built Valmet 611 engine. They are often used with snowplough equipment. Sisu has three main divisions with separate plants: trucks at Karjaa, terminal tractors at Helsinki and defense equipment at Hameenlinna.

Engine Valmet 611 DSA 6-cylinder turbocharged diesel 6,510cc 215bhp (157kW) **Transmission** Clutch: single dry plate; Gearbox: ZF S6-90 6F 1R synchromesh; Transfer Box ZF8043 single speed; Front Axle: Sisu DEA double reduction; Rear Axle: Sisu CTR double reduction **Frame** channel section ladder type **Brakes** dual circuit fully air-operated **Dimensions** wheelbase: 4,600 to 5,400mm; overall length: 7,080 to 8,280mm; overall width: 2,500mm; height to top of cab: 2,975mm; gross weight: 20,000kg; load capacity: 13,000kg **Performance** maximum speed: 88 to 94km/hr, according to axle ratio

Maker: Steyr-Daimler-Puch AG, Steyr

The old-established Steyr concern, originally armaments manufacturers, have built trucks since 1922, and are now Austria's leading commercial vehicle makers, with annual production of around 6,000 vehicles, and making up 35% of the heavy trucks on Austrian roads. The Plus range, with its distinctive wedge-shaped tilt cab, was introduced in 1968 and continues today. Eight different models of 4 × 4 are made, with engines varying from 170 to 330bhp, and there are also two 6 × 6 models with 260 or 330bhp engines. The standard bodies are tipper, with or without self-loading crane, tractor or concrete mixer, but various special bodywork can be supplied. Transmissions are a choice of ZF 8-speed or Fuller 12-speed gearboxes, with Steyr 2-speed transfer box. Three axle ratios are available.

Engine Steyr WD815.77 turbocharged 8-cylinder diesel 11,970cc 330bhp (240kW) **Transmission** Clutch: single dry plate; Gearbox: ZF 8F 1R or Fuller 12F 2R; Transfer Box: Steyr VG1200 dual ratio; Front axle: double reduction spiral bevel and planetary; Rear Axle: double reduction spiral bevel and planetary **Frame** channel section ladder type **Brakes** dual circuit fully air-operated with ALB (automatic load dependent braking force regulator) **Dimensions** wheelbase: 3,800mm; overall length: 6,276mm; overall width: 2,428mm; height to top of cab: 3,121mm; gross weight: 19,000kg; load capacity: 7,000kg **Performance** maximum speed: 76km/hr

Maker: Tata Engineering & Locomotive Co Ltd, Bombay

TELCO, Tata Engineering & Locomotive Company Ltd. is India's largest producer of heavy-duty commercial vehicles. In September 1945 Tata started manufacturing locomotives, their main product at that time. In 1954 the auto division embarked in technical and financial collaboration with Daimler Benz AG., West Germany. Up to 1969, Tata-Mercedes trucks have been made with an initial capacity of 3,000 vehicles in 1954. The collaboration with Daimler Benz ended in 1969 and since that date trucks have featured the Tata name only. Both normal-control and forward-control 4 × 2 and 4 × 4 trucks and 4 × 2 tractors are offered, in addition to a range of buses. More than half a million Tata vehicles are on the roads of India and in 57 other countries. Seventy per cent of all the trucks on Indian roads are Tata made.

Engine 6-cylinder diesel 4,788cc 112bhp (83kW) **Transmission** Clutch: single dry plate; Gearbox: GBS40 synchromesh 5F 1R; Transfer Box: 2 speed; Front Axle: FA104 single reduction spiral bevel; Rear Axle: single reduction hypoid **Frame** channel section ladder type **Brakes** air/hydraulic **Dimensions** wheelbase: 3,625mm; overall length: 6,100mm; overall width: 2,300mm; height to top of cab: 2,635mm; gross weight: 12,180kg; load capacity: 8,350kg **Performance** maximum speed: 72km/hr

Maker: Tatra NP, Koprivnice

Tatra is one of the oldest vehicle makers in Europe, as their ancestors, the Nesselsdorfer Wagenbau Fabriks Gessellschaft built their first truck (still preserved by the factory) in 1898. The name Tatra was adopted in 1919, when the town of Nesselsdorf became Koprovnice as a result of the independence of Czechoslovakia from the Austrian Empire. The Tatras are a celebrated range of mountains in the district. The current 815 range was introduced in 1983, and consists of 4 × 4, 6 × 6 and 8 × 8 trucks and tractors, all using the same V-8, V-10 or V-12 engines, and sharing a common cab. The 4 × 4 tipper illustrated is the shortest model in the range, but because of the heavy working conditions in which it is likely to be used, it has the most powerful available engine, the 315bhp V-12. With a drawbar trailer it can have a GCW of 38 tonnes.

Engine Tatra 3-390 V-12 air-cooled diesel 18,990cc 315bhp (235kW) **Transmission** Clutch: single dry plate; Gearbox: 5F 1R synchromesh; Transfer Box: 2 speed; Front Axle: single reduction spiral bevel; Rear Axle: single reduction spiral bevel **Frame** tubular backbone **Brakes** dual circuit fully air-operated **Dimensions** wheelbase: 3,700mm; overall length: 6,835mm; overall width: 2,500mm; height to top of cab: 2,900mm; gross weight: 16,000kg; load capacity: 6,785kg **Performance** maximum speed: 75 to 95km/hr

Maker: Terberg Benschop BV, Benschop

One of two 4 × 4 trucks made by Terberg, the F1150 is closely based on the Volvo F7 using the same cab, TD60 engine, clutch and gearbox. In appearance it is only distinguishable from the Volvo by its badging and higher ground clearance. A 12-speed ZF splitter gearbox is offered as an alternative to the standard 6-speed unit, and the axles are of Terberg design rather than Volvo. The F 1150 has a GVW of 16 tonnes, but a 19-ton 4 × 4 tipper chassis was introduced at the 1982 Amsterdam Truck Show. This is powered by the Volvo TD70 engine.

Engine Volvo TD60C 6-cylinder turbocharged diesel 5,480cc 154bhp (113kW) **Transmission** Clutch: Volvo single dry plate; Gearbox: ZF S6-65 6F 1R all-synchromesh; Transfer Box: Terberg VG-450 2 speed; Front Axle: Terberg TER-508 double reduction; Rear Axle: Terberg TER-1208 double reduction **Frame** channel section ladder type **Brakes** dual circuit fully air-operated **Dimensions** wheelbase: 3,500mm; overall length: 6,020mm; overall width: 2,500mm; height to top of cab: 2,780mm; gross weight: 16,000kg; load capacity: 10,600kg **Performance** maximum speed: 90km/hr

Maker: Terra Flex Ltd, Calgary, Alberta

Terra Flex has been designing and producing their vehicles for more than thirty years now. Their headquarters are in Calgary, Alberta and many of their tracked and wheeled vehicles find their way to customers working in the gas and oil exploration industry in that part of Canada. Beside a range of about ten basic types of tracked vehicles, Terra Flex manufactures two types of wheeled vehicles as well. Their smallest, the TF100TT, is a 12.2-ton central-articulated all-terrain truck. The TF300TT has a payload capacity of 1.35 tons with a gross weight of 26 tons. Terra Flex is a division of Bombardier Inc, one of the world's largest producers of light snow and tracked vehicles.

Engine Detroit Diesel 4-53 4-cylinder diesel 2,120cc 136bhp (101kW) **Transmission** Clutch: single dry plate; Gearbox: Clark 28,000 series 4F 1R powershift; Front Axle; Clark single reduction; Rear Axle: Clark single reduction **Frame** box section **Brakes** fully air-operated **Dimensions** wheelbase: 3,462mm; overall length: 6,760mm; overall width: 3,330mm; height to top of cab: 3,000mm; gross weight: 12,247kg; load capacity: 4,536kg **Performance** maximum speed: 47.3km/hr

Maker: S.A.R.L. Thomas Constructeurs, Portes les Valence

S.A.R.L. Thomas Constructeurs is a French manufacturer constructing four-wheel drive trucks and special vehicles. Their special vehicles are the Minicrabe, Super Hydrocrabe and Alpicrabe 280, all tool carriers some even available with four-wheel steer system. These vehicles often feature a German-made Schmidt snow-plough or snow-blower. Trucks are the Alpiroute 310, the Miniroute 190 and the bonneted TH1700. All use Renault engines, front and rear axles as well as Renault cabs. Thomas Trucks are used for fire fighting applications and are fitted with a French-made Camiva body.

Engine Renault MIDR 06.02.12, 6-cylinder turbocharged diesel 5,491cc 172bhp (127kW) **Transmission** Clutch: single dry plate; Gearbox: 8F 1R synchromesh; Transfer Box: two speed; Front Axle: 3MRDIF single reduction; Rear Axle: 3MRF single reduction **Frame** channel section ladder type **Brakes** dual circuit fully air-operated **Dimensions** wheelbase: 3,000mm; overall length: 4,915mm; overall width: 2,490mm; height to top of cab: 2,800mm; gross weight: 11,000kg; load capacity: 5,000kg **Performance** maximum speed: 81.35km/hr

Maker: UROVESA, Santiago de Compostela

UROVESA, URO Vehiculos Especiales S.A., is the youngest Spanish factory which entered its home truck-market recently. Like T.M.U. in Bilbao and I.P.V. in Lugo, Urovesa specialised in the design and manufacture of all-wheel drive trucks, to satisfy the increased demand for this type of vehicle in Spain. Although the factory has been operational for only a couple of years now, Urovesa is offering their customers four different types, namely the U12.08, U12.13, U14.09 and U14.10. All of these are deliverable with four different wheelbases, from 2,600mm up to 4,000mm. Uro trucks serve customers in transport, forestry, building and construction industries, as well as being used for fire fighting and emergency tasks.

Engine Perkins 6.354 6-cylinder diesel 5,800cc 115bhp (87kW) **Transmission** Clutch: single dry plate; Gearbox: Clark 285V, 5F 1R; Transfer Box: URT-1, two speed; Front Axle: single reduction, disengagable drive; Rear Axle: single reduction **Frame** channel section ladder type **Brakes** dual circuit fully air-operated **Dimensions** wheelbase: 2,800mm; overall length: 4,915mm; overall width: 1,985mm; height to top of cab: 2,550mm; gross weight: 11,900kg; load capacity: 6,000kg **Performance** maximum speed: 96km/hr

Maker: The Zeligson Co, Tulsa, Oklahoma

Zeligson has been custom retrofitting all-wheel drive ex-army trucks since 1946. The firm's customers can be found in many transportation sectors like pipeline projects, geophysical exploration, logging, mining, construction or utility. All their trucks are hand made to meet customers' requirements. Zeligson offers their vehicles with Continental engines but Cummins, Caterpillar or Detroit Diesel engines are also available for fitment. Fuller or Allison transmissions, Spicer or Rockwell transfer cases and Rockwell axles are used. Normal-control cabs are featured on the M and Z series. Forward-control cabs are used as well, like a one-man cab and a 4-men low-profile cab. Recently, the firm started installing fibreglass tilt hoods. Zeligson manufactures vehicles with 4 × 4, 6 × 6 and 8 × 8 drive layouts.

Engine Continental R6602, petrol 196bhp (146.2kW) **Transmission** Clutch: single dry plate; Gearbox: Spicer 6352, 5F 1R synchromesh; Transfer Box: Rockwell T138, two speed; Front Axle: Rockwell FM240H double reduction; Rear Axle: M240HX double reduction **Frame** channel section ladder type **Brakes** dual circuit fully air-operated **Dimensions** load capacity: 5,000kg

Three Axle Trucks, 6 × 2, 6 × 4, 6 × 6

Up to the end of the First World War practically all trucks carried their loads on two axles, but the idea of using three or four axles to support a longer chassis and therefore obtain a bigger payload was considered quite early on. Foden produced designs for a 6-wheeled steam wagon in 1903, and two years later Victor Janvier built a twin-steer 6-wheeler in Paris. It had double chain drive to the rear wheels and a claimed load capacity of seven tons, which seems optimistic. Little was heard of it, but the twin-steer 6-wheeler, or 'Chinese six' as it was nicknamed, became popular in Britain in the 1930s, and is still made by two companies in Spain.

In 1920 the Goodyear Rubber Company made some experimental 6- and 8-wheeled trucks and buses in order to test their large pneumatic tyres, and a few years later the American manufacturers White and Six-Wheel had 6 × 2 trucks on the market. Foden announced a 6 × 2 steam wagon for 1927, and later that year another British steam lorry maker, Sentinel, brought out their DG6 on which the rear axles were coupled by chains, making it the first production 6 × 4. This layout was soon adopted by many truck makers, though in place of the chain coupling most used tandem bevel or worm drive. 6 × 2s were made as well, and the choice between the two depended on the type of work to be done and the terrain. A 6 × 2 is lighter and cheaper but for heavy loads such as

sand and gravel, and on rough ground or hilly country the additional traction afforded by 6 × 4 outweighs its drawbacks. On most 6 × 2s the third axle is unpowered, serving simply to support the load, and a number of these can be lifted when the truck is running empty, which saves fuel and tyre wear.

The maximum GVW for a three-axle truck in Britain is 24 tonnes, but in Spain it is 28.5 tonnes for a 6 × 4 with twin tyres on both rear axles, or 27 tonnes for the popular twin-steer Chinese sixes with only one twin-tyre axle. Axle spread is an important factor in some states of the USA, which is why a number of companies such as International make 'forward axle' models for those states which impose a minimum distance between front and the leading rear axle, for a given weight.

The 6 × 6 with all three axles driven, like the 4 × 4, was developed in response to military needs. During the 1930s the US Army ordered a number of 6-wheel-drive trucks, mainly from the smaller manufacturers such as Biederman and Corbitt, and during the Second World War the type was made in considerable numbers for load-carrying and artillery tractor work, in particular by Mack. Over the past ten years the 6 × 6 has become popular for certain civilian tasks, particularly in civil engineering where heavy loads of earth, sand or gravel have to be carried. As the demand for such trucks is not

very great they are often made by the smaller specialist manufacturers like Ginaf and Terberg. Alternatively, there are firms specialising in the conversion of 6 × 4 trucks to all-wheel-drive.

A Sentinel DG6 of 1930 with both rear axles driven, linked by chains.

Maker: Carelli SpA, Modena

Carelli specialize in low loading trucks for the transportation of machinery, building equipment, bulldozers and boats. Originally Fiat-powered, they now use Mercedes-Benz engines. As well as the 6 × 2 illustrated, Cambs are made in 8 × 4 and 10 × 4 forms, with half cabs as well as full width cabs. Like many Italian trucks they have right hand drive to assist the driver on narrow mountain roads.

Engine Mercedes-Benz OM410 6-cylinder diesel 9,570cc 192bhp (143kW) **Transmission** Clutch: ZF torque converter; Gearbox: Clark 4F 1R or ZF 6F 1R automatic; Rear Axle: single reduction hypoid **Frame** channel section ladder type **Brakes** dual circuit fully air-operated **Dimensions** wheelbase: 4,525mm; overall length: 9,240mm; overall width: 2,880mm; height to top of cab: 2,560mm; gross weight: 24,000kg; load capacity: 15,650kg **Performance** maximum speed: 67.6km/hr

Maker: Ginaf Automobielbedrijven BV, Veenendaal

This unusual vehicle has been developed by Ginaf using DAF components to provide a freighter for up to five cargo pallets for wide-bodied aircraft. Total space inside the van and trailer is 120m³. The truck is based on a DAF DKTL bus chassis with mid-mounted underfloor engine and a third axle ahead of the driving axle. The cab is from the current 2800 series and incorporates a roof-top sleeper. The close-coupled two-axle trailer is similar to those used with regular DAF vans.

Engine DAF 1160 6-cylinder diesel 11,630cc 194bhp (143kW) **Transmission** Clutch: torque converter; Gearbox: GB 340 5F 1R automatic; Rear Axle: single reduction hypoid **Frame** channel section ladder type **Brakes** dual circuit fully air-operated **Dimensions** wheelbase: 5,300mm; overall length: 11,000mm; overall width: 2,440mm; gross weight: (truck) 24,200kg; (truck + trailer) 36,200kg **Performance** maximum speed: 90km/hr

Maker: Hollming Oy, Suorama

Originally known as the Kestotankki, this unusual design is the work of Reijo Hirvonen, a designer of racing cars and a specialist in monocoque structures. The tanker body is self-supporting, and there is no conventional chassis frame, the cab and wheels being attached directly to the 18,000-litre tank. A choice of engines is offered, Volvo 235 to 275bhp, or MAN 280 to 320bhp for hillier operating conditions. With the former a Volvo 16-speed transmission is used, with the latter a ZF Ecosplit 16 speeder. The cab is a Volvo F7, non-tilting as the engine is mounted horizontally and well back, under the front part of the tank. The manufacturers, Hollming Oy, are a well-known shipbuilding and general engineering group who also make frameless drawbar trailers to be used in conjunction with the tanker. Total capacity of tanker and trailer is about 37,500 litres, or about 20% more than for a conventional vehicle of the same weight.

Engine Volvo THD 100DE 6-cylinder turbocharged diesel 9,600cc 284bhp (212kW) *or* MAN D2566 MKUL 6-cylinder turbocharged diesel 11,410cc 315bhp (235kW) **Transmission** Clutch: Fichtel & Sachs twin dry plate; Gearbox: Volvo SR 62 16F 2R constant mesh *or* ZF 16-S-130 16F 1R synchromesh; Rear Axle: Volvo EV 85B single reduction hypoid **Frame** self-supporting monocoque tank **Brakes** dual circuit fully air-operated **Dimensions** wheelbase: 5,650mm; overall length: 9,700mm; overall width: 2,480mm; height to top of cab: 2,388mm; gross weight: 23,500kg; load capacity: 15,500kg **Performance** maximum speed: 100km/hr

Maker: Maschinenfabrik Augsburg-Nürnberg AG, Munich

This is one of M.A.N.'s range of forward-control trucks made in 4-, 6- and 8-wheeled form, and also as tractors. There is a companion range of 4- and 6-wheelers up to 22 tonnes with underfloor engines, a design inherited from Bussing which M.A.N. acquired in 1971. The somewhat complex designation of this model indicates its specification as follows: 22 (tonnes GVW) 281bhp, F = forward control, N = trailing axle, L = air suspension, BL = leaf suspension (alternative). With the drawbar trailer illustrated the total permissible GCW is 38 tonnes. It is powered by a turbocharged 281bhp engine, and there is a similar looking model 22.321 with 321bhp engine. Day or sleeper cabs are available on most of these models.

Engine M.A.N. D2566 MKF/280 6-cylinder turbocharged diesel 11,413cc 281bhp (206kW)
Transmission Clutch: twin dry plate; Gearbox: ZF K-130 16F 2R constant mesh; Rear Axle: M.A.N. double reduction **Frame** channel section ladder type **Brakes** dual circuit fully air-operated
Dimensions wheelbase: 5,275mm; overall length: 9,840mm; overall width: 2,500mm; height to top of cab: 2,906mm; gross weight: 22,000kg; load capacity: 13,090kg **Performance** maximum speed: 93 to 119km/hr, according to axle ratio

Maker: Daimler-Benz AG, Stuttgart

This 6 × 2 chassis is part of a wide range of Mercedes-Benz 6-wheelers, made in single- and dual-axle drive form, and powered either by the 14,620 V-8 or 18,270cc V-10 engines. The 6 × 2 layout is suitable for local or long-distance haulage, and has the advantage that when the vehicle is running unladen the trailing axle can be lifted in the interests of reduced tyre wear and better fuel economy. A choice of four different wheelbases and four cabs is offered, and with a two-axle drawbar trailer a maximum GCW of 38 tonnes is possible. As well as general haulage, these 6 × 2 Mercedes-Benz are popular for tanker work, with or without drawbar trailer.

Engine Mercedes-Benz OM422 V-8 diesel 14,620cc 280bhp (206kW) **Transmission** Clutch: single dry plate; Gearbox: ZF 5F 1R all synchromesh; Rear Axle: single reduction spiral bevel **Frame** channel section ladder type **Brakes** dual circuit fully air-operated **Dimensions** wheelbase: 5,450mm; overall length: 9,075mm; overall width: 2,500mm; height to top of cab: 2,910mm; gross weight: 22,000kg; load capacity: 13,535kg **Performance** maximum speed: 112km/hr

Maker: Saab-Scania AB, Sodertalje

The R 142 M designation of this Scania indicates that it has the largest engine in the range, a 14-litre V-8, that is is intended for medium duty work (M), and that it has the R cab for long-distance travelling. Despite its engine size it has only two driven axles, which would point towards the carriage of bulky rather than very heavy loads. The long, three-axle drawbar trailer is typical of Swedish practice which allows the total length of a combination such as this to be up to 24 metres. The 6 × 2 layout is also available in the R 112 M, R 112 H, and R 142 H chassis, and there are also 6 × 4 versions of all these.

Engine Scania DS 14 V-8 turbocharged diesel 14,200cc 388bhp (285kW) *or* Scania DSC 14 01 V-8 turbocharged and intercooled diesel 14,200cc 420bhp (309kW) **Transmission** Clutch: dual dry plate; Gearbox: Scania GR 870 1 0F 1R synchromesh on 9 upper ratios; Rear Axle: single reduction spiral bevel *or* hypoid **Frame** channel section ladder type **Brakes** dual circuit fully air-operated **Dimensions** wheelbase: 5,915mm; overall length: 8,600mm; overall width: 2,300mm; height to top of cab: 2,570mm; gross weight: 23,000kg; load capacity: 15,900kg **Performance** maximum speed: 102km/hr

Maker: Autocar Trucks Division of White Motor Corporation, Greensboro, North Carolina (factory at Ogden, Utah)

Autocar is one of the oldest names in the American industry, having built their first car in 1897 and their first truck ten years later. Since 1953 they have been owned by White, and in recent years have concentrated on heavy-duty 6 × 4 or 6 × 6 chassis mainly for the construction industry. The DC series illustrated has a steel cab and bonnet, while the more stylish Construktor series uses fibreglass for these components. Autocars are largely custom built, and there are no standard specifications. Engines are all diesels, by Caterpillar, Cummins or Detroit, from 230 to 450bhp, normally aspirated or turbocharged, transmissions can be provided from all the main makers, four, five or six speed main gearboxes and three or four speed auxiliary boxes. Wheelbases run from 3,708 to 6,985 mm. While most Autocars are rigid 6-wheelers, some 4-wheelers are made, and both 4- and 6-wheelers are used as tractors for very heavy low-loading trailers. The Canadian plant makes a twin-steer rigid 8-wheel chassis.

Engine Caterpillar 3406 6-cylinder turbocharged diesel 14,600cc 325bhp (242.5kW) **Transmission** Clutch: twin dry plate; Gearbox: Fuller 6F 1R main, with 3 speed auxiliary; Rear Axles: Rockwell SSHP single reduction hypoid **Frame** channel section double plate ladder type **Brakes** dual circuit fully air-operated **Dimensions** wheelbase: variable; overall length: variable; overall width: 2,641mm; height to top of cab: 2,845mm; gross weight: 32,000kg; load capacity: 24,000kg **Performance** maximum speed: 75km/hr

Makers: Vauxhall Motors Ltd, Luton, Bedfordshire

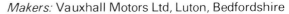

There are two 6 × 4s in Bedford's TM range. The long wheelbase (6,120mm) models are intended for general haulage work, while the 5,490mm chassis are suitable for heavy work such as the tipper illustrated. All TM 6-wheelers are designed for 26,000kg GVW, or 38,000kg GTW if a drawbar trailer is used. The regular, or narrow, cab is standardised, but the full width version is available as an option, as it is on the four-wheelers. Engines are the 8.2-litre Bedford Blue Series diesel, in normally-aspirated (154bhp) or turbo-charged (211bhp) forms. Standard transmission with the former engine is a Turner 6-speed gearbox with overdrive top, though an Eaton box is an alternative. The turbo-charged engines are used in conjuction with a ZF all-synchromesh 6-speed direct top gearbox.

Engine Bedford 8.2/150D Blue Series 6-cylinder diesel 8,198cc 154bhp (113.7kW) **Transmission** Clutch: single dry plate (twin plates with turbocharged engine); Gearbox: Turner 6F 1R synchromesh on upper five ratios; Rear Axles: Eaton single reduction spiral bevel **Frame** channel section ladder type **Brakes** dual circuit fully air-operated **Dimensions** wheelbase: 5,490mm; overall length: 8,184mm; overall width: 2,480mm; height to top of cab: 2,925mm; gross weight: 26,000kg; load capacity: 17,862kg **Performance** maximum speed: 100km/hr

Maker: Osterlund Inc, Harrisburg, Pennsylvania

Diamond Reo combines the names of two old-established truck makers, Diamond T and Reo, who were acquired by White and made under the name Diamond Reo until 1975. The name was then acquired by a former dealer, Loyal Osterlund, who revived production two years later at his own plant at Harrisburg. The Giant is made in four- and six-wheeled form, as a load-carrying truck or a tractor, and as with many American trucks, an additional tag axle can be fitted to the six-wheelers to make a four-axle rigid. The standard engine for all models is a 300bhp Cummins NTC 300, but alternative Cummins units of greater or less horsepower can be Fitted. One model, the C11664DD, uses an air cooled Deutz 320bhp diesel engine. Fuller tranmission is standard, while the rear axles are by Rockwell assembled to a Hendrickson spring tandem. The 6 × 4 Giant is particularly popular in the construction industry for concrete mixer and block carrier-work, and can also be used in conjunction with a medium-sized hydraulic crane, as well as for many kinds of general haulage work. In addition to the 6 × 4s, Diamond-Reo make one 6 × 6 chassis.

Engine Cummins NTC 300 6-cylinder diesel 13,948cc 300bhp (224kW) **Transmission** Clutch: Dana Spicer twin dry plate; Gearbox: Fuller RTOF 1160 8LL 10F 1R constant mesh; Rear Axles: Rockwell Standard SUHD single reduction hypoid tandem **Frame** channel section ladder type **Brakes** Rockwell dual circuit fully air-operated **Dimensions** wheelbase: 6,706mm; overall length: 8,585mm; overall width: 2,490mm; height to top of cab: 2,743mm; gross weight: 29,440kg; load capacity: 21,252kg **Performance** maximum speed: 92km/hr

Maker: Diesel Nacional SA, Monterrey

Like the other products of Diesel Nacional, the 6-wheeled Dinas are closely based on International designs. This link was strengthened in 1981 by the signing of a ten-year technical assistance and supply agreement between the two companies, by which International Harvester would provide a manufacturing licence, technical expertise and some specific components such as cab stampings to enable Diesel Nacional to manufacture several models of medium- and heavy-duty trucks including the Transtar. There are two models of Dina rigid 6-wheeler, the 661 G2 illustrated, and the larger 661 G3/3 which is powered by a 14-litre Cummins engine and has a 14-speed gearbox.

Engine Cummins V-8 diesel 8,200cc 202bhp (150.7kW) **Transmission** Clutch: single dry plate; Gearbox: 5F 1R; Rear Axles: single reduction tandem **Frame** channel section ladder type **Brakes** dual circuit fully air-operated **Dimensions** wheelbase: 5,436mm; overall length: 8,585mm; overall width: 2,490mm; height to top of cab: 2,090mm; gross weight: 20,865kg; load capacity: 14,696kg **Performance** maximum speed: 100km/hr

Maker: Chrysler Kamyon Imalatcilari AS, Cayirova-Gebze.

Chrysler set up their Turkish operation in 1964, making the D series of American Dodge trucks with angular cabs and bonnets which were simple to manufacture and repair. The same basic shape is still in production today, models including a 4×4 in station wagon or pick-up form, the 1.6-ton PD 250, 2.7-ton PD 350 and 8.5-ton PD 600AS, the last made in 4 × 2 or 6 × 4 versions. All use Perkins engines and Eaton or Spicer rear axles. In certain export markets these trucks carry the names De Soto or Fargo rather than Dodge.

Engine Perkins 6.354 6-cylinder diesel 5,800cc 128bhp (95.5kW) **Transmission** Clutch: Borg & Beck single dry plate; Gearbox: HEMA 5F 1R synchromesh; Rear Axles: Eaton 17220 2-speed hypoid tandem **Frame** channel section ladder type **Brakes** Rockwell hydraulic **Dimensions** wheelbase: 6,190mm; overall length: 9,158mm; overall width: 2,384mm; height to top of cab: 2,271mm; gross weight: 19,490kg; load capacity: 14,470kg **Performance** maximum speed 90km/hr

Maker: No 2 Automobile Works, Shiyan city, Hubei province

The EQ 155 is the 6-wheeled version of the EQ 140, it uses an updated engine, but cab, bonnet and wheels are identical to the 4-wheel version. The Dongfeng truck is made in a wide range of tailor-made versions including coach, semi-trailer, cattle truck, fire truck, environment-orientated vehicle and many other kinds of purpose-made vehicles.

Engine Dongfeng EQ6105 6-cylinder petrol 5,720cc 165bhp (121.3kW) **Transmission** Clutch: single dry plate; Gearbox: 5F 1R; Rear Axle: single reduction spiral bevel **Frame** channel section ladder type **Brakes** fully air-operated **Dimensions** wheelbase: c.6,000mm; overall length: 8,160mm; overall width: 2,470mm; height to top of cab: 2,396mm; gross weight: 13,908kg; load capacity: 8,000kg **Performance** maximum speed: 82km/hr

Maker: E.R.F. Ltd, Sandbach, Cheshire

The C Series is the senior line of E.R.F. and is made in rigid 3- and 4-axle models and also as a tractor (CP). The current SP cab was introduced in 1974, and is unique in being totally panelled in hot-pressed S.M.C. (sheet moulding compound), a fibreglass material which is used in conjunction with a welded steel frame, giving great strength and lightness as well as ease of panel replacement. The standard engine is the Cummins L10-250, and 9- or 10-speed gearboxes are offered, by Fuller and Spicer respectively. With the four wheeled trailer shown, the C36 has a GTW of 38 tonnes.

Engine Cummins L10-250 6-cylinder turbocharged diesel 10,000cc 243bhp (181.6kW) **Transmission** Clutch: twin dry plate; Gearbox: Fuller RTX 7609 9F 1R *or* Spicer SST8010 10F 1R synchromesh on all speeds except bottom and reverse; Rear Axles: fully floating single reduction tandem **Frame** channel section ladder type **Brakes** dual circuit fully air-operated **Dimensions** wheelbase: 5,386mm; overall length: 8,671mm; overall width: 2,495mm; height to top of cab: 2,782mm; gross weight: 24,390kg; load capacity: 18,000kg **Performance** maximum speed: 108km/hr

Maker: FAP Famos, Priboj

Like the four-wheeled FAP models, the 2626 uses a Mercedes-Benz design of cab in conjunction with a diesel engine built by the associated company, Famos, or a Mercedes-Benz diesel. Only one wheelbase is offered, but it can be used for general haulage as well as tipper work. GVW is 26,000kg, but in conjunction with a drawbar trailer, this can go up to 38,000kg. When the truck is operating on its own, and using the lowest of three rear axle ratios, it can climb a gradient of 39.5% in bottom gear.

Engine Famos 2FP 125B 6-cylinder diesel 11,040cc 256bhp (191kW) *or* Mercedes-Benz OM402 V-8 diesel 12,760cc 252bhp (188kW) **Transmission** Clutch: twin dry plate; Gearbox: 6F 1R all-synchromesh; Rear Axle: fully floating single reduction tandem **Frame** channel section ladder type **Brakes** dual circuit fully air-operated **Dimensions** wheelbase: 4,425mm; overall length: 7,185mm; overall width: 2,480mm; height to top of cab: 3,255mm; gross weight: 26,000kg; load capacity: 15,850kg **Performance** maximum speed: 62.5 to 77.1km/hr, according to axle ratio

Maker: Floor's Handel en Industrie BV, Wijchen

Floor's were originally a haulage firm who turned to the manufacture of trailers, followed by the importation and assembly of Mack trucks. In 1966 they turned out their first F.T.F. truck which used many Mack components, but now they use a variety of components including Detroit Diesel engines, Allison or Fuller Roadranger transmissions, and Motor Panels cabs. Both rigid chassis and tractors are made, the former in 6 × 2, 6 × 4, 6 × 6, 8 × 4, 8 × 8 and even 10 × 4, a most unusual axle layout. The 6-wheeler illustrated is intended for on/off highway use, particularly for hauling sand and gravel, and there is also an oilfield version.

Engine Detroit Diesel 6V-92T V-6 turbocharged diesel 9,050cc 324bhp (238kW) **Transmission** Clutch: torque converter; Gearbox: Allison HT750 DRD 5F 1R, automatic on upper four ratios; Rear Axles: double reduction tandem **Frame** channel section ladder type **Brakes** dual circuit fully air-operated **Dimensions** wheelbase: 5,512mm; overall length: 8,965mm; overall width: 2,900mm; height to top of cab: 3,200mm; gross weight: 50,000kg; load capacity: 33,000kg **Performance** maximum speed: 80km/hr

Maker: Sichuan Automobile Factory, Dazu city, Sichuan province

In 1983 the Sichuan Automobile Factory (situated near Chongqing) developed a heavy 18-ton truck, clearly under Roman-- influences. They even used the MAN-designation, the usual chinese designation should be Hongyan CQ 160 or 170. The name Hongyan means Red Rock, the place in Chongqing where the Communist 8th Route Army maintained their liaison office during the Sino-Japanese war. The Sichuan factory belongs to the Heavy Truck Corporation.

Engine Cummins NTC-290 6-cylinder diesel 290bhp (216kW) **Transmission** Clutch: single dry plate; Gearbox: 9F 1R; Rear Axle: double reduction tandem **Frame** channel section ladder type **Brakes** dual circuit, air assisted hydraulic **Dimensions** wheelbase: 5,200mm; overall length: 9,300mm; overall width: 2,500mm; height to top of cab: 3,064mm; gross weight: 30,000kg; load capacity: 18,000kg **Performance** maximum speed: 74km/hr

Maker: International Harvester Co, Chicago, Illinois (factory at Chatham, Ontario)

The Paystar is International's premium truck for heavy on/off highway applications. It is perhaps most widely used in the construction industry, but various special models are also used in oilfields for exploration, drilling and well servicing. The Weightwatcher is especially designed for ready-mix concrete work in western states, and has a set-forward front axle to conform to California bridge formula laws. It weighs about 920kg less than the regular Paystar, thanks to a special frame and aluminium cab. The standard engine on this model is a 270hp Detroit Diesel, with Fuller seven- or eight-speed transmissions. Paystars are made in International's Canadian plant at Chatham, Ontario, but all cabs come from the Spring-Ohio, body plant.

Engine Detroit Diesel 6V92TTA 6-cylinder turbocharged diesel 9,053cc 270bhp (201kW) **Transmission** Clutch: twin dry plate; Gearbox: Fuller RTO-1157 7 *or* 8F 1R constant mesh; Rear Axles: International single reduction tandem hypoid **Frame** channel section ladder type **Brakes** dual circuit fully air-operated **Dimensions** wheelbase: 5,842mm; overall length: 7,315mm; overall width: 2,440mm; height to top of cab: 2,750mm; gross weight: 25,500kg; load capacity: 18,000kg **Performance** maximum speed: 95km/hr

Maker: International Harvester Australia Ltd, Dandendong, Victoria

The ACCO C range of Australian Internationals is made in two six-wheeler models, a 6 × 2 and a 6 × 4. Engines are Cummins VT-190 turbocharged diesel V-8. Transmissions are 5- or 13-speed six or Cummins VT-190 turbocharged diesel V-8. Transmissions are 10- or 13-speed Fuller Roadranger constant mesh twin countershaft units. The truck illustrated has a Heuch refrigeration unit, and is used for wholesale delivery of food products to supermarkets. The radiator is protected by a 'roo bar', a very useful device in Australia where collisions with kangaroos and other wild animals are a frequent hazard.

Engine Cummins VT-190 V-8 turbocharged diesel 8,260cc 190bhp (142kW) **Transmission** Clutch: single dry plate; Gearbox: Fuller RT-613 13F 1R constant mesh *or* Fuller MT 653 5F 1R automatic constant mesh; Rear Axle: Rockwell single reduction tandem **Frame** channel section ladder type **Brakes** dual circuit fully air-operated **Dimensions** wheelbase: 4,540 or 5,350mm; overall length: 7,510 or 8,630mm; overall width: 2,438mm; height to top of cab: 2,700mm; gross weight: 21,160kg; load capacity: 14,500kg

Maker: Shanghai Heavy Motor Vehicle Factory, Shanghai

The Jiaotong (Communication) 15-ton truck has been made in small quantities since 1969. Production in 1980 was only 274 units. Several variants are made including the SH 361 tipper with 10 or 13 cu. metre capacity, and the SH 161-4 long-wheelbase truck. The chassis is also used for carrying crane, street sprinkler or fire engine body-work, and as a tractor for semi-trailers. One of the most impressive versions is the SXJ 50 oilfield rig made by the Shanghai No.1 Petroleum Machinery factory. In 1981 the factory introduced a new 18-ton chassis with half cab.

Engine Shanghai 6135Q-2 6-cylinder diesel 12,000cc 220bhp (164kW) or Hangchai 6130Q 6-cylinder diesel 11,150cc 210bhp (156.66kW) **Transmission** Clutch: twin dry plate; Gearbox: 6F 1R; Rear Axle: double reduction **Frame** channel section ladder type **Brakes** triple circuit fully air-operated **Dimensions** wheelbase: 5,800mm; overall length: 8,300mm; overall width: 2,600mm; height to top of cab: 2,970mm; gross weight: 26,000kg; load capacity: 15,000kg **Performance** maximum speed: 65km/hr

Maker: Kama Auto Zavod, Brezhnev

Introduced in 1976, the KamAZ range consisted of three models, all of 6 × 4 pattern. These were the cargo model illustrated, a tractor and a tipper, within three to four years time joined by sleeper cab versions featuring 500mm longer wheelbase. By 1982 there were 6 × 6 versions available, but instead of 8,000/10,000kg capacity these were capable of hauling only 5,000/7,000kg in off-road conditions. The KamAZ is a modern design, intended to take the Soviet truck industry through the 1980s and eventually to replace many of the existing models. It is made in a new factory at Brezhev, formerly Naberezhnie Chelny until the death of President Brezhnev in November 1982, in an area chosen by computer because it was close to supplies of oil, hydroelectric power, a river and a tyre factory. Planned production is 150,000 trucks per year, and 250,000 of the naturally-aspirated V-8 engines, as these are supplied by the KamAZ factory for use in other trucks such as the Ural-4320, ZIL-133GYa, and LAZ-4202 buses.

Engine KamAZ-740-V-8 diesel 10850cc 210bhp (154kW) **Transmission** Clutch: twin dry plate; Gearbox: 5F 1R with a splitter = 10F; Rear axles: double reduction **Frame** Channel section ladder type **Brakes** air-operated **Dimensions** wheelbase: 4,510mm; overall length: 7,435mm; overall width: 2,500mm; overall height: 2,910mm; gross weight: 15,305kg; load capacity: 8,000kg **Performance** maximum speed: 80km/hr

Maker: Kenworth Truck Co, Seattle, Washington

Kenworth is one of America's leading makers of premium trucks, and is best known for its conventional and cab-over tractors for long-distance hauling. To widen their market they introduced in 1971 a series of low-entry trucks for city work, originally known as the Hustler and later renamed the 700 series. These are made in Kenworth's Canadian plant at Quebec and Mexican plant at Baja California alongside the Peterbilt 310 which is the same design apart from differences in trim and badging. The standard engine is a 270bhp Detroit Diesel 6V92TTA, but other units by Detroit, Caterpillar or Cummins from 210 to 335bhp can be fitted. Like all Kenworths they are very much custom trucks built to purchasers' requirements. For example, the makers do not quote wheelbases but say "You name it, we'll deliver it, in one-inch increments from a super short tractor for pulling extra long trailers to maximum length straight trucks ..."

Engine Detroit Diesel 6V92TTA 6-cylinder turbocharged 2-stroke diesel 9,005cc 270bhp (201.5kW) **Transmission** Clutch: Spicer twin dry plate; Gearbox: Fuller RT910 10F 1R constant mesh; Rear Axle: Rockwell SQ-100 single reduction hypoid tandem; **Frame** channel section ladder type **Brakes** dual circuit fully air-operated **Dimensions** wheelbase: variable; overall length: variable; overall width: 2,340mm; height to top of cab: 2,280mm; gross weight: 23,000kg; load capacity: 15,000kg; **Performance** maximum speed: 95km/hr

Maker: Kenworth Truck Co, Seattle, Washington

Made in 6 × 4 and 6 × 6 versions, the Kenworth C510 is aimed mainly at the construction industry, although they are also used in logging, oilfield work, bulk haulage of sand and ashphalt or as tanker trucks. The standard engine is a Cummins 240hp turbocharged diesel, but Caterpillar and Detroit Diesels in in-line, V-6 and V-8 configurations are also available. Spicer or Fuller manual transmissions or Allison automatics are available, and as with other Kenworth trucks wheelbases are to the customer's request. Maximum GVW is 40,000kg for areas where such a high figure is allowed on only three axles. Heavier models are available, including the C520 and the C540 with engines up to 525bhp and capable of pulling up to 68,000kg. As the catalogue says, 'If your work needs more of a truck, we've got more of a Kenworth.' In 1984, production of the 500 series was transferred to the Foden factory at Sandbach which also belongs to Kenworth's owners, Paccar International Inc.

Engine Cummins L10-240 6-cylinder turbocharged diesel 10,000cc 240bhp (179kW)
Transmission Clutch: Spicer twin dry plate; Gearbox: Fuller RTO 11609B 9F 1R constant mesh;
Rear Axle: Eaton DS44OP single reduction spiral bevel tandem **Frame** channel section ladder
type **Dimensions** wheelbase: variable; overall length: variable; overall width: 2,475mm; height to
top of cab: 2,920mm; gross weight: 23,000 to 40,020kg; load capacity: variable **Performance**
maximum speed: 90km/hr

133

Maker: KMC Motors Ltd, Nicosia

KMC began truck production in 1973 with straight trucks and tractors of Dennis design, powered by Perkins 6.354 diesel engines. More recently they have turned to Dodge and M.A.N. for the basis of their vehicles, and now make a wide range of trucks and tractors in 4 × 2 and 6 × 4 form, as well as buses and trailers, both drawbar and semi-trailers. Engines are Dodge, M.A.N. or Detroit Diesel. Until recently KMC used Spanish Dodge cabs, but now use cabs of M.A.N. origin, as illustrated. KMCs are exported to more than twenty countries in the Middle East and Africa.

Engine M.A.N. D2156 6-cylinder diesel 10,344cc 215bhp (160.4kW) *or* Detroit Diesel 6V-71 6-cylinder diesel 6,900cc 228bhp (170kW) **Transmission** Clutch: single dry plate; Gearbox: ZF AK6-80 6F1R constant mesh *or* Allison MT654R 5F 1R automatic; Rear Axle: double reduction tandem **Frame** channel section ladder type **Brakes** dual circuit fully air-operated **Dimensions** wheelbase: 5,120mm; overall length: 7,335mm; overall width: 2,397mm; height to top of cab: 2,906mm; gross weight: 28,000kg; load capacity: 20,600kg **Performance** maximum speed: 80km/hr

Maker: Kremenchug Avto Zavod, Kremenchug

Introduced in 1965, the KrAZ-257 was updated to the B1 version in 1978, the main improvement being the adoption of a dual circuit braking system. It has a wooden framed cab and a semi-wooden dropside body. There are a number of variations on the basic model, including the 258V1 tractor and tippers designated 256B1 and 256B1S, the latter for Northern climates up to –60° Centigrade. The 256B1 illustrated was sold in Western Europe for a time under the name BelAZ, though in the Soviet Union this name is reserved for the heavy dump trucks. The YaMZ engines fitted to the KrAZ and other Russian trucks are made in the plant at Yaroslavl which formerly made YaZ trucks, the predecessors of the KrAZ. The 257 series has recently been supplemented by the more modern KrAZ-250.

Engine YaMZ-238 V-8 diesel 14860cc 240bhp (176kW) **Transmission** Clutch: twin dry plate ; Gearbox: 5F 1R with additional two speed reductor; Rear axles: double reduction **Frame** channel section ladder type **Brakes** dual-circuits air-operated **Dimensions** wheelbase: 6,450mm; overall length: 9,640mm; overall width: 2,650mm; overall height: 2,670mm; gross weight: 22,500kg; load capacity: 12,000kg **Performance** maximum speed: 68km/hr

Maker: Leyland Vehicles Ltd., Leyland, Lancashire

Leyland's Constructor range is made in 6 × 4 and 8 × 4 versions, the 6 × 4 replacing the Leyland Bison and the 8 × 4 the Scammell Routeman. Both use the T45 cab which was introduced on the Roadtrain tractors, and which has been gradually extended to all the heavy forward-control Leylands. In 1980 this cab, which was styled by Ogle Design Limited and is made by Motor Panels, won a Design Council Award. The cab on the 6-wheeled Constructor is slightly narrower than that on the 8-wheeler, but it has the same shape, panels and controls. The standard power unit for the Constructor 24.21 is the Leyland TL11A 209bhp turbocharged 6-cylinder, but a derated 181bhp TL11D is also available. In addition, for operators who run a fleet powered by proprietary engines and prefer standardisation, the 8-wheeled Constructor can be powered by Rolls-Royce or Gardner engines. Transmissions on the 6-wheelers are Fuller RT609 or Eaton D473.

Engine Leyland TL11A 6-cylinder turbocharged diesel 11,100cc 209bhp (156kW) **Transmission** Clutch: twin dry plate; Gearbox: Fuller RT609 9F 2R constant mesh; Rear Axle: double reduction **Frame** channel section ladder type **Brakes** dual circuit fully air-operated **Dimensions** wheelbase: 5,100mm; overall length: 7,362mm; overall width: 2,393mm; height to top of cab: 2,715mm; gross weight: 24,390kg; load capacity: 17,821kg **Performance** maximum speed: 90km/hr.

Maker: Leyland Vehicles Ltd, Leyland, Lancashire

Landtrain is the name given to the larger models of Leyland's bonnetted export trucks, of which the smaller are known as Landmasters. Landtrains are made in 4 × 2 or 6 × 4 versions, and both can be used as tractors as well as load-carrying trucks. GVWs range from 19 tonnes for the 4-wheeler rigid up to 65 tonnes for the heaviest articulated units. Engines are Cummins diesels of 250 to 290bhp, and six- or nine-speed gearboxes are used. The trucks are designed for long-distance operation over poor road surfaces and territories where refuelling and servicing facilities are few and far between. Fuel tanks can be as large as 155 gallons (700 litres). The makers claim that these are the first truck range from a European manufacturer specifically designed for the operating conditions of Africa, the middle East and South America. Landtrains for the East African market are assembled at Thika, Kenya.

Engine Cummins NTE-290 6-cylinder turbocharged diesel 14,000cc 290bhp (216kW) **Transmission** Clutch: Dana Spicer twin dry plate; Gearbox: Fuller RTO-9509B 9F 2R constant mesh; Rear Axle: Leyland double reduction **Frame** channel section ladder type **Brakes** dual circuit fully air-operated **Dimensions** wheelbase: 5,680mm; overall length: 9,337mm; overall width: 2,478mm; height to top of cab: 2,780mm; gross weight: 30,000kg; load capacity: 20,025kg **Performance** maximum speed: 100km/hr *(typical available specification for the truck illustrated)*

Maker: Mack Trucks Inc, Allentown, Pennsylvania (factory at Macungie, Pennsylvania)

Introduced in 1966, the Mack DM series is designed for very heavy duty work, and is ideally suited to on/off highway jobs, although regular highway trucks such as refuse collectors are built on this chassis. The standard DM is a 6 × 4, but there is a 6 × 6 variant known as the DMM, and in Canada a four-axle 8 × 6, the DMM 6006EX. Additional tag axles are also fitted to DMs, making a four- or five-axle truck. The latter can be used in conjunction with a six-axle trailer to form a 'Michigan centipede', a combination very popular in that State where there are restrictions on the weight loading on any one axle. A feature of the DM is its offset cab which places the driver directly behind the left front wheel giving excellent visibility for manoeuvring. A variety of engine options are available for the DM, including Mack in-line 6 or V-8, Caterpillar 3208 or 3406, or Cummins Formula 350, all diesels.

Engine Mack EM9-400 V-8 diesel 16,342cc 400bhp (298.4kW) **Transmission** Clutch: twin dry plate; Gearbox: Mack Maxitorque 6F 1R; Rear Axles: double reduction tandem **Frame** channel section ladder type **Brakes** dual circuit fully air-operated **Dimensions** wheelbase: 5,200mm; overall length: 8,420mm; overall width: 2,487mm; height to top of cab: 2,764mm; gross weight: 36,000kg; load capacity: 24,000kg **Performance** maximum speed: 82km/hr
(Typical available specification for the truck illustrated).

Maker: Mitsubishi Motors Corporation, Tokyo

6-wheeled Mitsubishis are made in 6 × 2 (FU) and 6 × 4 (FV) models, and there is also a normal-control 6 × 4 known as the NV. They are the largest Mitsubishi trucks made, and cover the GVW range from 21,400 to 27,600kg. A 14.8-litre V-8 engine is used, and there are four wheelbases available in the FU series, and three in the FV. The shortest is mainly used for tipper applications, as on the truck illustrated, while longer wheelbases can be used for concrete mixers, tankers or general cargo trucks. The engines, transmissions and a large proportion of other components are made in-house.

Engine Mitsubishi 8DC81A V-8 diesel 14,886cc 280bhp (206kW) **Transmission** Clutch: single dry plate; Gearbox: Mitsubishi 6F 1R, synchromesh on five upper ratios; Rear Axles: Mitsubishi single reduction hypoid tandem **Frame** channel section ladder type **Brakes** dual circuit vacuum operated hydraulic **Dimensions** wheelbase: 4,500mm; overall length: 7,235mm; overall width: 2,475mm; height to top of cab: 2,865mm; gross weight: 27,600kg; load capacity: 20,295kg **Performance** maximum speed: 88km/hr

Maker: Nissan Diesel Motor Co Ltd, Tokyo

This is one of the larger models in the Nissan range, powered by a 300bhp Nissan Diesel V-8 engine. There are three available wheelbases in the TWA52 range, 5,200mm for general haulage, 4,400mm for tipper work as illustrated, and 3,900mm for a tractor, the latter suitable for articulated units up to 42,000kg GCW. A choice of transmissions up to ten forward speeds is offered. There is also a 6 × 6 series of similar appearance, the TZA52, which can be used for dump truck work, or for off-highway transportation of heavy machinery, and as a logging truck in its articulated form. Maximum GCW of the TZA52 can be as high as 55,000kg.

Engine Nissan RD8 V-8 diesel 14,313cc 300bhp (224kW) **Transmission** Clutch: single dry plate; Gearbox: Nissan Diesel TMH612 6F 1R constant mesh; Rear Axles: Nissan single reduction hypoid tandem **Frame** channel section ladder type **Brakes** dual circuit fully air-operated **Dimensions** wheelbase: 4,400mm; overall length: 7,770mm; overall width: 2,480mm; height to top of cab: 2,570mm; gross weight: 25,500kg; load capacity: 18,060kg **Performance** maximum speed: 94km/hr.

Maker: Magyar Vagon es Gepgyar, Györ

The Raba name is derived from Raab which was the old name for Györ when the town was under Austrian rule. Vehicles have been made there intermittently since 1904, but the current range of M.A.N.-based heavy trucks has been built only since 1970. These now include 4 × 2 and 6 × 4 rigid chassis, and 4 × 2, 6 × 2 and 6 × 4 tractors, powered by 230 or 256bhp 6-cylinder engines built in the Raba factory under licence from M.A.N. Until 1983 cabs also came from M.A.N., but since then DAF cabs have been adopted. With the two-axle drawbar trailer illustrated the Raba K.26 has a maximum GCW of 38,000kg. Raba also make a 6 × 2 rigid chassis with trailing rear axle, the F.22 188-6.2.

Engine Raba-M.A.N. D2156 MT6 6-cylinder turbocharged diesel 10,350cc 256bhp (188kW) **Transmission** Clutch: Fichtel & Sachs single dry plate; Gearbox: Fuller RT9509 9F 1R constant mesh; Rear Axle: double reduction **Frame** channel section ladder type **Brakes** dual circuit fully air-operated **Dimensions** wheelbase: 4,950mm; overall length: 6,850mm; overall width: 2,490mm; overall height: 3,235mm; gross weight: 27,800kg; load capacity: 15,300kg **Performance** maximum speed: 85km/hr

Maker: Renault Vehicules Industriels, Venissieux, Rhone

The bonnetted Renault C260 trucks replaced the GBH series which was derived from a Berliet design dating back to 1967. They are made in 4 × 2, 4 × 4 and 6 × 4 versions, and also as a 4 × 2 tractor. All models are powered by a turbocharged 6-cylinder Renault engine, and share the same 9-speed all-synchromesh gearbox. There is a choice of three ratios on the double reduction rear axles on the 4 × 2 and 6 × 4 rigid chassis, and four ratios on the 4 × 2 tractor. Three wheelbases are available on the 6 × 4. The C260.26 is widely used with dump truck bodies or concrete mixers, as illustrated. This mixer is made by Recomat of Grenoble.

Engine Renault MIDS 06.20.45 6-cylinder turbocharged diesel 9,800cc 260bhp (192kW) **Transmission** Clutch: single dry plate; Gearbox: Renault B9 9F 1R synchromesh; Rear Axle: double reduction tandem **Frame** channel section ladder type **Brakes** dual circuit fully air-operated **Dimensions** wheelbase: 5,200 *or* 5,790 *or* 6,340mm; overall length: 8,685 *or* 9,795 *or* 10,865mm; overall width: 2,490mm; height to top of cab: 2,880mm; gross weight: 26,000kg; load capacity: 18,140 to 18,320kg **Performance** maximum speed: 85.3 to 99.5km/hr, according to axle ratio

Maker: Renault Vehicules Industriels, Venissieux, Rhone

The Renault 'R' range was introduced in 1980 as a replacement for the 'TR' models which had originally been made by Berliet before that company's take-over by Renault. The new range includes rigid and tractor models in two- and three-axle forms, powered by either a 306bhp in-line six or a 356bhp V-8 engine, both turbocharged. Both engines are available in the 4 × 2 rigid chassis and tractor, but only the six in the 6 × 4 illustrated. This is rated in solo form for 26 tonnes GVW, but with a fully-braked four-wheeled trailer, a GCW of 38 tonnes is possible. Without a trailer braking system, the limit is 29.5 tonnes. The resemblance to the Ford Transcontinental is no coincidence, as both trucks use the same cab, which is an ex-Berliet design.

Engine Renault MIDR 06.35.40 6-cylinder turbocharged diesel 12,002cc 306bhp (226kW)
Transmission Clutch: single dry plate; Gearbox: Fuller RTO 9513 13F 1R constant mesh; Rear Axles: double reduction tandem **Frame** channel section ladder type **Brakes** dual circuit fully air-operated
Dimensions wheelbase: 4,525, 4,775 or 5,275mm; overall length: 8,725, 9,025 or 10,275mm; overall width: 2,494mm; height to top of cab: 3,040mm; gross weight: 26,000kg; load capacity: 17,330kg **Performance** maximum speed: 110.9km/hr.

143

Maker: Intreprinderea de Autocamione Brasov, Brasov.

This is the smallest of three 6 × 4 Roman models, all of which are powered by the 10.3-litre 6-cylinder diesel engine built at Brasov under M.A.N. licence. This model is for 18.5-tonnes GVW, while the model 19.215 DF is for 26 tonnes, or 38 tonnes when a drawbar trailer is towed. Among variations are the 19.215DFK tipper, 12.CC 3 tanker and 19.AB 4 concrete mixer.

Engine D.2156HMN-8 6-cylinder diesel 10,334cc 215bhp (158kW) **Transmission** Clutch: single dry plate; Gearbox: ZF 6F 1R synchromesh; Rear Axles: double reduction tandem **Frame** channel section ladder type **Brakes** dual circuit air-assisted hydraulic **Dimensions** wheelbase: 4,935mm; overall length: 8,650mm; overall width: 2,500mm; height to top of cab: 3,020mm; gross weight: 18,500kg; load capacity: 11,510kg **Performance** maximum speed: 90km/hr

Maker: Magnis Truck Corporation (Pty) Ltd, Rosslyn, Alrode

A new name in South Africa's trucking is SAMAG. The first two letters of the name stand for South Africa, the last three letters form an African word, which means: strength. A Red bull decorates the grill of every Samag truck. This red bull is not only chosen as it is synonymous with strength and ruggedness, it has a much deeper meaning, as the "Red Afrikaaner" is well-known as a large South African breed of cattle. The company, called Magnis Truck Corporation (Pty.) Ltd., is responsible for the engineering, manufacturing, distribution and marketing of the Samag and Nissan Diesel truck ranges. Samag trucks are offered with normal and forward-control cabs. The normal-control cabs are similar to those featured on the Iveco range of normal-control trucks, while the forward-control cabs are similar to the cabs used on trucks belonging to the so called "Club of Four". All models are deliverable in truck and tractor versions with either 4 × 2 or 6 × 4 drive layout.

Engine ADE 407T 6-cylinder turbocharged diesel 11,410cc 280bhp (206kW) **Transmission** Clutch: single dry plate; Gearbox: Fuller RTOF14609B 8F 1R; Rear Axle: single reduction tandem **Frame** channel section ladder type **Brakes** dual circuit fully air-operated **Dimensions** wheelbase: 5,280mm; overall length: 7,393mm; overall width: 2,450mm; height to top of cab: 2,730mm; gross weight: 22,472kg; load capacity: 14,222kg **Performance** maximum speed: 115.2km/hr

Maker: Saab-Scania AB, Sodertalje

This is the most powerful of Scania's T range of bonnetted trucks, the E designation standing for extra heavy duty work, particularly on construction sites where off-road mobility is essential. It is powered by the 14.2-litre turbocharged DS14 engine, and is available with three alternative rear axle ratios. Two cabs are offered on the 142 E, the day cab illustrated and a sleeper cab which is normally used on the long-distance articulated models. Although the standard width of the T series is 2,490mm, narrower models are offered for the Swiss market, to conform with local width restrictions (in certain districts) stipulating a maximum of 2,300mm. Six wheelbases are offered, from 5,150mm for tractors, up to 7,150mm.

Engine Scania DSC 14 02 V-8 turbocharged and intercooled diesel 14,181cc 390bhp (287kW) *or* DSC 1401 420bhp (309kW) **Transmission** Clutch: twin dry plate; Gearbox: Scania GR8 71 10F 1R; Rear Axle: single reduction hypoid tandem **Frame** channel section ladder type **Brakes** dual circuit fully air-operated **Dimensions** wheelbase: 5,150mm; overall length: 7,375mm; overall width: 2,490mm; height to top of cab: 2,890mm; gross weight: 36,000kg; load capacity: 26,635kg **Performance** maximum speed: 92km/hr

Maker: Seddon Atkinson Vehicles Ltd, Oldham, Lancashire

The 300 series was introduced by Seddon Atkinson in 1978 as an intermediate range between the 16 tonne two-axle 200 and the larger 400s made in two-, three- and four-axle form. In 1983 they were replaced by the 301s which are made in a variety of models, 6 × 2, 6 × 4 and 8 × 4 rigids, and tractors in 4 × 2, 6 × 2 and 6 × 4 layouts. Cummins engines are used in all the 301s, the LT10-250 in the 6 × 4 and 8 × 4, and larger models in the tractors. Among a number of factory fitted options on the 6 × 4 are a sleeper cab and Power Take Offs from the gearbox. Three wheelbases are offered, one for tipper work and two for general haulage.

Engine Cummins LT10-250 6-cylinder turbocharged diesel 10,000cc 211bhp (152kW) **Transmission** Clutch: twin dry plate; Gearbox: Fuller RTX-6609 9F 1R constant mesh; Rear Axles: Seddon-Atkinson RA-472 single reduction hypoid **Frame** channel section ladder type **Brakes** dual circuit fully air-operated **Dimensions** wheelbase: 5,639, 6,401 *or* 7,239mm; overall length: 7,342, 9,321, *or* 10,698mm; overall width: 2,476mm; height to top of cab: 2,766mm; gross weight: 24,390kg; load capacity: 17,000kg **Performance** maximum speed: 94 to 108km/hr according to axle ratio

Maker: Oy Sisu Auto AB, Helsinki (factory at Karjaa)

Sisu began making trucks in 1931 and are now Finland's most important vehicle manufacturer, building 4-, 6- and 8-wheeled trucks, terminal tractors and buses. Scania has an 8.4% stake in the company. For many years they used Rolls-Royce and Leyland engines, but now standardise on Cummins and Valmet. Three basic ranges of truck are made, the medium-sized SK series, heavy forward-control SM series and bonnetted SL and SR series. There is also the 4 × 4 SA series which is chiefly made for military use. The SL-210 is the heaviest of the bonnetted models, which are made in 4 × 2, 4 × 4 and 6 × 2 forms as well. Cummins and Valmet engines are offered with this series, and Fuller transmissions. Although annual production of Sisu chassis does not exceed around 1,500, the company makes a high proportion of its own components, including frames, axles, cabs and suspension.

Engine Cummins LT 10-290 6-cylinder turbocharged and intercooled 10,000cc 294bhp (216kW) **Transmission** Clutch: twin dry plate; Gearbox: Fuller RTO 11613 13F 2R constant mesh; Rear Axle: Sisu BTT double reduction **Frame** channel section ladder type **Brakes** dual circuit fully air-operated **Dimensions** wheelbase: 5,170 or 5,570mm; overall length: 7,470 or 7,870mm; overall width: 2,500mm; height to top of cab: 2,835mm; gross weight: 26,000kg; load capacity: 16,500kg **Performance** maximum speed: 99 to 102km/hr, according to axle ratio

Maker: Steyr-Daimler-Puch AG, Steyr

Steyr makes a number of 6-wheel trucks, in 6 × 2, 6 × 4 and 6 × 6 versions. The 6 × 4 illustrated is available in three wheelbase lengths, of which the shortest is for a tractive unit or a concrete mixer. The 280 in the designation indicates the use of a 280bhp engine, one of three from 260 to 320bhp used in the heavier Steyr models. A 2F 4-speed gearbox with 2-speed transfer box is standardised. The truck illustrated carries a Liebherr concrete mixer.

Engine Steyr WD 615.65 6-cylinder diesel 9,726cc 280bhp (206kW) **Transmission** Clutch: single dry plate; Gearbox: ZF S112 8F 2R synchromesh; Rear Axle: double reduction **Frame** channel section ladder type **Brakes** dual circuit fully air-operated with ALB (automatic load dependent braking force regulator) **Dimensions** wheelbase: 4,275mm; overall length: 6,746mm; overall width: 2,429mm; height to top of cab: 3,004mm; gross weight: 32,000kg; load capacity: 23,800kg **Performance** maximum speed: 84km/hr.

Maker: Ural Auto Works, Miass

Introduced in 1964, this 6 × 4 truck was derived from the Ural-375 series of 6 × 6 models. As all 6 × 6 models used single tyres on rear axle, the double-tyred axles were gradually dropped on all models. Only one body is available, the dropside wooden body illustrated. Currently all trucks are fitted with super-balloons of 1100 × 400 size. The 377 can haul a trailer with a gross weight of 10 tonnes (5 tonnes off-road).

Engine ZIL-375Ya4 V-8 petrol 6,959cc 180bhp (132kW) **Transmission** Clutch: Twin dry plate; Gearbox: 5F 1R, not synchronized on low, additional two-speed reductor; Rear axles: double reduction **Frame** channel section ladder type **Brakes** dual circuit air/hydraulic **Dimensions** wheelbase: 4,925mm; overall length: 7,611mm; overall width: 2,500mm; overall height: 2,595mm; gross weight: 14,950kg; load capacity: 7,500kg **Performance** maximum speed: 75km/hr

Maker: Volvo Truck Corporation, Göteborg

The N10 is in the middle of the N series of normal control Volvo trucks, which includes the N7 made in 4 × 2 and 6 × 2 forms, the N10 4 × 2, 6 × 2 and 6 × 4, and the N12 with the same wheel arrangements but a more powerful engine. The N10 is available with a 275bhp TD 101G engine and the N12 with a 329bhp TD 121G or 385bhp TD 121F, both being 6-cylinder turbocharged diesels. Five wheelbase lengths are offered, enabling the N10 chassis to be used for a variety of work, from tippers on the shortest wheelbase length up to high-capacity general haulage trucks and vans. A variety of extras are available from Volvo Accessories, from radio and air-conditioning to genuine sheepskin seat covers and trim stripes in various colours. Like Scania, Volvo offer the N series in narrow cab forms for the Swiss market.

Engine Volvo TD 101G 6-cylinder turbocharged diesel 9,600cc 275bhp (202kW) **Transmission** Clutch: twin dry plate; Gearbox: Volvo R62 8F 1R all-synchromesh (with SR62 splitter, 16F 1R); Rear Axle: single reduction hypoid tandem **Frame** channel section ladder type **Brakes** dual circuit fully air-operated **Dimensions** wheelbase: 4,485 to 6,485mm; overall length: 7,160 to 10,740mm; overall width: 2,448mm; height to top of cab: 2,707mm; gross weight: 25,500 to 32,500kg; load capacity: 18,775 to 24,425kg **Performance** maximum speed: 85km/hr.

Maker: Shaanxi Automobile Factory, Qishan county, Shaanxi province

The new 13.5-ton SX161 is the 6×4 version of the all-wheel-drive SX 250. Recently this 5-ton 6 × 6 truck was named Dengpan, which means Mountain Climber. The 6 × 6 variant is already in production since the early seventies, but it is mostly in military use. A tractor variant can pull trailers with a load capacity of 15, 22 and 25 tons. The Shaanxi factory belongs to the Heavy-Truck Corporation.

Engine SX 6130Q 6-cylinder diesel 11,150cc 200bhp (148kW) **Transmission** Clutch: twin dry plate; Gearbox: 6F 1R; Rear Axle: double reduction **Frame** channel section ladder type **Brakes** dual circuit fully air-operated **Dimensions** wheelbase: 6,400mm; overall length: 9,742mm; overall width: 2,513mm; height to top of cab: 2,624mm; gross weight: 23,450kg; load capacity: 13,500kg **Performance** maximum speed: 70km/hr

Maker: Zavod Imieni Likhachev, Moscow

This is a development of the ZIL-133G (now G2), but it is in many ways a very different truck. In place of the 150bhp 5.9-litre petrol engine of the other truck, this one has a 210bhp 10.8-litre diesel made in the KamAZ works which is supplying a growing number of engines to the new generation of Russian trucks, at least until ZIL's own diesel engine and the new generation of YaMZ diesels of more contemporary specifications are in full production. The 133GYa has a different appearance too, thanks to a widened and lengthened bonnet, new wings and grille – overall length of the truck is increased due to a more sizable engine by 250mm. It also has a new 10-speed gearbox and modernised brakes. Because of increased power it can tow a 8,000kg trailer in addition to carrying its own load of 10,000kg. This truck can be seen as a middleman between thirsty petrol ZIL-130 trucks and the first generation of true diesel ZIL's with in-house built engines. At the moment the only variation is a tractor known as the ZIL-133VYa, but crane carrier and fire engine versions are planned for introduction shortly.

Engine KamAZ-740 V-8 diesel 10,850cc 210bhp (154kW) **Transmission** Clutch: twin dry plate; Gearbox: 10F 1R: Rear Axles: single reduction hypoid tandem **Frame** channel section ladder type **Brakes** air-operated **Dimensions** wheelbase: 6,010mm; overall length: 9,250mm; overall width: 2,500mm; overall height: 2,405mm; gross weight: 17,835kg; load capacity: 10,000kg; **Performance** maximum speed: 85km/hr.

Makers: Ateliers de Construction Mecanique de l'Atlantique, St. Nazaire

Production of A.L.M. trucks began in 1958 at Meaux by Ateliers Legueu, Meaux, hence the name, though they are now sometimes known under the name ACMAT, after the present manufacturers. 4 × 4 and 6 × 6 models are made, both using the same utilitarian-looking fibreglass bonnet and wings which have been unchanged since production began. A.L.M. vehicles are primarily military, being in use with the French Army and those of 26 other countries, but they also have a variety of civilian roles, particularly in desert countries. They are powered by Perkins 6- or 8-cylinder engines, and have two-speed transfer boxes, giving a maximum of 85km/hr in top gear and 45km/hr with the lower transfer ratio. The maximum climbable gradient when fully loaded is 50%. A.L.M. trucks are air transportable and parachutable. A 6 × 6 A.L.M. was the first truck home in the 1981 Paris-Dakar International Rally.

Engine Perkins 6.354D 6-cylinder diesel 5,800cc 138bhp (103kW) or Perkins V8-540 V-8 diesel 8,842cc 180bhp (134.3kW) **Transmission** Clutch: single dry plate; Gearbox: Type TR 540 5F 1R; Transfer Box: A.L.M. ACMAT Type AL 660 2-speed; Front Axle: A.L.M. ACMAT Type PAV 280 Gleason spiral bevel; Rear Axles: ACMAT double reduction tandem with Gleason spiral bevel **Frame** channel section ladder type **Brakes** dual circuit fully air-operated **Dimensions** wheelbase: 4,100mm; overall length: 6,943mm; overall width: 2,250mm; height to top of cab: 2,076mm; gross weight: 10,000kg; load capacity: 4,300kg **Performance** maximum speed: 85km/hr

Maker: Csepel Autogyar, Budapest

Csepel is one of the two major truck building concerns in Hungary, and has been in business since 1950. The D-566 entered production in 1971, and is part of a range of forward-control trucks of similar appearance, made in 4 × 2, 4 × 4 and 8 × 8 forms. Like many East European trucks they are made for both military and commercial use, with little difference in appearance. The D-566 is powered by a Raba-MAN 6-cylinder engine, made by Raba of Gyor under MAN licence, and also used in Raba's own trucks. Among features of the D-566 is central regulation of tyre pressures according to the terrain to be crossed. Payload varies from 5,000kg cross-country to 8,000 on roads, and the latter can be increased to 18,000kg when a trailer is used.

Engine Raba-MAN 6-cylinder diesel 10,680cc 200bhp (149.2kW) **Transmission** Clutch: single dry plate; Gearbox: 5F 1R; Transfer Box: 2 speed; Front Axle: double reduction; Rear Axles: double reduction tandem **Frame** channel section ladder type **Brakes** hydraulic **Dimensions** wheelbase: 4,300mm; overall length: 7,180mm; overall width: 2,500mm; height to top of cab: 2,670mm; gross weight: 17,000kg; load capacity: see text **Performance** maximum speed: 80km/hr

155

Maker: No.2 Motor Vehicle Factory, Shiyan, Hubei province

The Dongfeng (East Wind) EQ 240 (export name Aeolus) 6 × 6 cross country truck is the all-wheel-drive version of the EQ 140. Production began in 1976. A heavier version (EQ 245) with a payload of 3500kg has been developed recently. The EQ 240 is made as open truck with or without winch. The estimated annual production of the Dongfeng is about 1,000 units. Most of these vehicles are in military use.

Engine EQ6100 6-cylinder petrol 5,417cc 135bhp (99.3kW) **Transmission** Clutch: single dry plate; Gearbox: 5F 1R; Transfer box: two-speed; Rear Axle: full floating, hypoid gear reduction; Front axle: full floating hypoid gear reduction **Frame** channel section ladder type **Brakes** fully air-operated **Dimensions** wheelbase: 3,740mm; overall length: 6,352mm; overall width: 2,400mm; height to top of cab: 2,385mm; gross weight: 9,060kg (highway) 7,560kg (cross-country); load capacity: 4,210kg (highway) 2,710kg (cross-country) **Performance** maximum speed: 80km/h

Maker: Canadian Foremost Ltd., Calgary, Alberta

Foremost are specialists in the manufacture of off-road trucks for oilfield work, pipe laying and installation of electric power supplies in the most difficult terrain imaginable. They began by making tracked vehicles only, but now supplement these with a variety of wheeled trucks with load capacities from 10 to 70 tons. The Commander C is designed for loads up to 30 tons, while the companion model Super Commander C with 8 × 8 drive can handle up to 40 tons. A choice of Detroit or Cummins power is available. The frame is articulated behind the front axle for ease of steering which is hydraulically assisted. The huge low-pressure Goodyear Super Terra Grip tubeless tyres are ideal for transport across muskeg, mud, sand or snow. For oilfield work the Commander C is available with a heavy duty oilfield deck and winch. With special permit it is possible to operate a Commander C on public roads, though 57 tonnes on three axles is way above the normal limit, even in Northern Canada. The price of a Commander C is around $400,000.

Engine Detroit Diesel 8V71T V-8 diesel 9,300cc 350bhp (261kW) **Transmission** Gearbox: Clark 8F 4R; Transfer Box: Clark; Front Axle: Rockwell planetary drive; Rear Axle: Rockwell tandem planetary drive **Frame** channel section ladder type, articulated in centre **Brakes** fully air-operated **Dimensions** wheelbase: 8,130mm; overall length: 14,170mm; overall width: 3,500mm; height to top of cab: 3,580mm; gross weight: 56,800kg; load capacity: 27,200kg **Performance** maximum speed: 44km/hr

Maker: Sichuan Automobile Factory, Dazu city Sichuan province

In 1964 a Chinese delegation visited the Berliet factory in France, and as a result an important sales and licence manufacturing agreement was set up. In 1977 this factory started with the production of the Hongyan CQ 261, a Chinese licensed copy of the Berliet GBU. This truck had already been exported to China as Berliet GCH with steel cab instead of the GBU- canvas cab. G= camion, C= China and H= diesel. Berliet built 1,278 at the Bourg-en-Bresse factory for China. The standard CQ 261 uses the 200 hp 6150 engine, a tractor version named CQ 261Q25 the 250hp 6140Z engine. Besides, the factory also produces a long chassis tractor truck (CQ 261C25) and a 8 × 4 40 ton crane truck chassis (CQ 40D). Production in 1980 of the Hongyan CQ 261 was 500 trucks.

Engine Chongfa 6150 6-cylinder diesel 14,780cc 200bhp (148kW) **Transmission** Clutch: single dry plate; Gearbox: 5F 1R; Transfer Box: 2 speed **Frame** channel section ladder type **Brakes** dual circuit fully air-operated **Dimensions** wheelbase: 4,930mm; overall length: 7,974mm; overall width: 2,500mm; height to top of cab: 3,000mm; gross weight: 26,460kg (roads), 22,460 (cross country); load capacity: 12,260kg (roads), 8,266 (cross country) **Performance** maximum speed: 61km/hr

Makers: Isuzu Motors Ltd., Tokyo

This rugged and practical looking truck is part of Isuzu's all-wheel-drive range which includes two 4 × 4s and a 6 × 6. In conception the TW series dates back to the early 1950s when it was introduced as a military truck based on the American G.M.C. 2½-ton 6 × 6. It is virtually unchanged in appearance since then, although the diesel engine has been regularly improved. In its most familiar form it is employed as a tipper for bulk loads, but there are also models with self-loading crane and aerial platform. In addition there is a logging truck with a greatly increased wheelbase (7,010mm compared with 4,000mm for the regular version). The 4 × 4 Model HTS 11 is of similar appearance, and shares the same 150bhp 6-cylinder diesel engine.

Engine Isuzu 6BD1 6-cylinder diesel 5,785cc 150bhp (110kW) **Transmission** Clutch: single dry plate; Gearbox: Isuzu 5F 1R synchromesh on four upper ratios; Transfer Box: Isuzu dual ratio; Front Axle: single reduction spiral bevel; Rear Axle: single reduction tandem spiral bevel **Frame** channel section ladder type **Brakes** dual circuit vacuum assisted hydraulic **Dimensions** wheelbase: 4,000mm; overall length: 6,465mm; overall width: 2,295mm; height to top of cab: 2,430mm; gross weight: 14,000kg; load capacity: 9,330kg **Performance** maximum speed: 82km/hr

Maker: No.1 Motor Vehicle Factory, Changchun city, Jilin province

This truck is a copy of the Russian ZIL-157 and is made in the Cross-country Motor Vehicle sub-factory of the No.1 Motor Vehicle Factory in Changchun. The prototype was made in 1958 with headlamps set into the wings, but production models made from 1964 onwards used the CA 10 front end with external headlamps. Two variants are in current production, the CA 30 without winch and the CA 30A with winch. The chassis is used for many purposes both commercial and military, including engineering workshops, crane or drilling trucks and tractors for articulated trucks and buses. Production has varied according to demand, running from 3,000 to 7,000 annually. In 1980 3,354 trucks were delivered.

Engine Jiefang CA 30A 6-cylinder petrol 5,550cc 115bhp (86kW) **Transmission** Clutch: twin dry plate; Gearbox: 5F 1R; Transfer Box: 2 speed; Front Axle: single reduction spiral bevel; Rear Axles: single reduction spiral bevel **Frame** channel section ladder type **Brakes** air-operated **Dimensions** wheelbase: 5,340mm; overall length: 6,680mm (with winch, 6,922mm); overall width: 2,315mm; height to top of cab: 2,360mm; gross weight: 8,690kg; load capacity: 9,990kg (roads), 7,990kg (cross country) **Performance** maximum speed: 65km/hr

Maker: Kremenchug Avto Zavod, Kremenchug

This is the all-wheel-drive version of the KrAZ-257, and has the same wooden frame cab and square, utilitarian lines. It also uses the same YaMZ 14.8-litre V-8 diesel engine. The loaded truck can pull trailers of up to 30-tonnes gross weight, and it can also be supplied as a tractor for semi-trailers. Six different models of trailer and semi-trailer are made to use with the KrAZ-255. Variants include a logging truck (255L1) and a chassis for special applications (255B1). A centrally-mounted winch is a standard feature.

Engine YaMZ-238 V-8 diesel 14,860cc 240bhp (176kW) **Transmission** Clutch: twin dry plate; Gearbox: 5F 1R not synchronized on low; Transfer box: two speed; Front Axle: double reduction; Rear Axles: double reduction **Frame** channel section ladder type **Brakes** air-operated **Dimensions** wheelbase: 6,000mm; overall length: 8,645mm; overall width: 2,750mm; overall height: 2,940mm; gross weight: 19,415kg; load capacity: 7,500kg **Performance** maximum speed: 70km/hr

Maker: Kremenchug Avto Zavod, Kremenchug

Introduced in 1979, this truck is in the same category as the KrAZ 255 series, but has a much more modern appearance with all-metal cab and newer bonnet and grille. The engine is the same size but turbocharging gives it an additional 60bhp, and fuel consumption is greatly improved, being about 20% better at 50km/hr. The front axle is permanently engaged for 6-wheel-drive, unlike the earlier model. A mid-mounted winch is standard.

Engine YaMZ-238L V-8 turbocharged diesel 14,860cc 300bhp (221kW) **Transmission** Clutch: twin dry plate; Gearbox: 8F 1R; Transfer box: two speed; Axles: double reduction **Frame** channel section ladder type **Brakes** dual circuit air-operated **Dimensions** wheelbase: 6,000mm; overall length: 9,030mm; overall width: 2,722mm; overall height: 3,230mm; gross weight: 22,000kg; load capacity: 9,000kg **Performance** maximum speed: 80km/hr

Maker: Maschinenfabrik Augsburg-Nürnburg AG, Munich

M.A.N.'s semi-forward control 6-wheel dump truck is made in two versions, 6 × 4 and 6 × 6. This is the 6 × 6 model, as is indicated by its designation, 26-tonnes GVW 240bhp, D = three-axle vehicle, H = semi-forward control, A = all-wheel drive, K = tipper. This semi-forward control layout has been in the M.A.N. range since 1960, and for a while trucks of identical appearance were sold in France under the Saviem name. This arrangement was dropped when Saviem acquired Berliet, as the Berliet GBH range covered the same market as the M.A.N.s.

Engine M.A.N. D2566M 6-cylinder diesel 11,413cc 240bhp (1 / /kW) **Transmission** Clutch: single dry plate; Gearbox: ZF AK-690 6F 1R constant mesh, available with splitter box giving 12F; Transfer Box: 2 speed; Front Axle: double reduction planetary; Rear Axles: double reduction planetary tandem **Frame** channel section ladder type **Brakes** dual circuit fully air-operated **Dimensions** wheelbase: 4,775 or 5,200mm; overall length: 7,520 or 8,015mm; overall width: 2,490mm; height to top of cab: 2,692mm; gross weight: 26,000kg; load capacity: 18,770kg **Performance** maximum speed: 66.5 to 85km/hr, according to axle ratio

Maker: Daimler-Benz AG, Stuttgart

This is the largest of the Mercedes-Benz all-wheel-drive tipper range, which also includes the 4 × 4 1922AK and 1936AK. It is powered by the Mercedes-Benz 18-litre V-10 engine which was introduced in 1981. This engine has remarkable flexibility, delivering 1,100Nm of torque at just above idling speed, and its maximum 1,300Nm at 1,200rpm. This is particularly useful in the kind of operations for which this truck will be used, with frequent starting, low speeds and steep gradients. Note the protective bar in front of the radiator, and the extra cab protection above the windscreen.

Engine Mercedes-Benz OM423 V-10 diesel 18,423cc 335bhp (261kW) **Transmission** Clutch: single dry plate; Gearbox: ZF 16F 1R all-synchromesh; Transfer Box: VG 2000; Front Axle: single reduction spiral bevel; Rear Axle: single reduction spiral bevel **Frame** channel section ladder type **Brakes** dual circuit fully air-operated **Dimensions** wheelbase: 5,525mm; overall length: 7,125mm; overall width: 2,500mm; height to top of cab: 2,975mm; gross weight: 38,000kg; load capacity: 20,625kg **Performance** maximum speed: 91km/hr (highway), 64km/hr (cross country)

Maker: Oshkosh Truck Corporation, Oshkosh, Wisconsin

Oshkosh is one of America's leading specialist truck makers, and builds several distinct series of trucks for such varied applications as snow ploughs, concrete mixers, oilfield and general haulage, as well as fire engines for cities and airports, and military vehicles. The J Series is designed specifically for oilfield work, in which Oshkosh have been active since the 1920s. Three J models are made, all with 6-wheel-drive and large section tyres for travel on soft sand. For this reason, even though GVWs go up to nearly 50,000kg, only single tyres are used on the rear wheels. The J-2065 is in the middle of the range, and is powered by a 14.6-litre Caterpillar 6-cylinder engine, with a choice of Fuller nine-speed constant mesh, or Allison four-speed automatic transmissions. The largest model, the J-3080, has an 18-litre Caterpillar V-8 engine, and is unusual in that there are no brakes on the front wheels. All J Series can be used either as load carriers or as tractors with straight on low-loading trailers, in which case GCWs can be as high as 146,000kg.

Engine Caterpillar 3406-DIT 6-cylinder diesel 14,600cc 325bhp (240kW) **Transmission** Clutch: twin dry plate or torque converter; Gearbox: Fuller RTO-12509 9F 2R constant mesh or Allison HT-740D 4F 1R automatic; Transfer Box: Oshkosh 2 speed; Front Axle: Oshkosh single reduction hypoid; Rear Axles: Rockwell-Standard single reduction hypoid **Frame** channel section ladder type **Brakes** dual circuit fully air-operated **Dimensions** wheelbase: 4,953mm; overall length: 8,128mm; overall width: 2,794mm; height to top of cab: 3,175mm; gross weight: 38,556kg; load capacity: 27,129kg **Performance** maximum speed: 80km/hr

Maker: Avia n.p., Letnany, Prague

The distinctive Praga V3S was first built in 1952, and has changed little in appearance or specification since then. It has an air-cooled 6-cylinder Tatra engine, and is designed for loads of 5 tons on good roads, or 3 tons cross country. It has been used for a wide variety of civilian and military applications, including tippers, mobile workshops, cesspool emptiers and street sweepers. From 1967 to 1973 there was a companion 4 × 2 model, the S5T, which could also be had in short-wheelbase tractor form. The original Praga factory now makes components only, and the V3S is made in the former Avia aircraft and light truck factory. The latest model, the V3S-M1, is of similar appearance to the truck illustrated, but has headlamps mounted in the bumpers.

Engine Tatra T-912-4 6-cylinder air cooled diesel 7,410cc 118bhp (88kW) **Transmission** Clutch: single dry plate; Gearbox: 8F 1R; Transfer Box: 2 speed **Frame** channel section ladder type **Brakes** air-assisted hydraulic **Dimensions** wheelbase: 4,140mm; overall length: 6,900mm; overall width: 2,310mm; height to top of cab: 2,510mm; gross weight: 10,650kg; load capacity: 5,300kg (road) 3,500kg (cross country) **Performance** maximum speed: 75km/hr

Maker: Saab-Scania AB, Sodertalje

Scania make two models of all-wheel-drive truck, the 4 × 4 SBA 111, and the 6 × 6 SBAT 111S. Both were originally developed for military use, appearing in 1971, but they became available on the commercial market from 1977 onwards and have found many applications particularly in northern Scandinavia where there are few metalled roads. The SBAT 111S is powered by a Scania DS11 6-cylinder turbocharged diesel engine, and transmission is by Lysholm-Smith automatic torque converter. A ten-man crew cab is available in both military and civilian versions. The truck illustrated is fitted with Wirth mobile drilling equipment.

Engine Scania DS11 6-cylinder turbocharged diesel engine 11,020cc 290bhp (213kW)
Transmission Clutch: torque converter; Gearbox: Lysholm-Smith GA763 6F 1R automatic; Transfer Box: 2 speed; Front Axle: spiral bevel drive with planetary hub reduction; Rear Axles: spiral bevel drive with planetary hub reduction **Frame** channel section ladder type **Brakes** dual circuit fully air-operated **Dimensions** wheelbase: 5,030mm; overall length: 7,780mm; overall width: 2,474mm; height to top of cab: 2,788mm; gross weight: 19,000kg; load capacity: 9,000kg (road), 6,000kg (cross country) **Performance** maximum speed: 90km/hr

Maker: Fabryka Samochodow Ciezarowych, Starhovice

The 266 is the largest Star truck, and is made for the Polish Army as well as for commercial users. Its load capacity is 5,000kg on highways, and 3,500kg for off-road work. A wide variety of bodies are built on the 266 chassis, including some in the Jelcz factory such as the A3/578 tanker and the Jelcz 713 mobile repair workshop. Star 266s have been used for Himalayan and other expeditions, while an unusual version was a throne vehicle for the visit to Poland in 1979 of Pope John Paul II.

Engine Star S-359 6-cylinder diesel 6,842cc 150bhp (112kW) **Transmission** Clutch: single dry plate; Gearbox: ZF S6-45 5F 1R synchromesh on four upper ratios; Transfer Box: 2-speed; Front Axle: Gleason single reduction spiral bevel; Rear Axles: Gleason single reduction spiral bevel **Frame** channel section ladder type **Brakes** dual circuit air-assisted hydraulic **Dimensions** wheelbase: 3,595mm; overall length: 6,800mm; overall width: 2,500mm; height to top of cab: 2,640mm; gross weight: 10,850kg; load capacity: 5,000kg (road), 3,500kg (cross country) **Performance** maximum speed: 86km/hr (road), 50km/hr (cross country)

Maker: Tatra NP, Koprivnice

Tatra is one of the oldest vehicle makers in Europe, as their ancestors the Nesselsdorf Wagenbau Fabriks Gesellschaft built their first truck (still preserved by the factory) in 1898. The name Tatra was adopted in 1919, and the company became particularly famous for cars and trucks with tubular backbone frames. The current 815 range was introduced in 1983 and replaces the T148 bonnetted truck, and the T813 forward control trucks and tractors. The 815s follow Tatra tradition in having backbone frames, and in using an air cooled engine, in V8 (12,666cc), V10 (15,825cc) or V12 (18,990cc) forms. They are available as rigid trucks in two wheelbases, short for tippers, and long for general haulage bodies, and also as a tractor for semi trailers. The long wheelbase chassis has a conventional channel section frame in addition to the central tube. There is also special low cab chassis, the 815 PJ28 170 for use as a crane carrier or heavy drawbar tractor; this is made in 6 × 6 and 8 × 8 forms. The S3 illustrated is a three-way tipper, while the otherwise similar S1 is a rear tipper only.

Engine Tatra 3-929 V-10 air-cooled diesel 15,825cc 279bhp (208kW) **Transmission** Clutch: single dry plate; Gearbox: 5F 1R; Transfer Box: 2-speed; Front Axle: single reduction spiral bevel; Rear Axle: single reduction spiral bevel **Frame** tubular backbone **Brakes** dual circuit fully air-operated **Dimensions** wheelbase: 4,870mm; overall length: 6,980mm; overall width: 2,500mm; height to top of cab: 2,900mm; gross weight: 22,000kg; load capacity: 11,300kg **Performance** maximum speed: 88km/hr

Maker: Ural Auto Works, Miass

The Ural -375 series trucks were introduced in 1961, and have been made with little change since then, although now supplemented with a diesel version, the Ural-4320. This uses the new 10.85-litre V-8 KamAZ-740 engine that also powers the KamAZ forward-control trucks. The 375 is made in several models, the 375NM with dropside wooden body, the 375DM with all-metal body and dropping rear, the 375SM-1K1 and 375SNM tractors, also tropical and Northern climate (double glazing, insulation of cab and battery compartments) versions, capable of running in −60° Centigrade temperature. The tyre pressures on the 375D can be controlled while on the move, and a winch is generally standard equipment. Trailers can be hauled, up to 10 tonnes GVW on hard roads, or 7 tonnes across country.

Engine ZIL-375 V-8 petrol 6,959cc 180bhp (132kW) **Transmission** Clutch: twin dry plate; Gearbox: 5F 1R, no synchro on low; Transfer box: two speed; Axles: double reduction **Frame** channel section ladder type **Brakes** dual circuit hydropneumatically operated **Dimensions** wheelbase: 4,925mm; overall length: 7,355mm; overall width: 2,674mm; overall height: 2,680mm; gross weight: 13,450kg; load capacity: 5,000kg **Performance** maximum speed: 75km/hr

Maker: Ural Auto Works, Miass

After the new 11-litre KamAZ diesel was made in quantities big enough for supplying outside customers, there were several takers, including the builders of sizable Ural trucks. Ural diesel trucks are made now in several versions: two have regular cargo bodies (the one with a winch being 420kg heavier), a tractor 4420 for hauling 15 tonne semi-trailers and a special collective farm modification with tipper bodies on truck Ural-5557 as well as on drawbar trailer (shown). For easier starting in severe climates two 190 Ah batteries are installed instead of a single 140 Ah job as found on petrol-engined counterparts. The gearbox range is narrowed and the final drive ratio is down from 8,05 to 7,32. Fuel consumption has improved from 45 to something like 30 litre per 100km. A trailer of up to 7,000kg capacity remains towable across country.

Engine KamAZ-740 V-8 diesel 10,850cc 210bhp (154kW) **Transmission** Clutch: dual dry plate; Gearbox: 5F 1R, not synchronized on low; Transfer box: two speed; Axles: double reduction **Frame** channel section ladder type **Brakes** dual circuit hydropneumatically operated **Dimensions** wheelbase, 4,925mm; overall length: 7,366mm; overall width: 2,500mm; overall height: 2,870mm; gross weight: 13,795kg; load capacity: 5,000kg **Performance** maximum speed: 85km/hr

Maker: Zavod Imieni Likhachev, Moscow

The ZIL-157 was introduced in 1958 as a replacement for the generally similar-looking ZIL-151 which dated back to 1947. After three years an improved model 157K appeared, and in 1978 the present KD version was launched. It, the tractor version 157KDV and bare chassis 157KDE are still in demand, despite the introduction in 1967 of the ZIL-131, a more modern and more powerful, but not thirstier 6 × 6 truck with similar design and uses. For soft ground, a pressure regulator lowers the tyre pressure to 7 p.s.i., and the truck can move at up to 10km/hr with this pressure. A tractor model is also made.

Engine ZIL-157KD 6-cylinder petrol 5,355cc 110bhp (81kW) **Transmission** Clutch: single dry plate: Gearbox: five speed 5F 1R, no synchro on low; Transfer box: two speed; Axles: single reduction spiral bevel **Frame** channel section ladder type **Brakes** air-operated **Dimensions** wheelbase: 4,785mm; overall length: 6,922mm (without winch 6,685mm); overall width: 2,315mm; overall height: 2,360mm; gross weight: 8,690kg; load capacity: 5,000kg (3,000kg across country) **Performance** maximum speed: 65km/hr

Maker: Zavod Imieni Likhachev, Moscow

Introduced in 1967, the ZIL-131 is a second generation 6 × 6 truck, and supplemented the ZIL-157K which remains in production. The new truck has a more powerful V-8 engine instead of the 6-cylinder unit of the 157K, and this gives it an extra 500kg on the payload when moving across country (but equal 5,000kg on the roads). Extra power allows to haul a 6,500kg trailer instead of ZIL-157KD's 5,000. The respective figures for off-road work are 4,000 and 3,600kg. Like the ZIL-157K, the 131 is made as a tractor (131V) and is also supplied in chassis form for special bodies including fire engines.

Engine ZIL-131 V-8 petrol 5,966cc 150bhp (110kW) **Transmission** Clutch: single dry plate; Gearbox: 5F 1R, no synchro on low; Transfer box: two speed; Axles: double reduction **Frame** channel section ladder type **Brakes** air-operated **Dimensions** wheelbase: 4,600mm; overall length: 7,040mm (without winch 6,900mm); overall width: 2,500mm; overall height: 2,480mm; gross weight: 10,185kg; load capacity: 3,500kg **Performance** maximum speed: 80km/hr

The four-axle truck, or rigid 8-wheeler as it is often known in Great Britain, is a logical step from the three-axle. The first design for such a vehicle appeared in a French magazine in 1910. Not only did it have eight wheels, but petrol-electric drive with separate electric motors in each wheel! It is unlikely that it was ever built, and the first production rigid eight wheeler was made by Sentinel in 1929 when they added an extra steering axle to their DG6 6 × 4 steamer, increasing the payload from 12 to 15 tons. In 1930 a new Road Traffic Act in Britain laid down specific weight limits for various axle layouts—12 tons for two axles, 19 tons for three, and 22 tons for four. As the additional axle only accounted for about one ton of additional weight, and the payload could be increased by two to three tons, the 8-wheeler made sense to operators, and within a few years most of the makers of heavy trucks in Britain, such as A.E.C., Leyland, Foden, E.R.F., Albion and Scammell, were offering a 15-ton rigid 8-wheeler. They were much less popular on the Continent until quite recently, and virtually unknown in America until the 1970s when some firms such as Oshkosh and Kenworth who cater to the oil industry began to make a few for carrying specialised drilling equipment.

The heyday of the British 8-wheeler lasted for about thirty years from the early 1930s to 1964 when new legislation permitting 32 tons GVW for articulated vehicles made these seem a more desirable proposition than the 28-ton rigid 8, particularly as the latter was less manoeuvrable. From being the premium trucks for general haulage, the 8-wheeler was relegated to specific jobs such as fuel tanker and bulk tipper work. Nevertheless they have remained in the range of most British makers of heavy trucks, and are now also made by many European manufacturers, especially for the British and Swiss markets. In Holland they are especially popular for site work, with a GVW limit of 33 tonnes.

Apart from the 8 × 2s favoured in Spain, the majority of 8-wheelers are driven on the two rear axles. However the increasing need for heavy cross-country capabilities has bred a number of 8 × 6 and 8 × 8 trucks, particularly in Holland where Ginaf and Terberg (8 × 8) compete with imported Mercedes-Benz 8 × 4s and M.A.N. 8 × 8s. For really heavy cross-country work, the Canadian Foremost Magnum Four 8 × 8 has no rival with its 425bhp Detroit Diesel V-12 engine and 70-ton payload.

One of the lesser-known British makers of the 1930s was Armstrong-Saurer, but like many of their contemporaries they also entered the 8-wheeler market. It would be nearly forty years before their Swiss parent firm also made four-axle trucks, by which time Armstrong-Saurer had long vanished into limbo.

Maker: Comercial Pegaso SA, Madrid

The original Pegaso rigid 8-wheeler was made in 1965, and was one of the first of this axle layout on the Continent, although it had been popular in Britain for many years. Spanish 8-wheelers are unusual in that most of them drive on one axle only, with the single-tyred trailing axle either steered or self-steering. There are four 8 × 2 models in the current Pegaso Tecno range, two with 310bhp turbocharged engines, and two with 340bhp turbocharged and intercooled engines. Each can be rated for 36,250 or 38,000kg. There is also one 8 × 4, the 2431K. Day or sleeper cabs are available. Many different types of load are carried by Pegaso 8-wheelers, but among the most common are livestock and liquid fuel.

Engine Pegaso 9156.73 6-cylinder turbocharged diesel 11,945cc 310bhp (228kW) **Transmission** Clutch: single dry plate; gearbox: ZF 16S-130 16F 2R synchromesh *or* Fuller RTXF-1161313 13F IR constant mesh; Rear Axle: double reduction **Frame** channel section ladder type **Brakes** dual circuit fully air operated **Dimensions** wheelbase: 8,085mm; overall length: 10,740mm overall width: 2,450mm; height to top of cab: 3,300mm; gross weight: 36,250kg load capacity: 23,000kg **Performance** maximum speed: 96 to 125km/hr, according to gearbox and rear axle ratio

Maker: Renault Vehicules Industriels, Madrid

The Spanish manufacturer of Barreiros built heavy trucks from 1958 to 1978 in Madrid and during the latter years under control of Chrysler España SA, hence the Dodge badge on models offered from 1978 onwards. In 1983 the French giant RVI bought out Barreiros-Dodge again and the same truck models came on the market as Renault products. The most powerful truck had a 350hp turbo-diesel and was marketed in either 4 × 2, 6 × 2 or 8 × 2 configuration, but retaining the slightly modified Barreiros-Dodge cab. In 1984 however, also the same basis-models started to appear with Renault's own more modern boxshaped sleeper cab.

Engine Type BSS-36 6-cylinder turbo diesel 315hp (235kW) **Transmission** Clutch: twin dry plate; Gearbox: Fuller RTX-11609A 9F 1R constant mesh; Rear Axle: double reduction **Frame** channel section ladder type **Brakes** dual circuit fully air-operated **Dimensions** wheelbase: 7,970mm; overall length: 10,327mm; overall width: 2,482mm; gross weight: 35,000kg **Performance** maximum speed: 120km/hr

177

Maker: Daf BV, Eindhoven

DAF introduced an 8-wheeler chassis in the mid-1970s, and this type has become an important part of the company's range since then. 8 wheelers are currently made in both the 2800 and 3300 series, in two wheelbases, with day or sleeper cabs. GVWs vary according to regulations in different countries, 30 tonnes in the UK, 32 tonnes in Switzerland and 33 tonnes in the Netherlands. The 2800 illustrated has a tanker body in the shorter wheelbase.

Engine DAF DKSI1160 6-cylinder turbocharged and aftercooled diesel 11630cc 353bhp (260kW) **Transmission** Clutch: single dry plate; Gearbox: ZF 16S-130 8F 1R with splitter = 16F 2R; Rear Axles: DAF 2699 single reduction hypoid **Frame** channel section ladder type **Brakes** dual circuit fully air operated **Dimensions** wheelbase: 5,675 or 6,425mm; overall length: 8,870 or 10,200mm; overall width: 2,452mm; height to top of cab: 2,970mm; gross weight: see text; load capacity: c.22,600kg **Performance** maximum speed: 100km/hr.

Maker: E.R.F. Ltd, Sandbach, Cheshire

The traditional rigid 8-wheeler has long been an important part of E.R.F. production, the first having been made in 1935. The current C Series version has the same SP cab panelled in hot-pressed SMC fibreglass as the other E.R.F.s, but it is available with a wider choice of engines than the 6-wheelers, these being the Gardner 6LXDT, Cummins L10-250 and Rolls-Royce E220 or E265L, though the R R units are very much to special order only. Gearboxes are 9- or 10-speed. Two wheelbase lengths are available, both for tipper or general use, though the shorter would normally be used with tipper bodywork, especially for carrying sand or gravel.

Engine Cummins L10-250 6-cylinder turbocharged diesel 10,000cc 243bhp (181.6kW) **Transmission** Clutch: twin dry plate; Gearbox: Fuller RTX7609 9F 1R *or* Spicer SST8010 10F 1R constant mesh; Rear Axle: single reduction **Frame** channel section ladder type **Brakes** dual circuit fully air-operated **Dimensions** wheelbase: 6,655 or 7,239mm; overall length: 9,634 or 10,551mm; overall width: 2,495mm; height to top of cab: 2,782mm; gross weight: 30,500kg; load capacity: 21,000kg **Performance** maximum speed: 108km/hr
(typical available specification for the truck illustrated)

Maker: Foden Trucks, Sandbach, Cheshire

Rigid 8-wheelers have been an important part of the Foden range since the mid-1930s, and this continues under the new regime of ownership by Paccar Incorporated. The S108 is designed for 30 tons GVW, and is available with a Perkins (ex-Rolls-Royce) 265 Li engine in the base model, and a choice of thirteen other engine options, by Caterpillar, Cummins, Gardner and Perkins. A Fuller 9-speed gearbox is standardised, and Spicer 10- or Fuller 14-speed boxes are optional. The standard wheelbase is 6,510mm, but the frame rail length can be specified to give any legal wheelbase or rear overhang. Day or sleeper cabs are offered.

Engine Perkins 265 Li 6-cylinder turbocharged diesel 12,170cc, 265bhp (198kW) **Transmission** Clutch: twin dry plate; Gearbox: Fuller RTX 11609B 9F 1R constant mesh; Rear Axles: Eaton DS 401P single reduction hypoid tandem **Frame** channel section ladder type **Brakes** dual circuit fully air-operated **Dimensions** wheelbase: 6,510mm; overall length: 8,823mm; overall width: 2,497mm; height to top of cab: 2,911mm; gross weight: 30,490kg; load capacity: 22,210kg **Performance** maximum speed: 94 to 115 km/hr, according to axle ratio.
(typical available specification for the truck illustrated)

Maker: International Harvester Co, Chicago, Illinois (factory at Springfield, Ohio)

The International S range is a very wide one, from the Model 1654 shown on page 38 up to tractors and heavy construction trucks such as the four-axle dump truck illustrated. This is basically a 6-wheeler, with an additional non-drive tag axle ahead of the rear tandem, and is typical of American practice in four axle trucks. This layout is found on many makes although often the additional axle is fitted by an outside firm and is not a factory option. Tag axles are more common than the twin steering axles popular in Europe, though the latter are offered by some manufacturers, including International on the Paystar (page 182), Kenworth, Oshkosh and Canadian Mack. The S Series construction trucks are made with set-back front axles, as illustrated, or set forward to meet regulations in certain States. Engine options include various models of Cummins and Detroit Diesel. In the background of the photograph is an International Paystar 8 × 4, one of International's construction truck range.

Engine Cummins PT-270 6-cylinder diesel 14,010cc 266bhp (196kW) **Transmission** Clutch: single dry plate; Gearbox: Fuller RTO 1157DL 9F 2R constant mesh; Rear Axle: Dana RA-472 single reduction hypoid tandem **Frame** channel section ladder type **Brakes** dual circuit fully air-operated **Dimensions** wheelbase: 4,584mm; overall length: 6,858mm; overall width: 2,440mm; height to top of cab: 2,750mm; gross weight: 26,500kg; load capacity: 18,800kg **Performance** maximum speed: 120km/hr
(typical available specification for the truck illustrated)

Maker: International Harvester Co, Chicago, Illinois (factory at Chatham, Ontario)

The Paystar range includes the heaviest International trucks for the construction and oil industries. They are largely custom-built trucks and can be had in 4 × 4, 6 × 4, 6 × 6 and 8 × 4 versions, with tag axles or twin steering tandems, and front axles set back or forward according to the regulations in the States in which they are to operate. The truck illustrated is unusual in having twin steering axles in conjunction with a conventional bonnet, but this is necessitated by the exceptional length of wheelbase. The truck is about to load a large stationary air compressor. No fewer than twenty engine options are available with the Paystar series, including one International unit (the DT-466 210bhp), and others from Cummins and Detroit Diesel. Transmissions run from 5- to 15-speeds.

Engine Cummins NTCC-400 6-cylinder diesel 14,000cc 400bhp (298.4kW) **Transmission** Clutch: single dry plate; Gearbox: Fuller RTO 1157DL 9F 2R constant mesh; Rear Axles: International single reduction hypoid tandem **Frame** channel section ladder type **Brakes** dual circuit fully air-operated **Dimensions** wheelbase: variable; overall length: variable; gross weight: 58,000kg; load capacity: 46,000kg **Performance** maximum speed: 70km/hr
(typical available specification for the truck illustrated)

Maker: International Harvester Australia Ltd, Dandenong, Victoria

Unlike the parent firm in the USA, the Australian International factory makes a number of forward-control rigid 8-wheelers for highway use, similar in conception to British 8-wheelers. The T-2600 range is at the top of Australian International's programme, and supplements the smaller ACCO models. Two-, three- and four-axle models are made, with GVWs from 14,090 to 27,240kg, and up to 45,000kg GCW with drawbar trailer. International or Cummins diesel engines are used, with outputs up to 300bhp. Four rigid 8s are listed, with engines ranging from the 7.61-litre 210bhp International DT-466C on the TK-2650 illustrated, up to the 14-litre 300bhp Cummins Formula 300 BC11 in the TK-2670. The truck illustrated is operated by the Australian Operations Division of ICI.

Engine International DT-466C 6-cylinder diesel 7,610cc 210bhp (156kW) **Transmission** Clutch: twin dry plate; Gearbox: Fuller RT-613 13F 3R constant mesh; Rear Axle: Rockwell SP-40 single reduction tandem **Frame** channel section ladder type **Brakes** dual circuit fully air-operated **Dimensions** wheelbase: 6,550mm; overall length: 9,600mm, overall width: 2,490mm; height to top of cab: 2,720mm; gross weight: 27,240kg; load capacity: 21,400kg

Maker: IVECO- Magirus AG, Ulm

The 8 × 4 IVECOs are re-badged versions of the Magirus-Deutz range, and UK market models are powered, as before, by an aircooled V-8 Deutz diesel engine. A ZF 6-speed constant mesh gearbox is fitted, with the option of a front-mounted splitter giving 12 forward speeds. In Britain the 8 × 4 IVECO is mainly used as a tipper, but in Switzerland where 8-wheelers are popular for general haulage there are more powerful versions in two wheelbase lengths, with 320bhp 15,945cc V-10 engines. There are also 6 × 2 and 6 × 4 models powered by the V-8 engine, which are not available on the UK market.

Engine Deutz F8L 413 V-8 air-cooled diesel 11,310cc 228.5bhp (170.5kW) **Transmission** Clutch: Fichtel & Sachs single dry plate; Gearbox: ZFAK 6-80 6F 1R constant mesh (12F 2R with splitter); Rear Axle: double reduction **Frame** channel section ladder type **Brakes** dual circuit fully air-operated **Dimensions** wheelbase: 6,330mm; overall length: 8,375mm; overall width: 2,500mm; height to top of cab: 2,720mm; gross weight 30,490kg; load capacity: 22,075kg **Performance** maximum speed: 88 to 95km/hr, according to axle ratio

Maker: Kenworth Truck Co, Seattle, Washington

The Kenworth K-184 chassis is unusual for the USA in having twin steering axles in the European manner. Its advantages are that it offers maximum payload capacity and platform length within legal highway limits. It has a short BBC of 1,939mm, and yet a full sleeper cab is featured. A self-equalizing front suspension provides even front axle load distribution and reduced front axle tyre loads. As with most Kenworths a variety of engine options are available, Detroit Diesels from 270 to 435bhp and Cummins from 350 to 450bhp. Transmissions can be Fuller or Spicer 5 to 15 speeds, or Allison automatic with or without transmission retarders. The Kenworth K-184 has been particularly successful in oilfield service work, but is also used for sand and acid transport, and for general haulage work.

Engine Detroit Diesel 6V-92TTA 6-cylinder diesel 9,038cc 307bhp (229kW) **Transmission** Clutch: twin dry plate; Gearbox: Fuller RTO 1157DL 9F 2R constant mesh; Rear Axles: Rockwell *or* Eaton single *or* double reduction tandems **Frame** Channel section ladder type **Brakes** dual circuit fully air-operated **Dimensions** wheelbase: variable; overall length: variable; gross weight: from 28,113kg; load capacity: from 18,000kg **Performance** maximum speed: 90km/hr
(typical available specification for the truck illustrated)

Maker: Leyland Vehicles Ltd, Leyland, Lancashire

The 8-wheeled Leyland Constructors are part of the heavy duty range all of which use the T45 cab which was introduced on the Roadtrain tractors. They replace two models formerly made by the Leyland group, Leyland's own Octopus and the Scammell Routeman. Three models of 8-wheeler are made, the 30.21 illustrated which is powered by a Leyland TL11A turbocharged engine, the 30.25 powered by a Cummins LT10-250 turbocharged engine, and the 30.19 powered by a Gardner 6LXCT turbocharged engine. All these are rated at 30 tonnes GVW. Three wheelbase lengths are offered, in both tipper and haulage models. Leyland four axle trucks are assembled by Scammell at Watford, and are sold on the export market under the name Scammell S.26.

Engine Leyland TL11A 6-cylinder turbocharged diesel 11,100cc 220bhp (164kW) **Transmission** Clutch: twin dry plate; Gearbox: Spicer SST8010-SA SFIR constant mesh; Rear Axles: double reduction tandem **Frame** Channel section ladder type **Brakes** dual circuit fully air-operated **Dimensions** wheelbase; 6,395mm; overall length: 8,450mm; overall width: 2,470mm; height to top of cab: 2,868mm; gross weight: 30,490kg; load capacity: 22,400kg **Performance** maximum speed: 88 to 109km/hr, according to axle ratio.

Maker: Daimler-Benz AG, Stuttgart (factories at Arbon and Wetzikon, Switzerland)

Four-axle Mercedes-Benz trucks are currently assembled in Switzerland for domestic use and for export to countries where rigid 8-wheelers find a ready market. They are made in the former Saurer and F.B.W. factories by a company set up in December 1982 under the title N.A.W. (Nutzfahrzeuggesellschaft Arbon & Wetzikon). In this company Saurer hold a 45% share, Daimler-Benz 40% and F.B.W. 15%. As well as 8 × 4 trucks N.A.W. also make the Mercedes-Benz 3850 6 × 6 heavy tractor and certain specialised passenger vehicles such as airport buses.

The 8 × 4 Mercedex-Benz are made in nine models, powered by 14.6 litre V-8 or 18.3 litre V-10 engines, and in five wheelbase lengths. GVW is restricted to 33 tonnes for the Swiss market, but can be as high as 35 tonnes elsewhere. The truck illustrated has a tipper body by Lanz & Marti of Sursee, Switzerland.

Engine Mercedes-Benz OM422A V-8 turbocharged diesel 14,620cc 330bhp (243kW) **Transmission** Clutch: single dry plate; Gearbox: ZF 16S-130 4F 1R with splitter = 8F 2R; Rear Axles: double reduction tandem **Frame** channel section ladder type **Brakes** dual circuit fully air-operated **Dimensions** wheelbase: 5,200mm; overall length: 7,500mm; overall width: 2,500mm; height to top of cab: 3,045mm; gross weight: 33,000kg; load capacity: 23,400kg **Performance** maximum speed: 87 to 112km/hr, according to axle ratio

Maker: R.F.W. Truck Manufacturing Co, Chester Hill, New South Wales

R.F.W. make a number of four axle chassis with a wide range of optional specifications to customers' requirements. The 8 × 4 illustrated is a water carrier used for spraying road surfaces in open cast mines and quarries. The extra wide body (3,200mm) allows for a tank capacity of 40,000 litres. It is powered by a Cummins NTC-400 engine, but a Caterpillar 3406 or Detroit Diesel 6V92TA can also be used in this chassis. Alternative applications are as a heavy duty aircraft refuelling tanker or coal hauler. For customers requiring greater traction, R.F.W. make an 8 × 8 chassis powered by a 475bhp Detroit Diesel 8V92TA engine. A recently-supplied 8 × 8 explosive carrying truck has a GVW of 60 tonnes.

Engine Cummins NTC-400 6-cylinder turbocharged diesel 14,000cc 400bhp (298.4kW) **Transmission** Clutch: torque convertor; Gearbox Allison HT750DRD 5F 1R automatic; Rear Axle: single reduction **Frame** channel section ladder type **Brakes** triple circuit fully air-operated **Dimensions** wheelbase: variable; overall length: variable; overall width: 3,600mm; height to top of cab: N/A; gross weight: 54,545kg; load capacity: about 40,000kg **Performance** maximum speed: 70km/hr

SCANIA P 112H   S   ○○●●

Maker: Saab-Scania AB, Sodertalje

With increasing demand for four-axle trucks in Europe, Scania added an 8 × 2 chassis to their P 112H range in 1980, and followed this up with an 8 × 4 which made its first appearance at the 1982 Geneva Show. Both models use the same basic components including the DS11 11-litre turbocharged engine, but the 8 × 4 uses a rocking beam tandem rear axle bogie. They are designed for GVWs up to 33 tonnes although at the time of writing regulations in Switzerland, where many of these trucks are sold, impose a limit of 28 tonnes. Models sold in Switzerland have narrower cabs to comply with the 2.3m maximum width regulations.

Engine Scania DS11 6-cylinder turbocharged diesel 11,000cc 280bhp (206kW) **Transmission** Clutch: single dry plate; Gearbox: Scania GR870 10F 1R all synchromesh; Rear Axle: single reduction hypoid tandem **Frame** channel section ladder type **Brakes** dual circuit fully air-operated **Dimensions** wheelbase: 7,215mm; overall length: 10,010mm; overall width: 2,480mm; height to top of cab: 2,790mm; gross weight: 33,000kg; load capacity: 20,220kg **Performance** maximum speed: 112km/hr

189

Maker: Seddon Atkinson Vehicles Ltd, Oldham, Lancashire

The 8 × 4 Seddon Atkinson 400 was introduced in 1975, and effectively replaced the Atkinson Defender 8-wheeler.

It was replaced during 1982 by an equivalent 8-wheeler in the 401 series, and supplemented by an 8 × 4 version of the 301. The latter uses a Cummins LT10-250 engine, while the 401s use Gardner and Rolls-Royce engines. All the 8-wheelers use a nine speed Fuller constant mesh gearbox. Two wheelbases are available, for tipper bodies and for general haulage. A sleeper cab and Power Take Offs from the gearbox are among the factory fitted options. The 301 illustrated has Norde rubber suspension on the rear axles, bodywork by Northern Assemblies, and a Hiab crane.

Engine Cummins LT10-250 6-cylinder turbocharged diesel 10,000cc 241bhp (180kW) **Transmission** Clutch: twin dry plate Gearbox: Fuller RTX 7609 9F 1R constant mesh; Rear Axles: Seddon Atkinson RA472 single reduction hypoid **Frame** channel section ladder type **Brakes** dual circuit fully air-operated **Dimensions** wheelbase: 7,391 or 7,874mm; overall length: 8,887, 9,370 or 10,286mm; overall width: 2,476mm; height to top of cab: 2,767mm; gross weight: 30,490kg; load capacity: 22,085kg **Performance** maximum speed: 86 to 112km/hr according to axle ratio

Maker: Oy Sisu Auto AB Helsinki (factory at Karjaa)

Sisu make two distinct versions of their bonnetted 8-wheeler, the 8 × 4 illustrated, with a trailing axle ahead of the tandem driving rear axles, and an 8 × 2 with a more conventional axle spread, two at the front and two at the rear, with the rearmost axle only driving. The layout illustrated is quite common in America, but rare in Europe. Both versions are available in three models, the SR260, SR300 and SR320, the figures representing the approximate kilowatt output of the Cummins engines. Despite their very different appearance, the SR chassis has a great deal in common with the forward control SM series (see page 226), with identical engine location, axles, steering and suspension. As Pat Kennett wrote in *Truck* magazine, the chassis goes a long way down the line before it knows whether a bonnetted or forward control cab will be mounted on it.

Engine Cummins NTE-350 6-cylinder turbocharged diesel 14,000cc 355bhp (261kW)
Transmission Clutch: twin dry plates; Gearbox: Fuller RT014613 13F 2R constant mesh; Rear Axle: Sisu BTE double reduction **Frame** channel section ladder type **Brakes** dual circuit fully air-operated
Dimensions wheelbase: 6,400mm or 6,630mm; overall length: 8,740 or 8,970mm; overall width: 2,500mm; height to top of cab: 2,975mm; gross weight: 33,500kg; load capacity 25,000kg
Performance maximum speed: 96 to 129km/hr, according to axle ratio

Maker: Steyr-Daimler-Puch AG, Steyr

8-wheelers have been part of the Steyr range since the introduction of the present 91 series in 1968. Six models are currently made, with either 9.7-litre 6-cylinder or 11.97-litre V-8 engines, and 9- or 13-speed gearboxes by ZF and Fuller respectively. The 330 in the designation of the truck illustrated indicates a 330bhp V-8 engine. A four-spring or two-spring rear bogie is available, the latter allowing the rearmost axle to be lifted when the truck is running unladen. Because of local regulations, Steyr 8-wheelers are popular in Switzerland; the tipper illustrated is operated by Leo Schilling of Baden.

Engine Steyr WD 815.60 V-8 turbocharged diesel 11,970cc 330bhp (240W) **Transmission** Clutch: single dry plate; Gearbox: ZF S130 4F 1R + splitter synchromesh *or* Fuller RT9513 13F 2R constant mesh; Rear Axle: double reduction **Frame** channel section ladder type **Brakes** dual circuit fuly air-operated with ALB (automatic load dependent braking force regulator) **Dimensions** wheelbase: 5,450mm; overall length: 7,736mm; overall width: 2,435mm; height to top of cab: 3,000mm; gross weight: 32,000kg; load capacity: 22,340kg **Performance** maximum speed: 76km/hr

Maker: Volvo Truck Corporation, Göteborg

Volvo have made a rigid 8 chassis since 1974, initially for the UK market but now sold in several countries where four-axle trucks are popular. The FL10 was introduced in September 1985 as part of Volvo's new range of 4-, 6- and 8-wheel trucks covering the field from 12 to 30 tonnes for rigid chassis and up to 38 tonnes for articulated vehicles. The four-axle FL10 is made only in 8 × 4 form, but the less powerful FL7 is available as an 8 × 2 or 8 × 4. In the model numbers of the new range, F stands for forward control, L for low cab, and the figures for approximate engine capacity in litres. The FL10, which supplements but does not replace the former F10, is an intermediate model which combines the size of the F7 with the power and performance of the F10. All FL10s are powered by Volvo's 299bhp TD101F turbocharged and intercooled engine.

Engine Volvo TD101F 6-cylinder turbocharged and intercooled diesel 9,600cc 299bhp (223kW) **Transmission** Clutch: twin dry plate; Gearbox: 8F 1R synchromesh (with optional splitter, 16F 2R) Rear Axles: single reduction hypoid tandem **Frame** channel section ladder type **Brakes** dual circuit fully air-operated **Dimensions** wheelbase: 6,590 to 7,910mm; overall length: 8,400 to 11,000mm; overall width: 2,490mm; height to top of cab: 2,860mm; gross weight: 30,490kg; load capacity: 22,000kg **Performance** maximum speed: 80 to 109km/hr, according to axle ratio

Maker: Flextruck Ltd, Breslau, Ontario

This unusual truck was originally made under the equally unusual name of Rubber Railway, under which title about 100 trucks were made from 1970 to 1976. After a change of ownership and name the design was revived in 1979, and is now made in two forms, the 8 × 6 illustrated, and a rear-engined 10 × 6 intended for the ready-mix concrete business. The most distinctive feature of the Flextruck design is the frame which is articulated at the centre; a turn of the steering wheel directs hydraulic fluid into one or other of two cylinders which connect front and rear frames, and thus effects steering without turning the front wheels in the usual way. The standard engine is a Detroit Diesel V-8, but other units can be specified. Other details of the specification including axle spread can be varied according to customers' requirements.

Engine Detroit Diesel 8V71TT V-8 diesel 9,300cc 305bhp (227.5kW) **Transmission** Clutch: Spicer twin dry plate; Gearbox: Spicer 1007-3A 7F 1R; Front Axle: Rockwell SRD double reduction; Rear Axle: Rockwell SSHD double reduction **Frame** channel section articulated at centre **Brakes** fully air-operated **Dimensions** wheelbase: 5,613mm; overall length: 10,668mm; overall width: 2,438mm; height to top of cab: 2,540mm; gross weight: 40,480kg; load capacity: 24,840kg **Performance** maximum speed: 88km/hr

Maker: Canadian Foremost Ltd, Calgary, Alberta

The Magnum 4 is the largest wheeled truck made by Canadian Foremost, in a range that starts with the two-axle Delta 2 for 10 ton loads, and includes the 15-ton Delta 3, and 30- and 40-ton Commander C and Super Commander C. While these are used for a variety of general oilfield work, the Magnum 4 is specifically designed for transporting the huge pipes needed for pipeline construction. Like the Commander's the Magnum's frame is articulated at the centre. The Goodyear Super Terra Grip tubeless tyres have dimensions of 66 × 43in (1,676 × 1,092mm). Although it looks small in the photograph, the offset cab seats two men in tandem. The standard engine in the Magnum 4 is a Detroit Diesel 12V71-T, but a Cummins KT1150 is an option. In addition to their Calgary headquarters, Foremost have a US sales office at Houston, Texas, conveniently located for the Texas oilfields.

Engine Detroit Diesel 12V71-T V-12 diesel 13,950cc 465bhp (347kW) **Transmission** Gearbox: Clark 8000 8F 4R; Front Axles: Rockwell SPR-440 double reduction tandem hypoid; Rear Axles: Rockwell SPR-440 double reduction tandem hypoid **Frame** channel section ladder type, articulated in centre **Brakes** fully air-operated **Dimensions** overall length: 16,300mm; overall width: 4,000mm; height to top of cab: 2,900mm; gross weight: 104,400kg; load capacity: 66,300kg **Performance** maximum speed: 36.9km/hr

Maker: Ginaf Automobielbedrijven BV, Veenandaal

Ginaf's 8-wheel-drive trucks are made in two models, the F.351 illustrated with normally-aspirated 11.63-litre Daf diesel engine for 33,000kg GVW, and the F.480 with a slightly longer wheelbase, turbo-charged engine and 36,000kg GVW. Both are mainly used as tippers for on/off-highway work, but they can carry other bodywork such as telescopic crane or concrete mixer. Like all other current Ginaf trucks they use Daf cabs.

Engine Daf DKTD 1160 6-cylinder turbocharged diesel 11,630cc 256bhp (188kW) **Transmission** Clutch: F & S single dry plate; Gearbox: ZF AK6-90 6F 1R, with double ratio transfer = 12F 2R; Transfer Box: ZF VG8500 dual ratio; Front Axles: TR Ginaf VG 75; Rear Axles: Rockwell M240HX **Frame** channel section ladder type **Brakes** dual circuit fully air-operated (Westinghouse compressor) **Dimensions** wheelbase: 5,240mm; overall length: 7,370mm; overall width: 2,480mm; height to top of cab: 3,070mm; gross weight: 33,000kg; load capacity: 22,550kg **Performance** maximum speed: 75km/hr

Maker: Irtex/Ponticelli Freres, Paris

Irtex is the result of an association between French and foreign companies, each of them experts in the transportation and handling of heavy loads. Construction of the vehicles is undertaken by Ponticelli Bros. in Paris, France. One of the Irtex products is the PEA, a 8 × 8 carrier using a Mercedes-Benz OM404 engine, ZF torque converter and transfer case, axles by SOMA and a Daf cab. Another 8 × 8 vehicle is the BB, a tractor manufactured in 1981, and ever since operating for one of Irtex's members, Sainert in Spain. To the company's earlier products belong the W8-SA 6 × 6 tractor and the T40A 8 × 6 tank carrier. The T40A was for military purposes, while all the other former and recent Irtex tractors and carriers normally serve in geophysical exploration tasks. Presently a dump truck is listed to be in production as well. The DCB22 can carry a 22.5 to 29.5 ton payload depending on the bucket chosen. The dump body installed is made by Bennes Marrel in France.

Engine Mercedes-Benz OM404 V-12 diesel 20,900cc 450bhp (336kW) **Transmission** Clutch: ZF WSK400 torque converter; Gearbox: 8F 1R Transfer Box: ZF 4S150GPA, two speed Front Axle: two SOMA double reduction axles; Rear Axle: two SOMA double reduction axles **Frame** channel section ladder type **Brakes** dual circuit fully air-operated **Dimensions** wheelbase: 10,200mm; overall length: 11,100m; overall width: 3,350mm; height to top of cab: 3,500mm; gross weight: 60,000kg; load capacity: 35,000kg **Performance** maximum speed: 57.5km/hr

Maker: Maschinenfabrik Augsburg-Nurnburg AG, Munich

Like other German truck manufacturers, M.A.N. introduced an 8-wheeler especially for markets where regulations favoured such a layout, in particular Holland, Switzerland and Britain. The range includes two models of 8 × 4, a short wheelbase tipper and a longer wheelbase truck for general haulage, while a more specialised model is the VFAK 8 × 8 tipper chassis. (V=second steering axle, F=forward control, A=all wheel drive, K (Kipper)=tipper). This 34 tonne truck is made in Munich, but tippers of larger capacity, up to 48 tonnes, are made by M.A.N.'s special vehicle division, OAF-Gräf und Stift in Vienna. It has optional drive to the two front axles and a battery of cross axle and inter-axle differential locks. It is aimed particularly at the Dutch and Danish markets.

Engine M.A.N. D2566MKF 6-cylinder turbocharged diesel 11,413cc 280bhp (206kW) **Transmission** Clutch: single dry plate; Gearbox: Fuller RTO 11613 5F 1R; Front Axles: double reduction; Rear Axles: double reduction **Frame** channel section ladder type **Brakes** dual circuit fully air-operated **Dimensions** wheelbase 6,000mm; overall length: 8,235mm; overall width: 2,500mm; height to top of cab: 3,239mm; gross weight: 34,000kg; load capacity: 23,000kg **Performance** maximum speed: 70km/hr

Maker: Minsk Avto Zavod, Minsk

This is the most powerful all-wheel-drive cargo truck made in the USSR. In production since 1976, it is descended from a line of 8 × 8 designs made in the MAZ factory since the early 1960s. Primarily intended for military purposes, these trucks are also widely used for civilian work whenever heavy hauling is called for, particularly over rough ground. They can be used solo or with drawbar trailers; maximum payload with a four-axle trailer is 60,000kg. Special versions are used for carrying large diameter pipes or as logging trucks. Among its special features are twin two-seater cabs, eight independently sprung wheels fitted with 1500 × 600-635 tyres, and an automatic gearbox.

Engine D12A-525A V-12 diesel 38,800cc 525bhp (386kW) **Transmission** Clutch: Torque converter; Gearbox: 3F 1R automatic; Transfer Box: two speed; Axles: double reduction **Frame** channel section ladder type **Brakes** air/hydraulic **Dimensions** wheelbase: 7,700mm; overall length: 11,657mm; overall width: 2,975mm; overall height: 2,950mm; gross weight: 44,150kg; load capacity: 20,000kg **Performance** maximum speed: 60km/hr

Maker: Oshkosh Truck Corporation, Oshkosh, Wisconsin

The Dragon Wagon concept was originally developed by the Lockheed Missiles & Space Company, and made by them from 1974 to 1980. The patents were then acquired by Oshkosh, and a totally new Dragon Wagon with much lower profile cab and different engine appeared in 1981. The distinctive feature of the design is a centre-articulated frame which can yaw up to 32° and roll up to 6° in either direction. In effect it consists of two modules each of which drives on all four of its wheels. As well as carrying goods the rear module can be fitted with a 5th wheel for semi-trailer work, in which form it can cope with a load of 45 to 65 tons on good roads. It can be a medium-mobility truck for 22.5 ton loads, or a high-mobility truck with excellent off-road performance with a 12.5 ton load. The Dragon Wagon illustrated is in military paint, but just as the Lockheed version was used for commercial purposes, so Oshkosh expect theirs to find customers in businesses such as oil exploration.

Engine Detroit Diesel 8V-92A V-8 turbocharged diesel 12,060cc 445bhp (332kW) **Transmission** Clutch: torque converter; Gearbox: Allison HT704D 4F 1R automatic; Transfer Box: Oshkosh 2 speed; Front Axles: single reduction tandem; Rear Axles: single reduction tandem **Frame** channel section, articulated at centre **Brakes** dual circuit fully air-operated **Dimensions** wheelbase: 7,139mm; overall length: 10,442mm; overall width: 2,438mm; height to top of cab: 2,591mm; gross weight: 34,473kg; load capacity: see text **Performance** maximum speed: 83km/hr

Maker: Titan Véhicules Spéciaux, Villefranche-sur-Saone

This Titan company is a French manufacturer of all-wheel-drive vehicles, and should not be confused with the German Titan GmbH of Appenweier, makers of heavy road tractors. At present the French Titan company, which has been well known in the fields of dump bodies and trailers, and which built their first complete truck in 1982, produces 6 × 6 and 8 × 8 rigid trucks, and a 6 × 6 articulated dump truck. Besides these all-wheel-drive models, Titan make 8 × 4 tractors especially for military purposes. Most Titans are based on Terberg components, and the company also imports complete Terberg trucks which are sold on the French market as Titans. In other cases Titan trucks feature Renault engines, gearboxes and cabs, with axles by SOMA or Terberg, and Terberg frames. Annual production is about 100 units. In addition to France, Titans are sold in several African countries.

Engine Volvo TD121G 6-cylinder turbocharged diesel 329bhp (242kW) **Transmission** Clutch: twin dry plate; Gearbox: Volvo R70, 8F 1R synchromesh Transfer Box: MAN G801, two speed; Front Axle: Terberg hub reduction tandem or SOMA hub reduction tandem; Rear Axle: Terberg hub reduction tandem or SOMA hub reduction tandem **Frame** channel section ladder type **Brakes** dual circuit fully air-operated **Dimensions** wheelbase: 5,900mm; overall length: 8,235mm; overall width: 2,500mm; height to top of cab: 3,200mm; gross weight: 55,000kg; load capacity: 21,000kg **Performance** maximum speed: 80km/hr

Maker: Floor's Handel en Industrie BV, Wijchen

This is one of the very few 10 × 4 chassis made for general hauling, though the layout is more familiar on specialist concrete mixer chassis. The F.T.F. can be used for this work, but is also seen as a tipper. The drive is taken to the two leading rear axles, the final one being a tag axle to support the chassis. Most components, including the Detroit Diesel 6V-71 engine and Fuller Roadranger transmission, are shared with the 8-wheelers in the F.T.F. range. Detroit Diesel 8V-92 engine and Allison automatic transmission are options.

Engine Detroit Diesel 6V-71N V-6 diesel 6,976cc 230bhp (169kW) **Transmission** Clutch: twin dry plate; Gearbox: Fuller Roadranger RTO 9513 13F 1R constant mesh; Rear Axles: double reduction tandem **Frame** channel section ladder type **Brakes** dual circuit fully air-operated **Dimensions** wheelbase: 6,520mm; overall length: 9,260mm; overall width: 2,490mm; height to top of cab: 3,050mm; gross weight: 45,000kg; load capacity: 28,000kg **Performance** maximum speed: 85km/hr

Maker: Ginaf Automobielbedrijven BV, Veenendaal

Introduced in 1984, the F520 DKX is Ginaf's first five axle truck, and a keen competitor of the similar Terberg F3000. The three leading axles steer, and the middle axle, which is the only unpowered one, can be pneumatically raised by about 30cm, allowing the same off-road performance as any 8 × 8 vehicle. On the road, the fifth axle allows the F520 to operate up to a maximum GVW of 58, 100kg, or 8,000kg more than a four axle truck. It is powered by a DAF 11,630cc turbocharged engine with piston cooling and intercooling, and, like other current Ginafs, has Holland's first locally designed and made steerable planetary hub reduction axles. These are made by Ginaf using DAF components, while the rear axles are DAF made. Because Ginaf employ so many components of DAF origin, including cabs, they can be serviced by the international network of DAF dealers and service stations.

Engine DAF DKX1160 6-cylinder turbocharged and intercooled diesel 11,630cc 365bhp (243kW) **Transmission** Clutch: Fichtel & Sachs single dry plate; Gearbox: ZF 16S 130 16F 2R synchromesh; Transfer Box: Mercedes Benz VG2000 3W 2-speed; Front Axles: Ginaf APG20 double reduction; Rear Axles: DAF 2699T double reduction **Frame** channel section ladder type **Brakes** dual circuit fully air-operated **Dimensions** wheelbase: 5,338mm; overall length: 8,220mm; overall width: 2,480mm; height to top of cab: 3,070mm; gross weight: 58,100kg; load capacity: 45,500kg **Performance** maximum speed: 70km/hr

Maker: Terberg Benschop BV, Benschop

Like Ginaf and the now defunct RAM, Terberg began by selling reconditioned ex-US Army trucks soon after World War II. As the supply of original components dried up they incorporated an increasing proportion of modern parts of European origin, and became truck manufacturers in their own right. Mercedes-Benz engines and cabs were used for a while, but more recently Terberg have standardised on Volvo components. Among their many products are 6 × 6, 8 × 8 and 10 × 8 chassis which are used mainly for heavy aggregate transport. The F3000 steers with three of its five axles, only the central one being unpowered. Maximum legal GVW in the Netherlands for a five axle truck is 58,100 kg. Like other heavy Terberg trucks, the F3000 uses a Volvo F12 cab.

Engine Volvo TD 121G 6-cylinder turbocharged diesel 11,970cc 320bhp (235kW) **Transmission** Clutch: Volvo twin dry plate; Gearbox: Fuller RTO-14613 13F 2R constant mesh; Transfer Box: Mercedes-Benz VG2000 2-speed; Front Axles: Terberg/Soma hub reduction tandem; Rear Axles: Terberg/Soma hub reduction tandem **Frame** channel section ladder type **Brakes** dual circuit fully air-operated **Dimensions** wheelbase: 6,850mm; overall length: 9,030mm; overall width: 2,489mm; height to top of cab: 3,250mm; gross weight: 58,100kg; load capacity: 45,000kg **Performance** maximum speed: 80km/hr

Maker: Fahrzeugfabrik Willy Scheuerle, Pfedelbach

The Scheuerle company makes the largest prime movers in the world, capable of transporting indivisible loads weighing up to 400 tonnes. They use hydrostatic drive to independently sprung half axles, each carrying two wheels. Thus the truck illustrated has 14 axles and 28 wheels. Most Scheuerles work at very low speeds, but one recently introduced model is capable of 65km/hr fully loaded, so can be licenced for use on the German *autobahnen*. The truck illustrated is a special order for an American customer for the transport of large cylinders, and is a load carrier rather than a tractor like most earlier Scheuerles. It is powered by two Cummins VTA 171OC V-12 engines totalling 1600bhp driving nine of the 14 axles, six for slow motion and three for higher speeds. Maximum speed when carrying a full payload of 290 tonnes is 24km/hr, while empty the Scheuerle can reach 40km/hr. These figures are for level running – at a gradient of 8% the laden speed is 6.4km/hr. All axle lines except the fourth are steered. The six slow motion axles are lifted automatically when the vehicle is running unladen.

Engine Two Cummins VTA 171OC V-12 turbocharged diesels 28,040cc 800bhp (596.8kW) each **Transmission** Clutch: none; Gearbox: none (hydrostatic drive to nine axles); Driven axles: NAF. Non-driven axles: Sauer EZP 16242V. **Frame** box section central main beam with box section outriggers **Brakes** hydrostatic on driven axles **Dimensions** overall length: 18,750mm; overall width: 4,500mm; gross weight: 370,000kg; load capacity: 290,000kg **Performance** maximum speed: see text

Articulated Trucks

The articulated truck, or tractor and semi-trailer, first appeared in 1898 when the British Thornycroft company attached a two-wheeled trailer to one of their new short-wheelbase steam wagons. The combination won a Premier Award at the 1898 Liverpool Heavy Vehicle Trials, but no more were made, nor were any other vehicles of this kind seen for more than ten years. The first company to offer articulated trucks for sale was the Knox Automobile Company of Springfield, Massachusetts who offered a 3-wheel tractor in 1909. Designed by Charles Hay Martin, it featured a turntable carried by semi-elliptic springs attached directly to the rear axle of the tractor so that the weight of the semi trailer was carried by the tractor rear wheels, and the much lighter weight of the tractor was carried by separate lighter springs. The tractor frame could also be of lighter construction than otherwise. Powered by 40hp 4-cylinder engines, these Knox-Martin tractors could pull five or ten ton loads at up to 10 mph, or with altered gearing they could do 33 mph when coupled to fire apparatus.

A four-wheeled tractor was introduced in 1915 and made until well into the 1920s. The British Scammell tractor went into production in 1921; it used the same principle as the Knox, and as the axle loading did not exceed 6 tons on any one axle it was permitted to travel at 12 mph, instead of the 5 mph to which other tractors, mostly steam traction engines, were subject. The Scammell had a rated payload of 7 tons compared with 5 for a rigid truck of comparable power, though it frequently carried much more. It had few rivals in Britain until the late 1920s, but in America several firms, in particular Mack and White, had articulated trucks in regular production by 1923. Scammell built two exceptional tractors which with special trailers could pull 100 ton loads, in 1929, and carried on with steady development of their 4 × 2 tractors up to the 1960s.

The articulated truck was more widespread in America than in Europe in the years before the Second World War, and by the late 1930s refinements such as sleeper cabs were not uncommon on the powerful Macks, Whites, Kenworths and Internationals which were already starting to take long-distance freight haulage away from the railways. Where state laws permitted them, double bottoms (a drawbar trailer behind a semi-trailer) were frequently used, and the twin-axle semi-trailer also made its appearance. The 6 × 4 tractor was very rare before the war, but the need to haul aircraft components, and sometimes complete aircraft, led to 6 × 4s being made by firms like Kenworth and Peterbilt, and they soon became part of the ranges of most American firms offering heavy trucks.

1910

In Europe the 'artic' was much slower to become widespread, most manufacturers sticking to large rigid 6-wheelers, and in Britain, 8-wheelers, though artics became progressively more popular in the 1950s, and with more powerful engines and increased GVWs they had become the most logical solution by the 1960s. From 1964 onwards the maximum permissible GVW in Britain was 32½ tonnes. Although opposed by environmental groups the British transport industry in late 1982 obtained government approval to have this figure raised to bring the country into line with the rest of Europe, where a 38 tonne limit generally prevails. Some countries allow more, the limit in Belgium being 40 tonnes, Italy 44 tonnes, and Holland 50 tonnes. Since 1982 British manufacturers have produced a variety of tractors to cope with 38 tonne loads, in 6 × 2 twin steer, or 6 × 4 models, and export models are made by some companies which can easily pull up to 44 tonnes.

In America the general limit is 80,000lbs (36.8 tonnes), but some states permit a much higher limit so long as the weight is spread over a sufficient number of axles. The most notable example is Michigan, where a GCW of 153,000lbs (70.38 tonnes) is permitted, but axle weight limits necessitate up to 11 axles for such a load. This might be made up by a 3-axle tractor, 5-axle semi-trailer and 3-axle drawbar trailer behind, or a 5-axle rigid truck pulling a 6-axle drawbar trailer. Several of the axles can be lifted when the truck is running empty. These rigs are mostly used for carrying sand and gravel, or steel, and only operate within the state of Michigan.

All American manufacturers offer forward-control (cab-overs) and bonnetted (conventional) tractors, as buyers are about evenly divided as to the merits of the two layouts. The conventional is thought to give a more comfortable ride and to give greater protection in the event of a head-on collision, but obviously loses out in states where overall length limits apply. Generalisations are dangerous, but rather more conventionals are bought by owner operators, and cab-overs by fleet operators. Both types can be had with special luxury packages for cab and sleeping compartments which are fitted out to the standard of a high quality mobile home.

Overleaf: 1910 Knox-Martin 3-wheeled tractor and beer-carrying semi-trailer.

Maker: Vauxhall Motors Ltd, Luton, Bedfordshire

The Bedford TL series was introduced in 1980; covering many of the same models as the TK series, it has a wider spread, from 5.7 to 16.3 tonnes GVW for rigid chassis, and including five tractors from 16.3 to 32 tonnes GCW. A total of seven engines are offered in the TL range, though the smaller ones are not available in the tractors. One of the major improvements in the TL is a re-designed cab with greater quietness and comfort. For major servicing it can be tilted forward, but routine maintenance can be carried out via panels behind the doors. There are five tractors in the TL range, the 1630 powered by a 5.4-litre engine, the 1930 illustrated powered by the 8.2-litre Blue Series or 5.4-litre Red Series engine, and the 2400, 2800 and 3200 (24, 28 and 32 tonnes), all using the 8.2-litre 210bhp Blue Series.

Engine Bedford 8.2/130D 6-cylinder diesel 8,198cc 127.5bhp (95.2kW) **Transmission** Clutch: single dry plate; Gearbox: Turner T5A 5F 1R synchromesh on upper four ratios; Rear Axle: Eaton 16 Series two speed single reduction spiral bevel **Frame** channel section ladder type **Brakes** dual circuit fully air-operated **Dimensions** wheelbase: 2,438mm; overall length: 4,457mm; overall width: 2,016mm; height to top of cab: 2,309mm; gross weight: 19,310kg; load capacity: 12,000kg **Performance** maximum speed: 100km/hr

Maker: Vauxhall Motors Ltd, Luton, Bedfordshire

When Bedford introduced their TM range in 1975 they offered maximum weight trucks in both rigid and articulated form, the latter for GCWs up to 32 tonnes. Later, models for 38 and 44 tonnes were added to the range for export markets, the latter available with a 6 × 4 tractor. Engines on the TM tractors can be the Bedford Blue Series 8.2-litre, Detroit Diesel 6V71DD 7-litre, Detroit Diesel 8V71DD 9.3-litre or Cummins E-290 14-litre. For 1983 the new 10-litre Cummins LT10 was also offered in the TM Series. Three cabs are available, the regular as illustrated, full width or sleeper. Transmissions vary according to engine fitted, and include Turner, Eaton, ZF, Fuller and Spicer units from 6 to 13 forward speeds, and an Allison automatic 5 speed with direct drive on top.

Engine Detroit Diesel 6V71DD V-6 diesel 6,981cc 222bhp (165kW) *or* Bedford Blue Series 8.2/210TD 6-cylinder turbocharged diesel 8,198cc 208bhp (155.5kW) **Transmission** Clutch: twin dry plate; Gearbox: Fuller RT609 direct top 9F 1R, *or* RTO609 overdrive top 9F 1R both constant mesh; Rear Axle: Bedford single reduction hypoid **Frame** channel section ladder type **Brakes** triple circuit fully air-operated **Dimensions** wheelbase: 2,769 or 3,000mm; overall length: 4,845 or 5,115mm; overall width: 2,480mm; height to top of cab: 2,925mm; gross weight: 32,520kg; load capacity: 17,500kg **Performance** maximum speed: 110km/hr

Maker: Ford Motor Co Ltd, Langley, Bucks

The Ford Cargo series was introduced in 1981 as a replacement for the long-lived D series of which more than 540,000 had been made since 1965. The Cargo covered an even wider range of models which has been extended still further since the year of introduction, and now covers rigid and articulated trucks from 6 to 32 tonnes GVW. There are twelve Cargo tractors, all with the same wheelbase but offering a wide range of engines from the Ford 130 and 150 for the lower end of the scale (17 to 21 tonnes) up to the 206bhp Deutz V6, 215bhp Perkins V8-640 and 240bhp Cummins LT10-250 for the 28 to 32 tonne models. Ford Cargo tractors can be fitted with a variety of Regular Production Options, including aerodynamic aids such as roofmounted air deflector and under bumper airdam. Cargo models are identified by a four-digit code. The first two denote the approximate GVW, and the last two the brake horsepower divided by ten. Thus the 3224 illustrated is a 32 tonner with 240bhp engine.

Engine Cummins LT10-250 6-cylinder turbocharged diesel 10,000cc 240bhp (186kW)
Transmission Clutch: single dry plate; Gearbox Fuller 11609A 9F 1R constant mesh; Rear Axle: Eaton single reduction hypoid **Frame** channel section ladder type **Brakes** dual circuit air/hydraulic **Dimensions** wheelbase: 3,000mm; overall length: 5,314mm; overall width: 2,280mm; height to top of cab: 2,495mm; gross weight: 32,000kg; load capacity: 20,000kg **Performance** maximum speed: 100km/hr

Maker: Hino Motors Ltd, Tokyo

The SH is part of Hino's new range of tractors, introduced in 1982, sharing the same three seater cab and made in 4 × 2 (SH) and 6 × 4 (SS) models. Two engines are available in the SH series, a 260bhp six, in the SH273 and a 320bhp V8 in the SH633. The former is for GCWs up to 38 tonnes, while the latter is for 40 tonnes. A nine speed synchromesh gearbox is standard on both models, but the SH273 can also be had with six speeds. Hino trucks are exported to 120 countries, and the company has assembly plants in Ireland, Portugal and Canada.

Engine Hino EK100 6-cylinder diesel 13,267cc 260bhp (191kW) *or* Hino EF750 V8 diesel 16,745cc 320bhp (235kW) **Transmission** Clutch: single dry plate; Gearbox: 6F 1R or 9F 1R synchromesh; Rear Axle: double reduction **Frame** channel section ladder type **Brakes** dual circuit fully air-operated **Dimensions** wheelbase: 3,200mm; overall length: 5,550mm; overall width: 2,490mm; height to top of cab: 3,060mm; gross weight: 38,000kg; load capacity: 26,000kg **Performance** maximum speed: 98 or 102km/hr according to gearbox

Maker: Kutaisi Avto Zavod, Kutaisi, Georgia

The KAZ factory began vehicle manufacture in about 1951, making trucks of ZIS (later ZIL) design. Today ZIL components are still largely used in the KAZ-608V tractor, but the design is that of the Georgian factory. It was introduced in 1967 as the KAZ-608 Kolhida, and improved in 1976 as the KAZ-608V. The tilt cab seats three and has sleeping accommodation. This tractor is the only model made in the Kutaisi factory. The name Kolhida comes from the territory on the Black Sea near the factory, which was the ancient land of Colchis, site of the Argonauts' expedition in search of the Golden Fleece, and birthplace of Medea.

Engine ZIL-130Ya5 V-8 petrol 5,966cc 150bhp (110kW) **Transmission** Clutch: single dry plate; Gearbox: 5F 1R no synchro on low; Rear Axle: double reduction **Frame** channel section ladder type **Brakes** air-operated **Dimensions** wheelbase: 2,900mm; overall length: 5,062mm; overall width: 2,360mm; overall height: 2,525mm; gross weight: 19,725kg; load capacity: 15,500kg **Performance** maximum speed: 70km/hr

Maker: Leyland Vehicles Ltd, Leyland, Lancashire

The Roadtrain was the first of the new generation of Leyland trucks to use the T45 cab which was styled by Ogle Design Limited and made by Motor Panels. This cab was tested in Concorde's wind tunnel, and gives about one third less drag than other production cabs. Engine options on the Roadtrain are Cummins L10-250 or L10-290 or Perkins (ex Rolls-Royce) 240Li, 265Li or 300Li. Leyland also make several 4 × 2 tractors in the Cruiser range, for GCW for 24 to 35 tonnes, powered by Leyland engines, and Cummins-powered 6 × 2 or 6 × 4 tractors. A Spicer SS10 10-speed splitter gearbox is standard.

Engine Cummins L10-250 6-cylinder turbocharged diesel 10,000cc 250bhp (186kW) **Transmission** Clutch: twin dry plate; Gearbox: Spicer SS10 10F 2R constant mesh; Rear Axle: double reduction **Frame** channel section ladder type **Brakes** dual circuit fully air-operated **Dimensions** wheelbase: 3,220mm; overall length: 5,460mm; overall width: 2,377mm; height to top of cab: 3,120mm; gross weight 38,000kg; load capacity: 17,500kg **Performance** maximum speed: 88 to 120km/hr, according to axle ratio

Maker: Liberecke Automobilove Zavody, Jablonec nad Nisou

This is the tractor model of the new Liaz range, which with the 100.05 16-tonne 4 × 2 truck, was introduced late in 1974 to supplement and eventually replace the old Skoda 706 series. It was powered by a 6-cylinder turbocharged diesel engine of 270 or 304bhp, but more recently an uprated engine with intercooling developing 320bhp has been added, the truck so powered being known as the 100.55. All Liaz models use British-made Holset turbochargers. The gearbox is a two-range 5-speed unit made by Praga. An additional tractor is the 6 × 2 known as the 122.47. All these Liaz vehicles comply fully with Western European Construction and Use regulations. The current range, with minor re-styling, and engines from 210 to 320bhp, is called the 110 series.

Engine MS 637 6-cylinder turbocharged diesel 11,940cc 270bhp (200kW) *or* MS 638 6-cylinder turbocharged diesel 11,940cc 304bhp (222.1kW) **Transmission** Clutch: twin dry plate; Gearbox: Praga 10 P 80 10F 1R synchromesh; Rear Axle: double reduction **Frame** channel section ladder type **Brakes** dual circuit fully air-operated **Dimensions** wheelbase: 3,750mm; overall length: 6,350mm; overall width: 2,500mm; height to top of cab: 2,715mm; gross weight: 38,000kg; load capacity: 24,000kg **Performance** maximum speed: 110km/hr

Maker: Antoine Lohéac, Grand Couronne, Rouen

The Lohéac has a most unusual background, in that the trucks are built entirely for use by Antoine Lohéac's own tanker company, and none are sold to outside customers. Nevertheless more than 500 have been made; when production began in the early 1950s they were based on ex-US Army semi-forward control tractors made to the same design by International, Kenworth and Marmon-Herrington. Gradually M. Lohéac incorporated more of his own components including cabs, semi-trailers and even items usually bought out, such as silencers and fuel tanks. Engines were Berliets at first, but recently he has standardised on 280bhp Daf or 320bhp Scania units. No Lohéac has ever been scrapped, but simply rebuilt, so that the frames are still the old World War 2 American ones, as are the steering wheels. The snout-like bonnets bear some trace of their US Army ancestry, but bonnets and cabs are made at the Lohéac premises. Of fibreglass construction, they do not tilt, as M. Lohéac believes that tilt cabs are only useful on unreliable trucks! The great majority of the 500 made are articulated tankers, but a few 4 × 2, 4 × 4 and 6 × 6 rigids have been made as well.

Engine Daf DKS 1160E turbocharged 6-cylinder diesel 11,630cc 280bhp (206kW) *or* Scania DS14 turbocharged V-8 diesel 14,200cc 320bhp (238.7kW) **Transmission** Clutch: single dry plate; Gearbox: Fuller RT-9509A 9F 1R constant mesh; Rear Axle: Eaton single reduction spiral bevel **Frame** channel section ladder type **Brakes** dual circuit fully air-operated **Dimensions** wheel base: N/A; overall length: N/A; overall width: N/A; height to top of cab: N/A; gross weight: 38,000kg; load capacity: 22,000kg **Performance** maximum speed: 105km/hr

Maker: Minsk Avto Zavod, Minsk

The MAZ plant has been making trucks since 1947, and in 1965 they broke new ground with their 500 series which were the first forward-control Russian trucks to be made in any numbers. Straight trucks and tractors were made, originally with 180bhp V-6 engines, replaced in 1973 by 240bhp V-8s. The all-metal three-seater tilt cab can be had with a single-bunk sleeper, as illustrated. Various semi-trailers are available with the 504B tractor, including a tanker and a hydraulically-operated tipper.

The MAZ-5429 has been produced since 1978 and has a three-place cab instead of a two-place one like found on MAZ-504V. Some, called MAZ-5430, are fitted with hydraulic apparatus for a tipper semitrailer.

Engine YaMZ-236 V-6 diesel 11,150cc 180bhp (132.4kW) **Transmission** Clutch: twin dry plate; Gearbox: 5F 1R; Rear Axle: double reduction **Frame** channel section ladder type **Brakes** dual circuit fully air operated **Dimensions** wheelbase: 3,950mm; overall length: 5,620mm; overall width: 2,500mm; height to top of cab: 2,720mm; gross weight: 24,100kg; load capacity: 13,500kg **Performance** maximum speed: 85km/hr

Maker: Minsk Avto Zavod, Minsk

Three years after the turbocharged flagship of the MAZ range, the 6422 tractor, was launched, came a slightly de-tuned 4 × 2 tractor 5432. It has a similar two-seat, two-bunk sleeper cab with a number of contemporary features which separate it from 504V and 5430 tractors, produced in parallel to date. Mechanical improvements include a 8-speed box instead of a 5-speeder and multi-featured braking system similar to that in the model 6422. For this truck was designed a two-axle 20-tonner semi-trailer MAZ-9397 (21,000kg in the case of a version with aluminium body).

Engine YaMZ-238P V-8 turbocharged diesel 14,860cc 280bhp (206kW) **Transmission** Clutch: twin dry plate; Gearbox: 8F 1R; Rear Axle: double reduction **Frame** channel section ladder type **Brakes** dual circuit fully air operated **Dimensions** wheelbase: 3,550mm; overall length: 6,050mm; overall width: 2,500mm; height to top of cab: 2,870mm; gross weight: 34,000kg; load capacity: 20,000kg **Performance** maximum speed: 88km/hr

Maker: Daimler-Benz AG, Stuttgart

There are several models of two-axle Mercedes-Benz tractor, for GCWs of between 30 and 38 tonnes, operating with two- or three-axle trailers. The 1633S illustrated is powered by a 14.6-litre V-8 engine, in three versions, the naturally aspirated 017422 (276bhp), the turbocharged 017422A (330bhp), use the turbocharged and intercooled 0174226A (375bhp). Gearboxes are either ZF 5-speed or Mercedes-Benz 8-speed, both being all-synchromesh boxes. Four cabs are offered, two lengths of day cab and two sleeper. All tilt for maintenance. For heavier loads there are a number of three-axle tractors in 6 × 2, 6 × 4 or 6 × 6 form. With low-loading trailers, these can pull up to 110 tons GCW.

Engine Mercedes-Benz OM422 V-8 diesel 14,620cc 276bhp (206kW) **Transmission** Clutch: single dry plate; Gearbox: ZF 5 S-110GP 5F 1R all-synchromesh; Rear axle: double reduction **Frame** channel section ladder type **Brakes** dual circuit fully air-operated **Dimensions** wheelbase: 3,500mm; overall length: 5,995mm; overall width: 2,500mm; height to top of cab: 3,260mm; gross weight: 38,000kg; load capacity: 22,000kg **Performance** maximum speed: 111km/hr

Maker: Comercial Pegaso SA, Madrid

This is one of Pegaso's range of articulated trucks which are widely used for long-distance haulage in Spain. This particular model uses a 12-litre 310bhp Pegaso turbocharged diesel engine, but larger tractors are powered by a turbocharged and intercooled version developing 340bhp. Gearboxes are ZF 16 speed synchromesh or Fuller 9 or 13 speed constant mesh. GVWs are normally 38 tonnes, but the most powerful 6 × 4 tractor can be used with a low-loading trailer for a GCW of 80 tonnes. Pegaso trucks are sold in many of the world's markets, being particularly well-represented in Africa and Latin America. They are also sold in Poland, Rumania, Bulgaria, Greece and several Middle Eastern countries.

Engine Pegaso 9156.73 6-cylinder turbocharged diesel 11,945cc 310bhp (228kW) **Transmission** Clutch: single dry plate; Gearbox: ZF 165-130 16F 2R synchromesh *or* Fuller RTXF-1161313 13F 1R constant mesh *or* Fuller RTXF-11609A 9F 1R constant mesh; Rear Axle: double reduction **Frame** channel section ladder type **Brakes** dual circuit fully air-operated **Dimensions** wheelbase: 3,500mm; overall length: 5,985mm; overall width: 2,450mm; height to top of cab: 3,215mm; gross weight: 38,000kg; load capacity: 19,000kg **Performance** maximum speed: 86 to 125km/hr according to gearbox and axle ratio

Maker: Steyr-Daimler-Puch AG, Steyr

Ten road tractors are made in Steyr's 91 series, with engines ranging from 6½-litres and 145bhp to the most powerful Steyr engine, the 11,970cc 330bhp V-8. The latter powers 6 × 4 as well as 4 × 2 tractors. The 1291.280 illustrated is one of the most popular models as its engine gives adequate power for most operations, yet is not as heavy on fuel. In fact it proved to be the most economical among its international competition when tested by the German magazine *Lastauto Omnibus*, with an overall figure of 34 litres per 100km.

Engine Steyr WD 615.67 6-cylinder diesel 9,726cc 280bhp (206kW) **Transmission** Clutch: single dry plate; Gearbox: ZF 6F 1R all synchromesh *or* Fuller RTO 9513 13F 1R constant mesh; Rear Axle: double reduction **Frame** channel section ladder type **Brakes** dual circuit fully air-operated with ALB (automatic load dependent braking force regulator) **Dimensions** wheelbase: 3,500mm; overall length: 6,096mm; overall width: 2,428mm; height to top of cab: 2,985mm; gross weight: 38,000kg; load capacity: 16,000kg **Performance** maximum speed: 113km/hr

Maker: Volvo Truck Corporation, Göteborg

The Volvo F10/12 series was introduced in 1977 as a replacement for the long-running and popular F88/89 models which had been made since 1965. They feature a completely new cab with its own suspension system of four coil springs each with a telescopic shock absorber which insulate the cab from the frame, and greatly improved air-conditioning. They are made in 4 × 2, 6 × 2 and 6 × 4 versions, as rigid trucks or tractors, with a choice of 250 or 300bhp engines on the F10s, and 330 or 385bhp on the F12s, all with turbocharging and the option of intercooling on the F12. In 1979 the Globetrotter version was introduced, with new higher cab which acted as an aerofoil and gave an illuminated space for the operator's name, and improved cab comfort. This supplements the regular cab version, but does not replace it. The photograph shows an F12 Globetrotter with intercooler attached to a 3-axle refrigerated van trailer.

Engine Volvo TD120F 6-cylinder turbocharged and intercooled diesel 12,000cc 385bhp (283kW) **Transmission** Clutch: twin dry plate; Gearbox: Volvo SR70 12F 1R constant mesh; Rear Axle: single reduction hypoid **Frame** channel section ladder type **Brakes** dual circuit fully air-operated **Dimensions** wheelbase: 3,200mm; overall length: 5,480mm; overall width: 2,480mm; height to top of cab: 3,468mm; gross weight: 44,000kg; load capacity: 28,000kg **Performance** maximum speed: 108km/hr

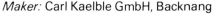

Maker: Carl Kaelble GmbH, Backnang

Kaelble is an old-established company, founded in 1884 and making trucks since 1926, which has specialised in ultra-heavy road tractors, dump trucks and hot ingot and slag transporters, although they also made ordinary goods-carrying trucks up to the mid-1960s. The articulated truck illustrated is intended for cross-country transportation of heavy equipment, crawler tractors, cables etc., and is particularly suited for major road works, and installation of gas and electricity supplies. The tractor is powered by a 320bhp Mercedes-Benz engine, and for extra-heavy loads a second tractor can be used at the rear. This faces backwards, but as they have the same gear ratios in reverse as forward it can be operated satisfactorily in conjunction with the front tractor. The unit can also be driven out of confined spaces without needing to turn round.

Engine Mercedes-Benz OM 403 10-cylinder diesel 15,950cc 320bhp (235kW) **Transmission** Clutch: torque converter; Gearbox: ZF 4F 4R automatic; Transfer Box: ZF; Front Axle: double reduction, planetary gears in wheel hubs; Rear Axle: double reduction, planetary gears in wheel hubs **Frame** channel section ladder type **Brakes** dual circuit, fully air-operated **Dimensions** wheelbase: 4,000mm; overall length: 7,255mm; overall width: 3,750mm; height to top of cab: 4,120mm; gross weight: 60,000kg; load capacity: 45,000kg **Performance** maximum speed: 50km/hr

Maker: E.R.F. Ltd., Sandbach, Cheshire.

Introduced in 1984, the CP range represents a new philosophy at E.R.F. The letters stand for C-type, Preferred specification, and in place of the wide variety of options offered on earlier E.R.F. tractors, the CP concentrates on the combination of Cummins engines, Fuller gearboxes and Eaton rear axles. Other components, such as Gardner engines and Kirkstall axles, are available, but at extra cost, and it is thought that about 75% of orders will be to the 'preferred specification.' Four different Cummins engines are available, 250, 290, 320 and 350bhp, while gearboxes can be either nine or thirteen speeders. Drive systems are 4 × 2, 6 × 2 twin steer, or 6 × 4, and day or sleeper cabs are available. Thus, even within the preferred specification a great variety of models can be had. The most powerful models are designed to cope with GCWs up to 40 tonnes, though restricted to 38 tonnes for operation in the UK. Illustrated is a twin steer 6 × 2 tractor with sleeper cab and Crane Fruehauf trailer.

Engine Cummins NTE-320 6-cylinder turbocharged diesel 14,000cc 320bhp (238.7kW) **Transmission** Clutch: twin dry plate; Gearbox: Fuller RTX 11609A 9F 1R constant mesh; Rear Axle: Rockwell single reduction **Frame** channel section ladder type **Brakes** dual circuit fully air-operated **Dimensions** wheelbase: 3,800mm; overall length: 5,903mm; overall width: 2,484mm; height to top of cab: 3,040mm; gross weight: 38,000kg; load capacity: 24,000kg **Performance** maximum speed: 113 to 120km/hr according to axle ratio

Maker: Fiat SpA, Turin

IVECO offer a wide range of tractors, including several models of 4 × 2, and three twin-steering axle 6 × 2s, the 190.30, 220.30 and 220.38. These are derived from the Fiat 170/190/220 series and use either a 13,798cc six or 17,174cc V-8 engine, both turbocharged. The new Turbostar version of the latter develops 420bhp making it the most powerful European tractor. Air suspension is featured on the centre and rear axles. A Fuller constant mesh gearbox with 12 forward speeds plus a crawler is standardised. Top gear on the 220.38 is an overdrive (0.87:1), but the more powerful Turbostar has direct drive in its ZF or Fuller gearboxes.

Engine Fiat-IVECO 8280.22 V-8 turbocharged diesel 17,174cc 381bhp (279.68kW) **Transmission** Clutch: Fichtel & Sachs single dry plate; Gearbox: Fuller Multimesh RTO 14613 13F 1R constant mesh; Rear Axle: double reduction **Frame** channel section ladder type; **Brakes** dual circuit fully air-operated **Dimensions** wheelbase: 3,780mm; overall length: 6,025mm; overall width: 2,500mm; height to top of cab: 3,109mm; gross weight: 38,000kg; load capacity: 22,000kg **Performance** maximum speed: 109.6km/hr

Maker: Oy Sisu Auto AB, Helsinki (factory at Karjaa)

Introduced in 1983 the SM range is the flagship of Sisu trucks, particularly the long distance 6 × 2 and 6 × 4 tractors which compare very well with their counterparts made in Germany, France or Britain. As well as these the SM range includes 6 × 2, 6 × 4 and 8 × 2 rigid chassis. Cummins engines are used, the NTE290, NTE370 and NTE400 in conjunction with Fuller gearboxes and Sisu's own hub reduction axles. Gross weight for tractor/trailer units is up to 52 tonnes, with 70 tonnes available with rigid trucks and drawbar trailers. The illustration shows a standard sleeper cab, but Sisu offer a luxury version, like International's Eagle. Called the Finlandia it has a special paint job, airconditioning and refrigerator.

Engine Cummins NTE-400 6-cylinder turbocharged and intercooled diesel 14,000cc 405bhp (298kW) **Transmission** Clutch: Spicer twin dry plate; Gearbox: Fuller RTO-14613 13F 2R constant mesh; Rear Axle: Sisu CTR double reduction **Frame** channel section ladder type **Brakes** dual circuit fully air-operated **Dimensions** wheelbase: 4,700mm; overall length: 6,840mm; overall width: 2,500mm; height to top of cab: 3,125mm; gross weight: up to 52,000kg; load capacity: about 35,000kg **Performance** maximum speed: 96 to 117km/hr, according to axle ratio

Maker: Seddon Atkinson Vehicles Ltd, Oldham, Lancashire

Introduced in 1981, the 401 was the first of the second generation of Seddon Atkinson trucks replacing the 400 after six years of successful service, and benefiting from technology acquired from International Harvester who took over Seddon Atkinson in 1974. In 1983 Seddon Atkinson introduced a lighter tractor, the 301, and these together make up the current tractor range which is available in 4 × 2, 6 × 2 and 6 × 4 versions for GCWs from 17 to 38 tonnes. The 301s are powered by Cummins engines, the LT10-250 or LTA10-290, while the 401 can be supplied with a variety of Cummins, Gardner or Perkins engines. Areas of high corrosion risk in the cab including the grille, quarter panels and wheel arches, are made of SMC (sheet moulded compound), while doors, roof, side and under floor panels are of Zintec coated steel. The 6 × 2 tractor illustrated is powered by a Cummins E320 engine, and is used to transport wood from the operator's saw mills to major customers such as the National Coal Board. With a Redmond semi-trailer, GCW of the outfit is 38 tonnes.

Engine Cummins E320 6-cylinder turbocharged diesel, 14,000cc 308bhp (230kW) *or* Perkins 300Li 6-cylinder turbocharged diesel, 12,170cc 288bhp (215kW) **Transmission** Clutch: twin dry plate; Gearbox: Fuller RTX11609A 9F 1R constant mesh; Rear Axle: Rockwell S180E single reduction hypoid **Frame** channel section ladder type **Brakes** dual circuit fully air-operted **Dimensions** wheelbase: 3,810mm; overall length: 6,126mm; overall width: 2,426mm; height to top of cab: 3,376mm; gross weight: 38,000kg; load capacity: 25,000kg **Performance** maximum speed: 120km/hr

Maker: Ashok-Leyland Ltd, Madras

In 1955 Ashok-Leyland Ltd. was established in technical collaboration with Leyland Motors Ltd. of the United Kingdom. But during the first twenty years, the Ashok-Leyland vehicles did not feature any resemblance at all with the truck and buses made by their overseas collaborator. This changed during the mid-seventies, and today several Ashok-Leyland models are similar to the vehicles made by British Leyland until a few years ago. An example is the 4 × 2 Tusker Turbo tractor, which in fact is the well-known Marathon. The Beaver, Comet, Hippo, Taurus and Tusker belong to Ashok-Leyland's current program. They are deliverable in truck and tractor version, with 4 × 2 or 6 × 4 drive layouts. Only the Comet is available with four-wheel drive. Beside this line of trucks, Cheetah and Viking single-deck buses and Titan double-deck buses are made. The four plants, situated in Ennore, Hosur, Bhandara and Alwar turned out 125,000 vehicles in thirty years.

Engine Ashok-Leyland ALI680, 6-cylinder diesel 11,093cc 180bhp (132.5kW) **Transmission** Clutch: single dry plate; Gearbox: Ashok-Leyland 5F 1R constant mesh; Rear Axle: hub reduction tandem **Frame** channel section ladder type **Brakes** dual circuit fully air-operated **Dimensions** wheelbase: 5,980mm; overall length: 9,110mm; overall width: 2,409mm; height to top of cab: NA gross weight: 26,416kg; load capacity: 16,261kg

Maker: International Harvester Australia Ltd, Dandenong

Atkinson began their Australian operations in 1962, and gradually developed a distinctive type of truck with cabs of local design and manufacture, and a high proportion of American components. When International Harvester acquired the parent Seddon Atkinson firm in Britain, the Australian branch was integrated into IHC's Australian operations, and now makes the flagships of the International fleet. The F4870 6 × 4 is the only Atkinson tractor made, but there is also a rigid 8 × 4 chassis, the K4970. The tractor can be supplied in many forms, with options of eight engines, thirteen transmissions, ten rear axles, eight rear suspensions, three front axles and a variety of detail options. The latter include a 'roo bar' as illustrated, frame reinforcements, Jacobs' engine brake and severe service kit. The F4870 is used for a variety of long-distance transport, in particular tankers and livestock trucks, and can pull a road train with two trailers.

Engine Cummins Formula 300 BC11 6-cylinder diesel 14,000cc 300bhp (224kW) **Transmission** Clutch: single dry plate; Gearbox: Fuller RT-11509 9F 1R constant mesh; Rear Axle: Rockwell SP-40 single reduction hypoid tandem **Frame** channel section ladder type **Brakes** dual circuit fully air-operated **Dimensions** wheelbase: 3,840mm; overall length: 6,680mm; overall width: 2,499mm; height to top of cab: 3,300mm; gross weight: 45,000kg; load capacity: 28,000kg **Performance** maximum speed: 110km/hr
(typical available specification for the truck illustrated)

Maker: Volvo White Truck Corporation, Greensboro, North Carolina (factory at Ogden, Utah)

Autocar is one of the oldest names in the American industry, having built their first car in 1897 and their first truck ten years later. In 1953 they were acquired by White, and both makes are now part of Volvo White. Autocars and some White models are made at Ogden, Utah, while Volvo White's main factory is at Dublin, Virginia. For many years all Autocars have been conventional trucks aimed mainly at the construction industry, although the AT models are regular over-the-highway tractors. They are made in two versions, the AT 64B with set back axle and the AT 64F (illustrated) with set forward axle. The ATs use the 400bhp Cummins engine, while the DK and DS models have 300bhp Cummins engines. The DK series are made as either trucks or tractors, and the lighter DS as a truck only. The standard specification includes Cummins engines, Fuller transmission and Rockwell axles, but other components can be specified on request.

Engine Cummins NTC-400 6-cylinder turbocharged diesel 14,000cc 400bhp (298.4kW) **Transmission** Clutch: Spicer twin dry plate; Gearbox: Fuller RTOF-14613 13F 1R constant mesh; Rear Axles: Rockwell SQ-100 single reduction hypoid tandem **Frame** channel section ladder type **Brakes** dual circuit fully air-operated **Dimensions** wheelbase: 5,486mm; overall length: 7,010mm; overall width: 2,642mm; height to top of cab: 2,772mm; gross weight: 36,800kg; load capacity: 24,000kg **Performance** maximum speed: 120km/hr

Maker: Volvo-White Truck Corporation, Greensboro, North Carolina (factory at Ogden, Utah)

The DC Series of conventional construction trucks are built in three models, a 4 × 2 and two 6 × 4s, short wheelbase for tractors as illustrated, and longer wheelbase for haulage work. There are, in fact, a variety of wheelbases available within each group, and such is the bespoke nature of Autocar's work that almost any length can be specified by the customer. The 'B' suffix indicates a set back front axle, while 'F' indicates a set forward axle, as required to comply with axle loading regulations in certain states. Caterpillar, Cummins or Detroit Diesel engines can be specified, in sizes from 230 to 450bhp. GCWs with low-loading machinery trailers as illustrated, can be upwards of 50,000kg. The DC series also includes 4 × 4 and 6 × 6 rigid chassis. For many years Autocars were made in the Philadelphia suburb of Ardmore, Pennsylvania, then moved out to the country at Exton, but from 1980 they have been made in one of Volvo-White's truck plants at Ogden, Utah.

Engine Caterpillar 3408 turbocharged V-8 diesel 17,995cc 450bhp (335.7kW) **Transmission** Clutch: twin dry plate; Gearbox: Fuller 6F 1R main, with 3-speed auxiliary; Rear Axle: single reduction spiral bevel tandem **Frame** channel section double plate ladder type **Brakes** dual circuit fully air-operated **Dimensions** wheelbase: variable; overall length: variable; overall width: 2,642mm; height to top of cab: 3,073mm; gross weight: 60,000kg; load capacity: 40,000kg **Performance** maximum speed: 64km/hr
(typical available specification for the truck illustrated)

Maker: DAF Nederland Bedrijvswagen BV, Eindhoven

This bonnetted tractor is one of DAF's N2800 range, which also includes 6 × 4 rigid chassis for a variety of on/off road work, especially the transport of earth, sand, gravel etc. Three versions of the 11.6-litre 6-cylinder engine are available in the N2800 series, the naturally-aspirated DKA 1160 (230bhp), the turbocharged DKTD 1160 (256bhp) and the turbocharged and inter-cooled DKX 1160 (330bhp). The 6 × 4 tractor illustrated is engaged in log transportation, but these tractors are also popular for use with tipping semi trailers and with low loaders for road construction machinery. With the most powerful engine, GCWs can be as high as 140 tonnes. The N2800 models are not sold on the UK market.

Engine DAF DKA1160 6-cylinder diesel 11,630cc 230bhp (169kW) **Transmission** Clutch: single dry plate Gearbox: ZF 16S 130 8F 1R + splitter = 16F 2R synchromesh Rear Axles: double reduction **Frame** channel section ladder type **Brakes** dual circuit fully air-operated **Dimensions** wheelbase: 4,200mm; overall length: 6,880mm; overall width: 2,480mm; height to top of cab: 2,880mm; gross weight: 44,000kg; load capacity: 26,000kg **Performance** maximum speed: 100km/hr

Maker: DAF Nederland Bedrijvswagen BV, Eindhoven

Introduced in January 1982, the 3300 is the flagship of the DAF range, and replaces the 2800 DKS. It has the same 11.6-litre 6-cylinder engine, turbocharged and inter-cooled, but changes to the fuelling have increased power from 310 to 330bhp. The ZF Ecosplit range-change gearbox has eight forward speeds, which with the splitter give sixteen possible ratios. The 3300 is fitted with VISAR, a computerised system to advise the driver on optimum gear changes. Several different models of the 3300 are made, including 4 × 2, 6 × 2, 6 × 4, 8 × 2 and 8 × 4 rigids, 4 × 2 and 6 × 4 tractors. The 3300 can be had with the luxurious Space Cab whose high roof allows the driver to stand up while changing clothes. Other features include a 12 volt power point for a portable TV set, a shower and a coffee maker.

Engine DAF DKX1160 6-cylinder turbocharged diesel 11,630cc 330bhp (243kW) **Transmission** Clutch: single dry plate; Gearbox: ZF 16S 130 Ecosplit 8F 1R + splitter = 16F 2R synchromesh; Rear Axle: double reduction tandem **Frame** channel section ladder type **Brakes** dual circuit fully air-operated **Dimensions** wheelbase: 4,970mm; overall length: 6,500mm; overall width: 2,440mm; height to top of cab: 2,970mm; gross weight: 44,000kg; load capacity: 26,000kg **Performance** maximum speed: 110km/hr

Maker: Diesel Nacional SA, Monterrey

The Dina 800-series is the top of the line model offered by the Diesel Nacional plant in Sahagun, Mexico, and derived from the wellknown International Transtar 4370. It is available in tractor- or rigid truck with two or three axles and recently even a model incorporating a 3-axle tandem at the rear allowing a load up to 30 tons has been developed. This series tractors can also be specified with a normal sleepercab or a new 'Aerodyne'-style raised unit behind the cab for increased driver-comfort.

Engine Cummins Big Cam NTC-350, 6-cylinder diesel 350hp (261kW) **Transmission** Clutch: twin dry plate; Gearbox: Spicer As-1552 15F 2R; Rear Axle: Rockwell FF-931 single speed spiral bevel type **Frame** steel channel section ladder type **Brakes** full air **Dimensions** wheelbase: 5,659mm; overall length: 6,957mm; width: 2,451mm; gross weight: 54,432kg; load capacity: up to 30,000kg **Performance** maximum speed: 105mm/hr

Maker: Dong-A Motor Co Ltd, Seoul

Ha-Dong Hwan Motor Co Ltd was renamed Dong-A Motor Co Ltd in the seventies. The firm started assembling Nissan Diesel two and three axle normal control and forward control trucks for the South-Korean market. Nowadays, fire-fighting vehicles are made still using Nissan Diesel, as well Isuzu chassis. Trucks and tractors of 30 to 55 ton capacities are manufactured using forward control cabs of Dong-A's own design. Other products are highway and city buses, wheel discs and trailers of all sorts like dump, tanker, cargo, bulk cement, container, low bed and platform. Two plants are operational today, one in Pyung Taek, the other in Boo Pyung. Dong-A's headquarters are located in Seoul.

Engine RD8, V-8 diesel 14,313cc 300bhp (223.8kW) **Transmission** Clutch: single dry plate; Gearbox: TMH511, 5F 1R constant mesh; Rear Axle: single reduction hypoid tandem **Frame** channel section ladder type **Brakes** dual circuit fully air-operated **Dimensions** wheelbase: 3,700mm; overall length: 6,330mm; overall width: 2,420mm; height to top of cab: 2,860mm; gross weight: 23,230 GVW, 53,000 GCW; load capacity: 15,000kg **Performance** maximum speed: 95km/hr

Maker: Faun Werke, Lauf an der Pegnitz

Faun is an old-established company which was originally called Fahrzeugwerke Ansbach und Nurnburg AG, the first letters of which provided the name FAUN. Today they are active in a number of fields, with six factories, four in Germany, one in France and one in the USA. Among their vehicles are heavy road tractors for commercial and military use, crane carriers, dump trucks, fire engines and street sweepers. Most of their road tractors are for drawbar trailers, but among their tractors for semi-trailers is the HZ 36.40/45, available in 6 × 4 and 6 × 6 versions. It is powered by a Klockner-Humboldt-Deutz air-cooled V-12 engine, but Mercedes-Benz or Cummins engines can be fitted as alternatives. The gearbox is normally a 15-speed Fuller, but a ZF box is an option. Weights and payloads vary according to the type of semi trailer; with the two-axle trailer illustrated GCW is 38 to 105 tons, and payload 22 to 75 tons. With an eight-axle semi trailer these figures can be increased to 125 to 250 tons and 80 to 190 tons respectively. With drawbar trailers (see page 319), considerably heavier loads can be drawn.

Engine Deutz F12 L413F V-12 diesel 19,144cc 365bhp (268kW) **Transmission** Clutch: Fichtel & Sachs twin dry plate; Gearbox: Fuller RT-12515 15F 3R constant mesh: Rear Axle: double reduction **Frame** channel section ladder type **Brakes** dual circuit fully air-operated **Dimensions** wheelbase: 4,500mm; overall length: 8,360mm; overall width: 2,500mm; height to top of cab: 3,070mm; gross weight: 106,686kg; load capacity: see text **Performance** maximum speed: 63.9km/hr

Maker: Foden Trucks, Sandbach, Cheshire

The S106T is the largest of the Foden tractors, which are also available in 4 × 2 form as the S104. Standard engine in the S106T is a Cummins 10-litre, but under Foden's policy of offering many options, fourteen other power units can be specified, by Caterpillar, Cummins and Perkins (ex-Rolls-Royce). Optional engine equipment includes a Cummins variable-speed governor, hand throttle control and two-stage air cleaners. Seven transmissions are available, 9, 10 or 13-speeders, in addition to the standard Fuller 9-speed gearbox. As with other Foden trucks, the wheelbase can be varied to give any legal length. Maximum GCW on British roads is restricted to 38 tonnes, but the S106T can cope with GCWs up to 55 tonnes in its most powerful form. Day or sleeper cabs are available.

Engine Cummins LT10-250 6-cylinder turbocharged diesel, 10,000cc 250bhp (186kW)
Transmission Clutch: Lipe twin dry plate; Gearbox: Fuller RT7609 9F 1R constant mesh; Rear Axle: Rockwell SQ100 single reduction hypoid tandem **Frame** channel section ladder type **Brakes** dual circuit fully air-operated **Dimensions** wheelbase: 3,885mm; overall length: 6,133mm; overall width: 2,497mm; height to top of cab: 2,949mm; gross weight: 38,000kg; load capacity: 26,000kg
Performance maximum speed: 98 to 108.7km/hr, according to axle ratio

Maker: Ford Motor Company, Louisville, Kentucky

Introduced in 1978, the CL-9000 series is the largest Ford truck, and is suitable for GCWs up to 62,595kg in the 6 × 4 tractor illustrated, although the maximum normal rating on US highways is 80,000lb (36,800kg). This is the CLT-9000, and there is a companion 4 × 2 tractor known as the CL-9000. The usual diesel engines by Caterpillar, Cummins or Detroit Diesel are available, ranging from 270 to 600bhp in the CLT-9000. A feature of these trucks is the variety of cabs offered, five in all, from a very short 54 inch (1,371mm) BBC day cab suitable for long trailers, doubles or triples, through the 64 inch (1,626mm) regular day cab to three sleepers, the longest of which has a BBC measurement of 110 inches (2,794mm) and a double bed. The CLT-9000 has air suspension, including separate air ride for the cab alone that separates it from the action of the frame.

Engine Detroit Diesel 8V92TA V-8 turbocharged diesel 12,051cc 435bhp (324.5kW) **Transmission** Clutch: twin dry plate; Gearbox: Fuller RT-11610 10F 1R constant mesh; Rear Axle: Rockwell SLHD single reduction hypoid tandem **Frame** channel section ladder type **Brakes** dual circuit fully air-operated **Dimensions** wheelbase: 6,248mm; overall width: 2,490mm; height to top of cab: 3,048mm; gross weight: 37,194kg; load capacity: 24,912kg **Performance** maximum speed: 121km/hr
(typical available specification for the truck illustrated)

Maker: Ford Motor Company, Louisville, Kentucky

Introduced in 1981, the LTL-9000 is Ford's answer to premium conventional trucks from International, Kenworth and Peterbilt, and is made on the same assembly line as the forward-control CL-9000 which has been in production for several years. As with most American trucks a very wide range of options is available so that there is no standard specification. There are fourteen engine choices, seven Cummins, six Caterpillar and one Detroit Diesel, of which the most powerful is the 435bhp Detroit Diesel 8V92TA. Transmissions are Fuller, from 9 to 15 speeds. There is an enormous variety of optional cab equipment: exterior trim patterns, mirrors which can be lighted and/or heated, AM/FM radio with or without cassette tape, roof vent and so on. The radio speakers and controls can be extended to the sleeping compartment, as can the cab air conditioning. Fuel consumption is very good; with the Cummins NTC-400 engine and pulling a 30 ton load, the LTL-9000 can average 7 miles per Imperial gallon. There is also a 4 × 2 tractor, known as the LL-9000 using the same bonnet and cab, but with a smaller variety of engine options, up to a maximum of 350bhp.

Engine Caterpillar 3408 turbocharged 6-cylinder diesel 14,600cc 400bhp (298.4kW) **Transmission** Clutch: twin dry plate; Gearbox: Fuller RTO-11615 15F 3R constant mesh; Rear Axle: Rockwell SQHP single reduction hypoid tandem **Frame** channel section ladder type **Brakes** dual circuit fully air-operated **Dimensions** wheelbase: 5,182mm; overall length: 7,506mm; overall width: 2,490mm; height to top of cab: 2,820mm; gross weight: 37,194kg; load capacity: 24,912kg **Performance** maximum speed: 121km/hr

(typical available specification for the truck illustrated)

Maker: Freightliner Corporation, Portland, Oregon

The first Freightliners were built in 1940 by the trucking company, Consolidated Freightways of Salt Lake City, Utah, for their own use, and none went to outside customers until 1948. From 1951 to 1976 they were marketed by White and known as White Freightliners, but they now bear the original Freightliner name. The basic appearance of the forward-control model has changed little in the past twenty years, and it retains the lightweight aluminium construction that distinguished the first Freightliners. The FLT series is available in 4 × 2 and 6 × 4 configurations, though the majority are 6 × 4s as that is the most popular type in the USA. Straight trucks are made as well as tractors, though they make up only a small part of production. The usual engine options of Caterpillar, Cummins or Detroit Diesel are available, with Cummins being the most popular.

Engine Cummins Formula 300 6-cylinder turbocharged diesel 14,000cc 300bhp (223.8kW) **Transmission** Clutch: twin dry plate; Gearbox: Fuller RT-9509A 9F 1R constant mesh; Rear Axle: Rockwell SQHD single reduction hypoid tandem **Frame** channel section ladder type **Brakes** dual circuit fully air-operated **Dimensions** wheelbase: 4,292mm; overall length: 6,007mm; overall width: 2,482mm; height to top of cab: 2,921mm; gross weight: 38,200kg; load capacity: 23,000kg **Performance** maximum speed: 120km/hr
(typical available specification for the truck illustrated)

Maker: Freightliner Corporation, Portland, Oregon

Freightliner's conventional trucks were introduced in 1973, and were a complete breakaway from the exclusively forward control models made up to that time. They are mostly tractors, made in 4 × 2 and 6 × 4 versions, though a 6 × 4 straight truck is also available. Although different in appearance, 80% of the parts are interchangeable with those of the forward-control model including some of the aluminium sheet panels of the cab. They weigh only 100 to 200lb more than the forward-control tractors. Engine, transmission and rear axle options are the same, with the majority of engines being Cummins. As well as the main plant at Portland, Oregon, Freightliner has factories at Chino, California, Indianapolis, Indiana, Mount Holly, North Carolina and Vancouver, Canada. In 1984 a conventional model with set-back front axle was introduced, giving greater manoeuverability and a smaller turning circle. This was in addition to the regular tractor illustrated.

Engine Cummins Formula 300 6-cylinder turbocharged diesel 14,000cc 300bhp (223.8kW) **Transmission** Clutch: twin dry plate; Gearbox: Fuller RT-9509A 9F 1R constant mesh; Rear Axle: Rockwell SQHD single reduction hypoid tandem **Frame** channel section ladder type **Brakes** dual circuit fully air-operated **Dimensions** wheelbase: 4,648mm; overall length: 6,337mm; overall width: 2,482mm; height to top of cab: 2,819mm; gross weight: 39,100kg; load capacity: 23,000kg **Performance** maximum speed: 115km/hr

Maker: G.M.C. Truck & Coach Division, General Motors Corporation, Pontiac, Michigan

The GMC Astro 95 tractor has been made since 1969, with a major facelift on the 1980 models, to which the current design is similar. It is the top offering in the GMC range and is available with a variety of engine options from Caterpillar, Cummins and Detroit Diesel up to a maximum of 450bhp. All engines on the 1985 Astros are turbocharged, and most feature aftercoolers as well. The Astro cab features a Dragfoiler (GMC Patent) aerofoil as standard equipment. Cab interior trims are very varied, and come in Standard, Luxury and Royal Classic versions, the latter being fitted out to a very high standard indeed, including deep cut-pile carpeting on floor, engine housing and sleeper bulkhead. Royal Classic interiors are only available on the 87 inch BBC sleeper cab. Exterior colour schemes are available in 95 different combinations, and make the Astro a popular truck with owner-operators. In addition to complete trucks, the Astro is available as a glider kit

Engine Cummins NTC-400 6-cylinder turbocharged diesel 14,000cc 400bhp (298.4kW)
Transmission Clutch: twin dry plate; Gearbox: Fuller RT-11609A 9F 1R constant mesh; Rear Axle: Rockwell SLHD single reduction hypoid tandem **Frame** channel section ladder type **Brakes** dual circuit fully air-operated **Dimensions** wheelbase: variable; overall length: variable; overall width: 2,490mm; height to top of cab: 2,980mm; gross weight: 36,800kg; load capacity: 22,500kg
Performance maximum speed: 121km/hr
(typical available specification for the truck illustrated)

Maker: GMC Truck and Coach Division, General Motors Corporation, Pontiac, Michigan

Introduced in 1977, the General is the top of the range of GMC conventional trucks, and is made in two or three axle form as a rigid truck or tractor. Up to 1980 there was a companion model badged as the Chevrolet Bison, but since then heavy trucks have been made only as GMCs. Generals are available in 108 and 116 inch BBC measurements, and as sleeper and non sleeper models. The most popular engines are Detroit Diesels in the 92 series, from 293 to 468bhp. New options for 1985 are the 293bhp 6V-71TA and 343bhp 6V-92TA. Other available engines include the Cummins Big Cam III and L-10 Series, and Caterpillar 3406. GVW ratings on the Generals can be as high as 79,000lbs (35,934kg). The cab is made of aluminium, with fibreglass doors, bonnet and wings. Although not shown in the photograph, the General can be fitted with a roof-mounted Dragfoiler to improve air flow.

Engine Detroit Diesel 6V-92TA V-6 turbocharged diesel 9,039cc 343bhp (256kW) **Transmission** Clutch: twin dry plate; Gearbox: Fuller RT-11609 9F 1R constant mesh; Rear Axles: Rockwell SSHD single reduction hypoid tandem **Frame** channel section ladder type **Brakes** dual circuit fully air-operated **Dimensions** wheelbase: variable; overall length: variable; overall width: 2,490mm; height to top of cab: 2,850mm; gross weight: 35,834kg; load capacity: 24,000kg **Performance** maximum speed: 120km/hr
(typical available specification for the truck illustrated)

243

Maker: Hanyang Special-Type Automobile Factory, Wuhan city, Hubei province

Little known until today is the Hanyang range of heavy trucks, developed in the late seventies. Dumpers, crane trucks and truck tractors have been developed by this factory which is situated in the city of Wuhan in Central China. Recently, the cabs have been restyled under Japanese influence. Trucks are designated 460-470 series, trailers 930-950-960-970 series. The heaviest dumper is a 35 ton variant. The Hanyang factory belongs to the Dongfeng (Aeolus) Corporation. Truck models include 4 × 2, 6 × 4, 6 × 6 and 8 × 8 chassis, in addition to 4 × 2, 6 × 4 and 6 × 6 tractors. All are powered by Deutz air-cooled diesel engines.

Engine Deutz F8L413F air-cooled diesel 11,301 cc 228.5 bhp (170.4 kW) **Frame** channel section ladder type **Brakes** dual circuit fully air-operated

244

Maker: International Harvester Truck Division, Chicago, Illinois (factory at Springfield, Ohio)

The CO Transtar series of forward-control tractors have been made since the 1960s with constant updating and improvements, the most noticeable of which is the XL cab illustrated, which was introduced in 1980. As with the 9370 conventional, this has its luxury Eagle version with individual colour schemes and lavish appointments. Because of its low weight and aerodynamic form the XL cab is more fuel efficient than any of its comparable rivals. 9670s are made in 4 × 2 and 6 × 4 versions, with the usual engine options from 290 to 450bhp.

Engine Detroit Diesel 8V-92TTAC V-8 turbocharged diesel 12,051cc 365bhp (272.3kW) **Transmission** Clutch: twin dry plate; Gearbox: Spicer SST-1214-3A 14F 1R constant mesh; Rear Axle: Rockwell SQHD single reduction hypoid tandem **Frame** channel section ladder type **Brakes** dual circuit fully air-operated **Dimensions** wheelbase: 4,737mm; overall length: 6,210mm; overall width: 2,480mm; height to top of cab: 2,900mm; gross weight: 42,000kg; load capacity: 25,000kg **Performance** maximum speed: 120km/hr
(typical available specification for the truck illustrated)

Maker: International Harvester Co, Chicago, Illinois (factory at Springfield, Ohio)

Introduced in August 1984, the 9370 is International's latest offering in the premium conventional truck field, replacing the Transtar F4370 series. Although most 9370s are 4 × 2 or 6 × 4 tractors, there is a rigid 6 × 4 truck model as well. There are ten engine options from 300 to 475bhp, by Cummins and Detroit Diesel, and nine transmissions by Fuller or Spicer. As well as the standard cab in day or sleeper form, there is the Eagle luxury sleeper cab, with facilities that make it more like a motorhome than a truck. These include twin bunks, a fold-down desk, a wash basin with running water and a full length double wardrobe.

Engine Cummins Formula 300 6-cylinder turbocharged diesel 300bhp (223.8kW) **Transmission** Clutch: twin dry plate; Gearbox: Fuller RTO-11609 9F 1R constant mesh; Rear Axle: Rockwell single reduction hypoid tandem **Frame** channel section ladder type **Brakes** dual circuit fully air-operated **Dimensions** wheelbase: variable; overall length: variable; overall width: 2,490mm; height to top of cab: 2,768mm; gross weight: up to 54,431kg; load capacity: up to 40,000kg **Performance** maximum speed: 125km/hr
(typical available specification for the truck illustrated)

Maker: International Harvester Australia Ltd, Dandenong

The Australian International plant makes two ranges of tractors, the forward-control T-2600 series, and the bonnetted S-2600 series. The latter are available in eight chassis, three 4 × 2 and five 6 × 4, for GCWs between 27 and 45 tons, making them second only to the Atkinson F4870 in the Australian International range. Engine options include the 210bhp International DT-466B, and Cummins units of 230, 270, 300 and 350bhp. Transmissions are all Fuller, 9-, 10- or 13-speed constant mesh.

Engine Cummins NTC-350 BC 6-cylinder diesel 14,000cc 350bhp (261kW) **Transmission** Clutch: single dry plate; Gearbox: Fuller RTF-12509 9F 1R constant mesh; Rear Axle: Rockwell SP-40 single reduction hypoid tandem **Frame** channel section ladder type **Brakes** dual circuit fully air-operated **Dimensions** wheelbase: 5,380mm; overall length: 7,670mm; overall width: 2,299mm; height to top of cab: 2,690mm; gross weight: 45,000kg; load capacity: 28,000kg **Performance** maximum speed: 110km/hr

Maker: Kama Auto Zavod, Brezhnev

This is the tractor version of the KamAZ range and like the others is a 6 × 4, but with a shorter wheelbase. These tractors will make up an important part of total KamAZ production, as Russia is turning to articulated trucks in order to reduce axle loadings and thereby cause less damage to road surfaces which suffer anyway from great changes of temperature. From a maximum 9 tonnes per axle on older Russian trucks, the limit is being reduced to 6 tonnes on the new generation, of which the KamAZ range is the spearhead. There are several KamAZ tractors available, the most common being models 5410 and 54112. Despite only 300kg difference in tractors curb weight, the former can haul a 19 and the latter 26 tonne (for export 28 tonne) semi-trailer, bringing gross vehicle weight to 26,125kg in the first case and 33,325 in the second. Like other models, the KamAZ tractor is powered by a 210bhp V-8 engine, which is also manufactured in the KamAZ factory for use in other trucks. The KamAZ plant is located at Brezhnev, formerly Naberezhnie Chelny until the death of President Brezhnev in November 1982.

Engine KamAZ-740 V-8 diesel 10,850cc 210bhp (154kW) **Transmission** Clutch: twin dry plate; Gearbox: 10F 1R; Rear Axle: double reduction tandem **Frame** channel section ladder type **Brakes** dual circuit fully air-operated **Dimensions** wheelbase: 4,160mm; overall length: 6,160mm; overall width: 2,500mm; height to top of cab: 2,830mm; gross weight: 26,125kg; load capacity: 14,000kg **Performance** maximum speed: 80km/hr

Maker: Kenworth Truck Co, Seattle, Washington

Like the K-100, the conventional Kenworth W-900 has been made with little outward change for over twenty years, and indeed its radiator still bears some resemblance to that of the pre-World War 2 Kenworth of 1940. It is made in 4 × 2 and 6 × 4 form, though the former are comparatively rare. Engine options include all the popular proprietary diesel units from 230 to 525bhp. Sleeper cabs are available, and the W-900 is particularly popular with owner-operators who can have a wide variety of colour schemes provided by the factory, or design their own. GCWs, where permitted, can be as high as 82,800kg.

Engine Cummins NTC-300 turbocharged 6-cylinder diesel 14,000cc 300bhp (223.8kW)
Transmission Clutch: twin dry plate; Gearbox: Fuller RT-910 10F 1R constant mesh; Rear Axle: Rockwell SQ100 single reduction hypoid tandem **Frame** channel section ladder type **Brakes** dual circuit fully air-operated **Dimensions** wheelbase: variable; overall length: variable; overall width: 2,486mm; height to top of cab: 2,743mm; gross weight: 38,640kg; load capacity: 24,000kg
Performance maximum speed: 130km/hr
(typical available specification for the truck illustrated)

Maker: Kenworth Truck Co, Seattle, Washington

The T600A represents a dramatic breakaway in appearance from the typical Kenworth conventional, which has evolved gradually over the past 40 years. Bonnet, wings and cab are streamlined for maximum aerodynamic efficiency. Items like the fuel tank, air cleaner and battery box are all hidden away under the aerodynamic styling. The result is a truck 22% more fuel efficient than standard conventionals. The T600A is available with 36 inch and 60 inch VIT (Very Important Trucker) sleeper cabs, and the usual engine/transmission combinations by Cummins, Fuller and other well known manufacturers.

Engine Cummins NTC-300 6-cylinder turbocharged diesel 14,000cc 300bhp (223.8kW) **Transmission** Clutch: twin dry plate; Gearbox: Fuller RTO 11613 13F 1R constant mesh; Rear Axle: Rockwell single reduction hypoid tandem **Frame** channel section ladder type **Brakes** dual circuit fully air-operated **Dimensions** wheelbase: variable; overall length: variable; gross weight: up to 45,000kg; load capacity: up to 25,000kg **Performance** maximum speed: 130km/hr

Maker: Leyland Vehicles Ltd, Leyland, Lancashire

This is the articulated version of the Landtrain export truck, of which the rigid 6 × 4 is shown on page 139. Engine options include Cummins units from 250 to 290bhp, and six- or nine-speed Fuller or ZF gearboxes are used. Maximum GCW of this model is 65 tonnes, but where local regulations permit, the Landtrain can literally be used as such, with a full trailer behind the semi-trailer and a considerably higher GCW. These trucks are particularly popular in African countries, including Kenya, Nigeria and Zimbabwe. African market Landtrains are assembled in Kenya at Thika, near Nairobi.

Engine Cummins NTE-290 6-cylinder turbocharged diesel 14,000cc 290bhp (216kW)
Transmission Clutch: Dana Spicer twin dry plate; Gearbox: Fuller RTO-9509B 9F 2R constant mesh; Rear Axle: Leyland double reduction **Frame** channel section ladder type **Brakes** dual circuit fully air-operated **Dimensions** wheelbase: 4,770mm; overall length: 7,174mm; overall width: 2,478mm; height to top of cab: 2,780mm; gross weight: 65,000kg; load capacity: 45,000kg
Performance maximum speed: 100km/hr
(typical available specification for truck illustrated)

251

Maker: Mack Trucks Inc, Allentown, Pennsylvania (factory at Macungie, Penna.)

Mack is America's oldest truck manufacturer, having delivered their first model, a sight seeing bus, in 1902, followed by a line of trucks in 1905. Their AC or Bulldog model with dashboard radiator was made from 1916 to 1938, and another long-lived Mack is the R series, introduced in 1966 and still going strong twenty years later. Over the years it has been made in two and three axle form, as a rigid and articulated truck, but chiefly the latter. Generally Mack-built diesel engines have been used, although a few petrol units were offered in the early 1970s. The fibreglass bonnet, which tilts forward for servicing, is also used on the DM600 6 × 4 chassis, while a variant is the U series with offset cabs. Currently the R series is made in 4 × 2 and 6 × 4 tractor versions, as well as rigid 6 × 4s. Power units are various models of the Mack Econoline EM6 turbocharged diesel engine.

Engine Mack EME6-300 6-cylinder turbocharged diesel, 11,010cc 300bhp (224kW) **Transmission** Clutch: Spicer twin dry plate; Gearbox: Mack TRL1078 5F 1R synchromesh; Rear Axle: Mack SS 34C double reduction type **Frame** channel section ladder type **Brakes** dual circuit fully air-operated **Dimensions** wheelbase: 4,940mm; overall length: 6,223mm; overall width: 2,411mm; height to top of cab: 2,611mm; gross weight: variable according to trailer and load capacity **Performance** maximum speed: 90km/hr
(typical available specification for the truck illustrated)

Maker: Mack Trucks Inc, Allentown, Pennsylvania (factory at Macungie, Penna.)

Introduced in 1982, the Ultra Liner is the latest in a series of over the highway tractors by Mack which began with the G Series short cab models of 1959. It is available as a 4 × 2 (MH602) or 6 × 4 (MH603) tractor, and has a very well equipped cab with twin-size mattress sleeping accommodation, and air suspension at each rear corner. The Ultra-liner is available with a wide variety of engines, Mack Econodynes and units from the major diesel engine suppliers, Caterpillar, Cummins and Detroit Diesel. No fewer than thirteen rear axle ratios are available.

Engine Mack EME6-300 6-cylinder turbocharged diesel 11010cc 300 bhp (224kW) **Transmission** Clutch: Spicer twin dry plate; Gearbox: Mack TRL 1078 5F 1R synchromesh; Rear Axle: Mack ST 34C double reduction **Frame** channel section ladder type **Brakes** dual circuit fully air-operated **Dimensions** wheelbase: 4,200mm; overall length: 5,490mm; overall width: 2,426mm; height to top of cab: 3,188mm; gross weight and load capacity, variable according to trailer **Performance** maximum speed: 120km/hr
(typical available specification for the truck illustrated)

Maker: Marmon Motor Co, Garland, Texas

The Marmon Motor Co was founded in 1963, and ever since has specialised in high quality conventional and forward control tractors for long distance haulage. Today they build some of the highest quality vehicles on the market. Two series are made in each cab configuration, the F Series for fleet operators and the P Series (Premium) for owner-operators. The latter are more distinctively styled, with the Marmon badge standing proud of the grille surround, butterfly type aluminium front bumper, square headlamps and striking paint schemes. Cab equipment is also more lavish on the Premium models. Sleeper cabs are available on the Premium conventionals, and on all cab-overs. A variety of sleeper boxes are made for the conventionals, including single and double bunk, crawl-thru and walk-thru models. Cummins engines are standardised, but Caterpillar or Detroit diesels can also be specified, as can transmission by Allison, Fuller and Spicer.

Engine Cummins Big Cam Formula 300 6-cylinder turbocharged diesel 14,000cc 300bhp (223.8kW) **Transmission** Clutch: Spicer twin dry plate; Gearbox: Fuller RT 1160A 9F 1R; Rear Axle: Rockwell SQ100 single reduction tandem **Frame** channel section ladder type **Brakes** dual circuit fully air-operated **Dimensions** wheelbase: variable; overall length: variable; overall width: 2,430mm; height to top of cab: 2,829mm **Performance** maximum speed: 125km/hr

Maker: Marmon Motor Co, Garland, Texas

Like the conventionals, the cab-over (forward-control) Marmons are made in two series, F for fleet owners, and P (Premium) for owner operators. The tractor illustrated is one of the latter, and is instantly recognisable by the 'M' badge which stands proud of the grille surround, and also by the butterfly aluminium bumper and square headlamps. The cab-overs are made in three models, the numbers indicating the BBC measurement, the 60 day cab, 86 single sleeper, and 110 double sleeper cab. They are all 6 × 4s, with wheelbases from 3,124mm upwards. Standard engines are Cummins Formula 300 on the F Series, and NTC-400 on the Premium Series, but these can be varied according to customer preference.

Engine Cummins NTC-400 6-cylinder turbocharged diesel 14,000cc 400bhp (298.4kW)
Transmission Clutch: Spicer twin dry plate; Gearbox: Fuller RTO-14613 13F 1R constant mesh; Rear Axle: Eaton DS401P single reduction spiral bevel tandem **Frame** channel section ladder type
Brakes dual circuit, fully air-operated **Dimensions** wheelbase: 4,394mm; overall length: 5,857mm; overall width: 2,426mm; height to top of cab: 3,108mm; gross weight: 55,200kg; load capacity: 38,000kg **Performance** maximum speed: 115km/hr
(typical available specification for the truck illustrated)

Maker: Minsk Auto Zavod, Minsk

This is the first of a new range of MAZ-6000 trucks, and so far only this 6 × 4 tractor has been announced. It is of much more modern design than other MAZ products, with 320bhp turbocharged V-8 engine, 8-speed all-synchromesh gearbox and up to date cab with one-piece windscreen. It is claimed that this tractor will run for 320,000km before needing a major overhaul. For the 6422 the first modern in the USSR three-axle semi-trailer MAZ-9398 was created (load capacity 26,200kg), joined later on by TIR and container-carrying semi-trailers, the latter of 32,400kg capacity.

Engine YaMZ-238F V-8 turbocharged diesel 14,860cc 320bhp (235kW) **Transmission** Clutch: twin dry plate with air-operated servo; Gearbox: 8F 1R all-synchromesh; Rear Axle: double reduction **Frame** channel section ladder type **Brakes** air-operated **Dimensions** wheelbase: 4,300mm; overall length: 6,570mm; overall width: 2,500mm; overall height: 2,870mm; gross weight: 48,000kg; load capacity: 32,500kg **Performance** maximum speed: 85km/hr

Maker: Nissan Diesel Motor Co Ltd, Tokyo

The CWA52 is the largest of the Nissan truck range, and is made as a straight 6 × 4 truck in three wheelbases for ratings up to 25,500kg GVW, and as a tractor as illustrated, for GCW up to 45,000kg. Both models use the Nissan RD8 300bhp V-8 diesel engine. Of similar appearance is the less powerful CWA45 powered by the 11.67 litre 275bhp Nissan PE6T in-line 6-cylinder engine.

Engine Nissan RD8 V-8 diesel 14,313cc 300bhp (224kW) **Transmission** Clutch: single dry plate; Gearbox: 9F 2R constant mesh; Rear Axle: single reduction hypoid **Frame** channel section ladder type **Brakes** dual circuit fully air-operated **Dimensions** wheelbase: 5,250mm; overall length: 6,870mm; overall width: 2,490mm; height to top of cab: 3,270mm; **Performance** maximum speed: 93 to 116km/hr according to axle ratio

Maker: Pacific Truck & Trailer Ltd, Vancouver, British Columbia

Pacific was founded in 1947 by three former executives of the Hayes Manufacturing Company to manufacture trucks specifically for the logging industry of Northwestern Canada. They have specialised in this type of truck ever since, although they also make oilfield trucks and heavy road tractors for drawbar trailers. In 1970 they were bought by International Harvester of Canada who sold them off in 1984 to a Malaysian-based subsidiary of the British Inchcape Group. The P-12 is made as a rigid 6 × 4 dump truck, as a tractor or as an oilfield truck in rigid or articulated form, the oilfield models being known as Roughnecks. The standard engine is the Detroit Diesel 12V-71-N, but options include the more powerful 12V-71-T or several units by Cummins or Caterpillar. The regular transmission is an Allison CLBT-5960, but Clark automatics are also available. The tractor illustrated is hauling two bottom dump trailers in Northern Quebec.

Engine Detroit Diesel 12V-71-N V-12 diesel 13,951cc 475bhp (354.35kW) **Transmission** Clutch: torque converter; Gearbox: Allison CLBT-5960 5F 1R automatic; Rear Axle: Clark BD-91,000 single reduction hypoid tandem **Frame** channel section ladder type **Brakes** dual circuit fully air-operated **Dimensions** overall width: 3,810mm; height to top of cab: 3,226mm **Performance** maximum speed: 58km/hr

PETERBILT 362 USA

Maker: Peterbilt Motors Co, Newark, California

In 1939 T. A. Peterman, a Washington State lumberman, bought the former Fageol truck plant in Oakland, California, and began to produce a new line of trucks originally aimed at the logging industry. As Fageols had been informally described as 'Bill-Bilt' after their president, W. H. Bill, Peterman chose the name Peterbilt for his trucks. The flat-fronted cab of the Model 352, similar to that of the Kenworth K-100, was introduced in 1955 and has changed little up to the present day. Three versions were made, the 352 in 4 × 2 and 6 × 4 forms, and the 6 × 4 352H which was intended for the most powerful engines of between 400 and 600bhp. Generally similar in appearance, the 'H' had a larger cab, radiator and fan. The 352 series has recently been replaced by the 362s which are similar but have a one-piece windscreen.

Engine Caterpillar 3408PCTA V-8 diesel 17,996cc 450bhp (335.7kW) **Transmission** Clutch: twin dry plate; Gearbox: Fuller RTO-12513 13F 1R constant mesh; Rear Axle: Rockwell SQHD single reduction hypoid tandem **Frame** channel section ladder type **Brakes** dual circuit fully air-operated **Dimensions** wheelbase: variable; overall length: variable; overall width: 2,420mm; height to top of cab: 3,048mm; gross weight: 36,800kg; load capacity: 24,000kg **Performance** maximum speed: 120km/hr
(typical available specification for the truck illustrated)

Maker: Peterbilt Motors Co, Newark, California

The 359 is Peterbilt's conventional companion to the 362 cabover, and like it has been gradually improved over a number of years. It is available as a rigid 6 × 4 and as a tractor, with a choice of wheelbases to customers' requirements. The standard power unit is a Cummins FNTC 300 Big Cam, but like other American Class 8 trucks the Peterbilt 359 can be had with a variety of engines by the three diesel makers, Caterpillar, Cummins and Detroit, from 275 to 425bhp. Virtually all the popular transmissions by Allison, Fuller and Spicer are available, as are suspensions by Peterbilt, Hendrickson or Reyco. There is a choice of sleeper cabs, 36 or 63 inch, with standard or Classic II interiors. The latter features deep pile carpet, burnished chrome fitments and a choice of naugahyde or 100% nylon velour seats.

Engine Cummins FNTC 300 Big Cam 6-cylinder turbocharged and after cooled diesel 14,000cc 300bhp (223.8kW) **Transmission** twin dry plate; Gearbox: Fuller RT 11609A 9F 1R constant mesh; Rear Axle: Rockwell SQ100 single reduction hypoid tandem **Frame** channel section ladder type **Brakes** dual circuit fully air-operated **Dimensions** wheelbase: variable; overall length: variable; overall width: 2,490mm; height to top of cab: 2,780mm; gross weight: up to 50,000kg; load capacity: up to 30,000kg **Performance** maximum speed: 125km/hr
(typical available specification for the truck illustrated)

Maker: Magyar Vagon es Gepgyar, Gyor

The Raba name is derived from Raab which was the old name for Gyor when the town was under Austrian rule. Vehicles have been made there intermittently since 1904, but the current range of M.A.N.-based heavy trucks has been built only since 1970. These now include 4 × 2, 4 × 4, 6 × 2 and 6 × 4 rigid chassis, and 4 × 2, 6 × 2 and 6 × 4 tractors, powered by 230 or 256bhp 6-cylinder engines built in the Raba factory under licence from M.A.N. The cabs were built by M.A.N. until recently, but now DAF cabs are used on all Raba models.

Engine Raba-M.A.N. D-21 56 MTN6 6-cylinder turbocharged diesel 10,350cc 256bhp (188kW) **Transmission** Clutch: single dry plate; Gearbox: ZF AK-690 6F IR synchromesh (various Fuller Transmissions also available); Rear Axle: double reduction **Frame** channel section ladder type **Brakes** dual circuit fully air-operated **Dimensions** wheelbase: 4,450mm; overall length: 6,745mm; overall width: 2,490mm; height to top of cab: 3,235mm; gross weight: 38,000kg; load capacity: 23,600kg **Performance** maximum speed: 105km/hr

Maker: Trailers de Monterrey SA, Monterrey

Trailers de Monterrey are part of the Grupo Industrial Ramirez, and were well-known trailer manufacturers before they began to build vehicles, starting with buses and coaches in 1953. Heavy tractors followed in 1959 and a 4 × 4 pick-up a few years later. All these types remain in production today. The R-22 is the latest in a line of tractive units and is made only in 6 × 4 form, powered by a Mexican-built Cummins NTC-350 diesel engine with the option of the NTA-450 or Detroit Diesel 8V92. Most other components such as transmission, rear axle and suspension are of American type but Mexican manufacture, the local content of the Ramirez being nearly 100%. The fibreglass cab and tilt bonnet are of local design and manufacture.

Engine Cummins NTC-350 FFC 6-cylinder turbocharged diesel 14,000cc 350bhp (261.1kW) **Transmission** Clutch: twin dry plate; Gearbox: Spicer 1214-3A 14F 2R constant mesh; Rear Axle: Rockwell SSHD single reduction hypoid tandem **Frame** channel section ladder type **Brakes** dual circuit fully air-operated **Dimensions** wheelbase: 5,650mm; overall length: 7,340mm; overall width: 2,290mm; height to top of cab: 2,740mm; gross weight: 54,545kg; load capacity: 38,000kg **Performance** maximum speed: 110km/hr

Maker: R.F.W. Truck Manufacturing Co, Chester Hill, New South Wales

As well as making 4 × 4 and 6 × 6 rigid trucks R.F.W. can offer tractors for semi trailer work up to a GCW of about 50 tons. Detroit Diesel, Caterpillar or Cummins engines are the usual power options, mostly in the 230 to 275bhp range, though units developing up to 400bhp can be provided for really heavy work. Transmissions are mostly Allison automatics. The low-loading trailer illustrated, operated by Auto Quik Lift, is carrying a bulldozer, but they are frequently used for transporters of new cars, and also as livestock trucks.

Engine Caterpillar 3406 6-cylinder diesel 14,600cc 325bhp (242.4kW) **Transmission** Clutch: torque converter; Gearbox: Allison HT 750 DRD 5F 1R automatic; Rear Axle: Eaton 42D double reduction **Frame** channel section ladder type **Brakes** dual circuit fully air-operated **Dimensions** wheelbase: variable; overall length: variable; overall width: N/A; height to top of cab: N/A; gross weight: 50,800kg; load capacity: 35,000kg **Performance** maximum speed: 95km/hr

Maker: Leyland Vehicles Ltd, Scammell Motors Plant, Watford, Hertfordshire

The Scammell name has been famous since 1919 when they introduced their 7½ ton articulated truck. This type of vehicle has been prominent in their production ever since, and since their acquisition by Leyland in 1955 they have been responsible for the heaviest trucks in the Leyland range. Today their products fall into three distinct categories, rear-engined chassis for airport fire crash tenders 6 × 4 or 8 × 4 forward control trucks and tractors using the Leyland C40 cab and the S24 6 × 4 or 6 × 6 chassis which can operate either as a straight truck or as a tractor with semi-trailers or drawbar trailers. It is powered by the Cummins NTE-350 engine, turbo-charged and aftercooled, and is available with either manual or automatic gearboxes. As a straight truck it has a GVW or 30 to 44 tonnes, and with a semi-trailer, 50 to 150 tonnes. Among its many possible applications are tipper, concrete mixer, tanker or recovery vehicle in straight form, or for logging, heavy machinery transport, oilfield or road train in articulated form.

Engine Cummins NTE-350 6-cylinder turbocharged diesel 14,000cc 350bhp (261.1kW) **Transmission** Clutch: twin dry plate (with manual gearbox); Gearbox: Fuller RT-12515 15F 3R constant mesh *or* Brockhouse + Spicer 10F 2R torque converter + manual *or* Allison HT 650 DRD 5F 1R; Rear Axle: double reduction **Frame** channel section ladder type **Brakes** dual circuit fully air-operated **Dimensions** wheelbase: 5,534 *or* 6,210mm; overall length: 7,659 *or* 8,335mm; overall width: 2,856mm; height to top of cab: 3,078mm; gross weight: 150,000kg; load capacity: 110,000kg **Performance** maximum speed: 90km/hr

Maker: Saab-Scania AB, Sodertalje

This is the heaviest and most powerful of the Scania tractors, having the 390 or 420bhp 14.2-litre V-8 engine and extra heavy duty chassis. The latter has a flitched frame with a total thickness of 17.5mm, compared with the single frame 8mm steel of the M range of medium-duty trucks, and 9.5mm for the H heavy duty trucks. Day and sleeper cabs are offered on the normal control T models as well as on the forward control R range; while many tractors have sleeper cabs, this one which is hauling heavy machinery over relatively short distances does not. GCW with the five axle low-loading trailer could be as high as 175 tonnes.

Engine Scania DSC 14 02 V-8 turbocharged and intercooled diesel 14,181cc 390bhp (287kW) *or* DSC 14 01 420bhp (309kW) **Transmission** Clutch: twin dry plate; Gearbox: Scania GR870 10F 1R synchromesh; Rear Axle: double reduction hypoid + planetary **Frame** channel section ladder type **Brakes** dual circuit fully air-operated **Dimensions** wheelbase: variable; overall length: variable; overall width: 2,490mm; height to top of cab: 2,890mm; gross weight: 175,000kg; load capacity: 110,000kg **Performance** maximum speed: 70km/hr

Maker: Western Star Corp, Kelowna, B.C.

The Western Star division of White was set up in 1968 in order to make trucks specifically aimed at the Western United States and Canadian markets but in 1981 Western Star became an independent company. Their products sell chiefly in Canada, but they enjoy some penetration of the US and Australian markets. Western Stars were originally made only in conventional form, but a cab-over range was added in the late 1970s. They are mostly made as tractors, but 4 × 4 and 6 × 6 rigid chassis for the construction industry are also offered. Engines, from the main US diesel manufacturers, range from 195 to 525bhp, and GCWs up to 62,100kg. The Canadian-built tractor illustrated is a Gold Star limited edition model, of which only 120 were made in 1985. The total cost of tractor and trailer is almost $200,00.

Engine Cummins NTC-400 6-cylinder turbocharged diesel 14,000cc 400bhp (298.4kW)
Transmission Clutch: twin dry plate; Gearbox: Fuller RT-11610 10F 1R constant mesh; Rear Axle: Rockwell SSHD single reduction hypoid **Frame** channel section ladder type **Brakes** dual circuit fully air-operated **Dimensions** wheelbase: variable; overall length: variable; overall width: 2,413mm; gross weight: 44,000kg; load capacity: 28,000kg **Performance** maximum speed: 110km/hr
(typical available specification for the truck illustrated)

Maker: Volvo White Truck Corporation, Greenboro, North Carolina (factory at Dublin, Virginia)

White is one of the oldest truck makers in America, having delivered their first steam van to the Denver Dry Cleaning Co in 1901. Thy introduced petrol engined trucks in 1909 and diesels in 1949, and were also pioneers of the 6 × 2 and 6 × 4 layouts. They have bought up a number of firms, including Sterling in 1951 (discontinued in 1963), Autocar in 1953 (still made) Reo in 1957 and Diamond T in 1960 (merged into Diamond-Reo and subsequently sold off). In 1981 White was itself bought by Volvo, and at their new factory at Dublin, Virginia, certain Volvo models such as the F6, F7, N10 and N12 are made alongside Whites. The latter include the low cab Xpeditor 6 × 4 highway tractors in conventional and cabover forms. The High Cabover is made as a 4 × 2 or 6 × 4 tractor, with short or long cabs, the latter incorporating a two-bunk sleeper.

Engine Cummins F-300 6-cylinder turbocharged diesel 14,000cc 300bhp (223.8kW) **Transmission** Clutch: Spicer twin dry plate; Gearbox: Fuller RT 11609A 9F 1R constant mesh; Rear Axles: Rockwell SQ100 single reduction hypoid tandem **Frame** channel section ladder type **Brakes** dual circuit fully air-operated **Dimensions** wheelbase: 4,750mm; overall length: 6,198mm; overall width: 2,438mm; height to top of cab: 2,603mm; gross weight: 36,800kg; load capacity: 24,000kg **Performance** maximum speed: 120km/hr

Maker: Maschinenfabrik Augsburg-Nürnburg AG, Munich

This is the largest of M.A.N.'s tractive units, and is unusual among road tractors in having 6-wheel-drive. It is intended for hauling heavy loads in difficult conditions, such as the mountainous country in the photograph. The designation DFAT indicates its specification: D = three axles (Drei achsen), F = forward control, A = all-wheel drive, T = truck tractor. The tractor has a GVW of 32 tons and the engine develops 321bhp, hence the numbers 32.321. From early 1982 a more powerful model, the 40.440, became available in 6 × 4 (DFT) and 6 × 6 (DFAT) versions. These tractors are suitable, in certain conditions, for trailer loads up to 105 tonnes GCW.

Engine M.A.N. D 2566MKF 6-cylinder turbocharged diesel 11,413cc 320bhp (235kW)
Transmission Clutch: twin dry plate; Gearbox: ZF K-130 16F 2R constant mesh, *or* ZF S-130 16F 1R synchromesh *or* Fuller RTO-9513 13F 1R constant-mesh; Transfer Box: G-801 2-speed; Front Axle: M.A.N. double reduction; Rear Axle: M.A.N. double reduction **Frame** channel section ladder type **Brakes** dual circuit fully air-operated **Dimensions** wheelbase: 4,750mm; overall length: 7,200mm; overall width: 2,500mm; height to top of cab: 3,176mm; gross weight: 38,000kg (normal loads); load capacity: 28,250kg (normal loads) **Performance** maximum speed: 48.8 to 64.3km/hr, according to axle ratio

Maker: Nicolas Industrie SA, Champs sur Yonne

Nicolas is a well-known manufacturer of low-bed trailers who began to make tractors in 1979 in order to be able to offer a complete combination to their customers. They use Detroit Diesel, Cummins or Mercedes-Benz engines in conjunction with Fuller, Allison, Clark or ZF transmissions. Cabs are mostly the ex-Berliet design from Renault that was also used in the Ford Transcontinental, though some of the heaviest 8 × 8 Nicolas tractors have the same cab as the Mol TG 250. Most Nicolas tractors, which go by the name Tractomas, have been made for export markets including China, Nigeria, Tunisia and Great Britain, where the heavy transport contractors Sunter Brothers of Northallerton have bought a 6 × 4 ballasted with 20 tons of concrete, making a total tractor weight of just over 39 tons. Nicolas tractors can be used with drawbar trailers as well as semi-trailers.

Engine Daimler-Benz OM 404A V-12 turbocharged diesel 20,910cc 480bhp (358kW) **Transmission** Clutch: ZF WSK 400.59 torque converter; Gearbox: ZF 4.S.150. GPA 8F 1R; Front Axle: double reduction; Rear Axles: double reduction **Frame** channel section ladder type **Brakes** dual circuit fully air-operated **Dimensions** wheelbase: 5,425mm; overall length: 8,020mm; overall width: 3,000mm; height to top of cab: 3,860mm; gross weight: 200,000kg; load capacity: 125,000kg **Performance** maximum speed: 45km/hr

Maker: Tatra NP, Koprivnice

Introduced in 1983, Tatra's 815 range covers a considerable variety of trucks, rigid and articulated models, in 4 × 4, 6 × 6 and 8 × 8 versions. Tractors are made in one 4 × 4 and three 6 × 6 versions, all with set-back front axles. This layout is also used for long wheelbase 6 × 6 rigid chassis, but the short wheelbase tippers have set forward front axles. Tatras are unusual in making 6 × 6 tractors for over the highway haulage work, and they also make drawbar tractors with 6 × 6 (twin steer) or 8 × 8 drive. Tatra make about 15,000 heavy vehicles per year, of which 35% are sold in Czechslovakia, 40% in the Soviet Union, and 25% in 50 other countries around the world.

Engine Tatra 3-930 V-12 air-cooled diesel 19,000cc 315bhp (235kW) **Transmission** Clutch: single dry plate; Gearbox: 5F 1R; Transfer box: 2-speed; Front Axle: single reduction spiral bevel; Rear Axle: single reduction bevel **Frame** tubular backbone **Brakes** dual circuit fuliy air-operated **Dimensions** wheelbase: 4,220mm; overall length: 6,500mm; overall width: 2,500mm; height to top of cab: 2,900mm; gross weight: 45,000kg; load capacity: 22,500kg **Performance** maximum speed: 95km/hr

Maker: ARDCO Industries Inc, Houston, Texas

ARDCO offers two series of 10×10 vehicles designed and constructed for moving bulky or extra heavy loads, the K10×10 and N10×10. In both cases, a three-axle powered articulated tractor and two-axle powered trailer are combined to form a single vehicle with a length of approximately 21 metres. The combination has the ability to operate the tractor and trailer engines independently of each other. The K10×10 is constructed by using the same components used for the K6×6. The N10×10 is built around standard N6×6 components. Power comes from Detroit Diesel engines, type 8V71, providing 305bhp. at 2200 rpm. An Allison H750 gear box is fitted, and connected to a transfer case, which drives the planetary Rockwell axles. The photo shows the ARDCO N10×10 in action, transporting a Ford of the L line on one of Canada's muddy tracks. The technical information is for the N6×6, the tractor unit of the N10×10.

Engine Detroit Diesel 8V71 V-8 diesel 9,300cc 305bhp (227.5kW) **Transmission** Clutch: torque converter; Gearbox: HT750 Allison; Transfer Box: two speed; Front Axle: Rockwell planetary; Rear Axle: Two Rockwell axles, planetary **Frame** channel section ladder type, articulated **Brakes** hydraulic **Dimensions** wheelbase: 6,960mm; overall length: 10,820mm; overall width: 3,378mm; height to top of cab: 2,972mm; gross weight: 30,000kg; load capacity: 20,000kg **Performance** maximum speed: 40.2km/hr

Maker: Nicolas Industrie SA, Champs sur Yonne

This was the first Nicolas Tractomas 8 × 8 tractor to be sold by the company, and went to the Compagnie des Phosphates in Tunisia. It uses the same design of cab as the Mol TG 250 (formerly PRP-Willeme), though without the crew cab or sleeper section. Power for this model comes from a Detroit Diesel 16V-71N V-16 developing 608bhp, though other models of Detroit Diesel, or Cummins KTA-525 or KTA-600 can also be specified for the 8 × 8 Tractomas. Less powerful Cummins or Detroit Diesel engines are used in the 8 × 4 models. Among many options available on Nicolas tractors are ballast boxes so that they can be used as drawbar tractors, winches of 20 or 30 tonnes capacity, and air conditioning. Nicolas make about fifty tractors per year, and have also supplied one load-carrying chassis with drilling rig for North Africa, and a four-axle aircraft refuelling tanker made in conjunction with the French tank makers, Titan SA.

Engine Detroit Diesel 16V-71N V-16 diesel 18,601cc 608bhp (453.6kW) **Transmission** Clutch: Clark CL-8652 torque converter; Gearbox: Clark 16820 8F 4R; Front Axles double reduction; Rear Axles: double reduction **Frame** channel section ladder type **Brakes** dual circuit fully air-operated **Dimensions** wheelbase: 7,040mm; overall length: 9,645mm; overall width: 3,000mm; height to top of cab: 3,380mm; gross weight: 350,000kg; load capacity: 270,000kg **Performance** maximum speed: (unladen) 69km/hr

Dump Trucks

The expression 'dump truck' can cover a wide range of vehicles from the little site dumper with single-cylinder engine and one cubic yard body, up to massive trucks as tall as a two-storey house, powered by engines of 126 litres capacity. The former may be thought of as motorised wheelbarrows, while the latter have developed gradually from ordinary on-highway trucks, the first steps towards specialisation taking place in the 1920s. In America many second hand trucks were modified for construction work, being fitted with scow-end dump bodies which would empty when tipped without the need for a tailgate to contain the load when they were on the move. The Hug Company of Highland, Illinois made purpose-built trucks of this type, at first for road construction and then larger models for quarrying, but the real ancestors of the modern off-highway truck were the Mack AP 6-cylinder trucks built for the Boulder Dam project in 1932. They had 14 cubic yard bodies specially designed for rock carrying, very strong frames reinforced with massive fishplates, solid tyres at the rear and pneumatics at the front. Two years later the Euclid Crane Hoist Company of Cleveland entered the market with a 10/11-ton scow-end dump truck specifically built for the construction and quarrying industries. This Trac-Truck of 1934 was the first in a long line of off-highway trucks which have been made up to the present day.

The development of open-cast coal mining as well as quarrying and ever more ambitious civil engineering projects led to an increasing demand for heavy dump trucks, and during the next twenty years Euclid were joined by other firms such as Dart, Wabco and Lectra Haul. Euclid made a twin-engined 3-axle truck with 45 ton capacity in 1951, and a 3-axle tractor with 2-axle trailer and capacity of 120 tons in 1958. Even this has been dwarfed in recent years by the 200-ton Lectra Haul and 235-ton Wabco 3200B, while the record for the largest truck in the world was set by the monstrous Terex Titan built in 1974, with a capacity of 350 tons. This was a record breaker in every direction; its engine was a 3,300bhp GM Electromotive Diesel designed for powering railway locomotives, with a capacity of 169 litres; this engine alone weighed 16 tons. The tyres weighed more than $3\frac{1}{2}$ tons each, and towered above the cab of a Kenworth truck. Although theoretically a catalogued model (at a price of about $2\frac{1}{2}$-million dollars), only one Titan was made, and is still at work in an open-cast coal mine in British Columbia. One drawback of trucks as large as this is that they cannot be transported complete to their workplace, but have to be assembled on site, this job taking some 600 man hours and involving heavy specialised equipment.

Although these monster dump trucks are used all over

The Euclid Trac-Truk of 1934, the world's first off-highway dump truck to be designed from scratch. Its basic shape was still recognisable in the Euclids being made thirty years later.

the world, really large ones are only made in America and the Soviet Union. Smaller trucks of up to 50-tons payload are made in several countries including Britain, Germany, Italy and Japan, while the Scandinavian countries specialise in trucks with centre-articulated frames for maximum manoeuvrability. These remarkable machines originated as forestry tractors, or Forwarders as they are called, which are still made alongside the dump trucks. The best-known makers are Volvo-BM, and Nordstrom in Sweden, Moxy in Norway and Valmet in Finland. One British firm, D.J.B., also makes trucks on this principle, as does the Canadian Flextruck Limited, although the latter are not dump trucks but concrete mixers and general haulage trucks.

Maker: Astra SpA, Piacenza

Astra was founded in 1946 and began by reconditioning ex-army trucks. Their first dump truck was made in 1954, and they now make several models up to the 42-ton BM35 as well as military trucks and a front-discharge concrete mixer chassis, the BM303. The BM35 is powered by a Detroit Diesel V-12 engine, and like most dump trucks of this size it has automatic transmission, combined pneumatic/hydraulic brakes on the rear wheels and pneumatic on the front. It has triple reduction final drive, by spiral bevel differential and compound planetary reduction gear in the wheel hubs. Astra production runs at about 750 units per year, and they are exported to thirty countries.

Engine Detroit Diesel 12V-71N 65 V-12 diesel 13,948cc 456bhp (336kW) **Transmission** Clutch: Allison TC 690 torque converter; Gearbox: Allison CLBT 5960 6F 1R automatic; Rear Axle: triple reduction **Frame** box section with closed loop cross members **Brakes** dual circuit air/hydraulic **Dimensions** wheelbase: 3,500mm; overall length: 7,665mm; overall width: 3,900mm; height to top of cab: 3,880mm; gross weight: 64,000kg; load capacity: 38,000kg **Performance** maximum speed: 65.5km/hr.

Maker: Aveling Barford International Ltd, Grantham, Lincolnshire

Aveling Barford are Britain's oldest established makers of dump trucks, having made a small site dumper based on a Fordson tractor as early as 1933. The present range of large dump trucks dates from 1954 when the Leyland-powered SL was introduced, and has been steadily extended up to the present, when eight models are made, from the 17-ton RD 1017 with swivel seat for two way driving, up to the 50-ton RD 150. This is powered by a Detroit Diesel V-16 engine, and features an Allison torque converter automatic transmission and Nitroleo suspension. This consists of nitrogen/oil suspension units, one to each wheel. At the front the piston acts as a kingpin and the front wheel stub axles are attached to the bottom of each piston. Other dump trucks in the Aveling Barford range are the 25-ton RD 025 and 30-ton RD 030, both powered by the Cummins NT 855C engine, the RD 033 and RD 135, both powered by the Detroit Diesel 8V-92TA, and the 35 and 40-ton RD 035 and RD 040, both powered by the Detroit Diesel 12V-71 V-12 engine. In 1985 Aveling Barford began to manufacture the Nordstrom 666B articulated dump truck, under the designation RxD 025.

Engine Detroit Diesel 16V-71N V-16 diesel 18,600cc 608bhp (453kW) *or* Cummins KTA-1150C 6-cylinder turbocharged and aftercooled diesel 18,900cc 600bhp (447kW) **Transmission** Clutch: torque converter; Gearbox: Allison Torqmatic CLBT 6061 6F 1R automatic; Rear Axle: Double reduction **Frame** box section side members, I-section cross members at front, tubular at rear **Brakes** dual circuit air/hydraulic **Dimensions** wheelbase: 4,267mm; overall length: 9,195mm; overall width: 4,483mm; height to top of cab: 3,962mm; gross weight: 85,279kg; load capacity: 45,360kg **Performance** maximum speed: 62.7km/hr

Maker: Beijing No.3 General Machinery Factory, Beijing (Peking)

The Beijing BJ 370 20-ton dump truck was introduced in prototype form in 1977, powered by a Santong 6VE 110Q diesel engine. Later variants use imported engines, as the BJ 371; GM 6V-71N 238hp engine, BJ 372; Jelcz SW 680/17 242hp engine, BJ 373; Caterpillar 3306TA 245hp engine and the here described BJ 374 with Cummins NT 855C 250hp-engine. The Beijing Construction Machinery Corporation offers these trucks for export.

Engine Cummins 6-cylinder diesel 14,000cc 250bhp (186.5kW) **Transmission** Clutch: mechanical constant mesh gearbox with dog clutch; Gearbox: 6F 1R; Rear Axle: central double reduction **Frame** longitudindal member (U-shape with equal cross section) reinforced by L-section member **Brakes** internal expanding shoe type, air operated with dual line **Dimensions** wheelbase: 3,600mm; overall length: 7,210mm; overall width: 2,909mm; height to top of cab: 3,140mm; gross weight: 35,000kg; load capacity: 20,000kg **Performance** maximum speed: 36km/hr

Maker: Byelorussian Avto Zavod, Zhodino

The factory of BelautoMAZ at Zhodino, near Minsk, is the main producer of dump trucks for the Soviet Union, and has been building these since 1959. The model 540A is the base model, and has been in production since 1967. Like all BelAZ dump trucks apart from the largest model 549, it has a one-man cab. Special versions include the 540S for Northern climates, the 540T tropical version, and the 7510 coal truck with larger capacity body. A similar but larger (40,000kg capacity) model is the 548A which is powered by a turbocharged version of the YaMZ-240 engine developing 500bhp compared with 360bhp for the naturally-aspirated unit. This is also made in special versions for Northern climates and the coal industry. All BelAZ dump trucks have air/hydraulic independent suspension. The photo shows a BelAZ-540A next to the smallest Russian-made car, the ZAZ-966B.

Engine YaMZ-240 V-12 diesel 22,300cc 360bhp (265kW) **Transmission** hydromechanical, with a 4-wheel torque converter and a 3-speed semi-automatic box; Rear Axle: double reduction **Frame** channel section ladder type **Brakes** dual circuit air-operated **Dimensions** wheelbase: 3,550mm; overall length: 7,250mm; overall width: 3,480mm; overall height: 3,580mm; gross weight: 48,075kg; load capacity: 27,000kg **Performance** maximum speed: 55km/hr.

Maker: Byelorussian Avto Zavod, Zhodino

Byelorussian builders of super-heavy tippers have a new flag-ship in the shape of this 110-tonner, but already a few 180-tonners, fitted with a 12-cylinder engine, have been assembled since 1983. The base model is called 7519 (and its 100-tonner derivative, bearing a 39.5m³ body and more economical 6-cylinder engine, has the number 75191) and is not significantly bulkier than a 549, standing on a wheelbase lengthened by 850mm. The capacity of the body is up to 44m³ and curb weight to 85 tonnes. Pneumo-hydraulic rear suspension is no longer independent as on the model 549 and tyres of 33.00-51 size are fitted. A turbocharged diesel with its 25% greater capacity and 200 extra bhp consumes an impressive 400 litres of fuel per 100km at 30-35km/hr from a 1,000 litre tank. The productivity of a 110-tonner is, according to actual tests in opencast pits, up by 1.5-1.6 times in comparison with the model 549.

Engine 8CN 21/21 V-8 turbocharged diesel 58,300cc 1300bhp (956kW) generator GPA-800 (800kW) **Transmission** Clutch: none; Gearbox: electric drive with 360kW motors in each wheel; Rear Axle: planetary reduction from electric motors **Frame** Channel section ladder type **Brakes** dual circuit hydraulic **Dimensions** wheelbase: 5,300mm; overall length: 11,250mm; overall width: 6,100mm; overall height: 5,130mm; gross weight: 195,000kg; load capacity: 110,000kg **Performance** maximum speed: 50km/hr

Maker: Byelorussian Avto Zavod, Zhodino

This model replaces the 110-tonner model 7519 as the leader of the BelAZ range. Fitted with a 12 cylinder 21/21 series engine or a lower-revving 26/26 series from a diesel locomotive, this tipper has for the first time an AC current generator (of 1350kW) instead of the usual DC unit. Unexpectedly the huge locomotive powerplant necessitates an increase not only in length, width and height dimensions by 200-420mm, but also wheelbase by mere 50mm. The "locomotive version" is heavier by ten tonnes and loses the same amount in load capacity. Pneumo-hydraulic suspension, unlike on earlier models, is non-independent all around. Braking at the rear is by discs rather than drums. World's hugest, 40.00-57 size tyres are used and the Russian rubber industry was asked to produce these domestically, so with advancement in production of 7521s rubber imports can be gradually dropped.

Engine 12DM 21/21 V-12 turbocharged diesel 87,300cc 2300bhp (1690kW) generator 1350kW **Transmission** Clutch: none; Gearbox: electric drive with 560kW motor in each wheel; Rear Axle: planetary reduction from electric motors **Frame** channel section ladder type **Brakes** dual circuit hydraulic **Dimensions** wheelbase: 6,650mm; overall length: 13,500mm; overall width: 7,600mm; overall height: 6,030mm; gross weight: 325,000kg; load capacity: 180,000kg **Performance** maximum speed: 50km/hr

Maker: Benxi Heavy-type Automobile Factory, Benxi city, Liaoming province

Since 1980 the Benxi factory has assembled Wabco Haulpak 75B dumpers. This factory also produces dumpers and crane trucks on Jiefang, Linghe, Dongfeng and Huanghe basis. The 68-ton truck is in production for service in the open-cast mines in North China.

Engine Detroit 16V-71N 16-cylinder V diesel 18,600cc 608bhp (454kW) *or* Cummins VT-1710 12-cylinder V diesel 28,000cc 635bhp (474kW) **Transmission** Clutch: torqueconverter; Gearbox: 6F 1R; Rear Axle: double reduction **Frame** special alloy steel modified box section frame with integral front bumper and cross member **Brakes** dual circuit air/hydraulic **Dimensions** wheelbase: 4,060mm; overall length: 9,600mm; overall width: 4,010mm; height to top of cab: 4,390mm; gross weight: 109,504kg; load capacity: 68,000kg **Performance** maximum speed: xxkm/hr

Maker: Caterpillar Tractor Co, Peoria, Illinois (Factory at Decatur, Illinois)

The Caterpillar Tractor Company was formed in 1925 from a merger of two tractor manufacturers, Best and Holt, and soon became the world's largest maker of crawler tractors. They added proprietary engines to their products in 1932, and dump trucks in 1962. These are now made in four sizes, the 35-ton 769C, 50-ton 773B, 85-ton 777 and 150-ton 785, all powered by Caterpillar turbocharged and aftercooled diesel engines. The most powerful of these, used in the Model 785, develops 1380bhp and has a capacity of 51.8 litres. All four models have Caterpillar planetary automatic transmission, oil-cooled disc brakes, fully hydraulic steering and oil-pneumatic suspension cylinders. Caterpillar have a total of eleven factories in the United States but all the dump trucks are built at the Decatur plant, which was opened in 1955.

Engine Caterpillar 3412 V-12 turbocharged diesel 27,000cc 650bhp (485kW) **Transmission** Clutch: torque converter; Gearbox: Caterpillar 7F 1R automatic; torque converter drive on reverse and first gear; Rear Axle: double reduction **Frame** full box section with torque tube cross member, box section rear cross member **Brakes** dual circuit air/hydraulic **Dimensions** wheelbase: 4,191mm; overall length: 9,119mm; overall width: 4,064mm; height to top of cab: 3,835mm; gross weight: 83,301kg; load capacity: 45,360kg **Performance** maximum speed: 65km/hr

Maker: Intreprinderea de Autocamione Brasov, Brasov

DAC trucks are built in the same factory as Romans. Three distinct types are made under the DAC name, conventional 4 × 2s formerly known as Bucegi, a 6 × 6 5-tonner for military and commercial applications, and a range of 4 × 2 dump trucks, including the 90-61C for 50 ton payloads and the 170-100AC for 100 ton payloads. The latter is powered by a turbocharged V-12 diesel engine of 1,000bhp, with torque converter and electric drive. These are made under licence from the American Clark Corporation.

Engine 12V 331 TC42 V-12 turbocharged diesel 39,720cc 1,000bhp (735kW) **Transmission** Clutch: torque converter; Gearbox: electric drive 4F 4R; Rear Axle: double reduction **Frame** box section side members **Brakes** dual circuit hydro-pneumatic with retarder integral with transmission housing **Dimensions** wheelbase: 4,800mm; overall length: 10,250mm; overall width: 4,940mm; height to top of cab: 4,720mm; gross weight: 167,290kg; payload: 100,000kg **Performance** maximum speed: 53km/hr

Maker: Dart Truck Co, Kansas City, Missouri

Dart is one of America's oldest truck builders, having made their first half-ton 2-
cylinder truck in 1903. They entered the field
of heavy-duty mining trucks in 1937, and in
the early 1950s abandoned regular highway
vehicles to concentrate on rear- and bottom-
dump trucks. Today they make 4- and 6-
wheel rigid trucks and articulated bottom-
dump coal haulers, as well as front-end
loaders, log stackers and aircraft refuelling
chassis. The 3120 is the largest of three rear
dump trucks in the current Dart range from
85 to 120 tons capacity. It has six engine
options, Detroit Diesel or Cummins units
from 1,050 to 1,350bhp, and Allison torque
converter transmission. Unlike a number of
other dump trucks of comparable size, Darts
do not use electric final drive, but their own
mechanical system with triple reduction. As
well as being lighter, this system enables
ratios to be changed on site, as job conditions
warrant.

Engine Cummins KTA 2300-C1200 V-12 turbocharged diesel 37,720cc 1,200bhp (895.2kW)
Transmission Clutch: torque converter; Gearbox: Allison CLBT-9680 6F 1R automatic; Rear Axle:
Dart DS800, double reduction differential and final planetary reduction in each wheel **Frame** box
section side and cross members **Brakes** dual circuit air/hydraulic **Dimensions** wheelbase:
5,334mm; overall length: 11,836mm; overall width: 5,791mm; height to top of cab: 5,385mm;
gross weight: 188,244kg; load capacity: 108,864kg **Performance** maximum speed: 60km/hr.
(typical available specification for the truck illustrated)

Maker: Dart Truck Co, Kansas City, Missouri

Six wheel dump trucks are relatively rare, but Dart designed their Model 2085 in order to achieve superior performance on steep gradients or soft surfaces. It can carry its 85-ton load up a muddy 16.4% effective gradient, which is 23% better performance than a conventional 85-ton single drive-axle dump truck. The Model 2085's ten 21.00 × 35 inch tyres obtain only 71 pounds per square inch ground bearing pressure. Dart has been building tandem-drive dump trucks since 1950, but the Model 2085 is the largest made so far. Engine choices are Detroit Diesel 16V-92T or Cummins VTA-1710, 16 and 12 cylinders respectively and both developing 800bhp. Like the two-axle models, the 2085 uses Allison automatic transmission and Dart's own triple reduction final drive. Since 1958 Dart was part of Paccar Inc, who also own Kenworth and Peterbilt in the USA, and Foden in Great Britain, but in March 1984 they were acquired by Unit Rig & Equipment Co, makers of Lectra Haul dump trucks.

Engine Detroit Diesel 16V-92T V-16 turbocharged diesel 24,140cc 800bhp (596.8kW) *or* Cummins VTA-1710 V-12 turbocharged diesel 28,040cc 800bhp (596.8kW) **Transmission** Clutch: torque converter; Gearbox: Allison DP-8961 6F 1R automatic; Rear Axle: Dart DT550 double reduction differential and final planetary reduction in each wheel **Frame** Box section side and cross members **Brakes** dual circuit air/hydraulic **Dimensions** wheelbase: 6,858mm; overall length: 12,370mm; overall width: 4,547mm; height to top of cab: 4,064mm; gross weight: 129,158kg; load capacity: 77,112kg **Performance** maximum speed: 60km/hr.

Maker: DJB Engineering Ltd, Peterlee, County Durham

DJB Engineering was founded in 1973 by David John Bowes Brown, and has specialised in articulated dump trucks in 4 × 4 and 6 × 4 versions, though the latter can also be used as tractive units for logging, pipe carrying and similar work. There are three models in the 4 × 4 range, the D25C, D35C and D44, with payloads of 25, 35 and 44 tons respectively. All are powered by Caterpillar diesel engines and have Caterpillar automatic transmissions with torque converters. Axles, steering valves and many other components are also by Caterpillar. The frame is articulated behind the cab, with a hydraulic steering system that gives a turning circle of only 51ft 8ins (15,740mm). While four-wheel-drive is standard, the D25C and its sisters can be supplied with front-wheel-drive only, in which case the rear Caterpillar axle is replaced by a heavy-duty DJB tag axle. Variations on the standard dump truck include a water wagon (D25C WW) and a low profile cab (D25C LP) for operating in mines.

Engine Caterpillar 3306 PCTA 6-cylinder turbocharged diesel 10,447cc 255bhp (190kW) **Transmission** Clutch: torque converter; Gearbox: Caterpillar 980B 4F 3R; Front Axle: Caterpillar 966 double reduction; Rear Axle: Caterpillar 980B double reduction **Frame** (front) tapered box section with integral bumper (rear) enclosed full box section **Brakes** triple circuit air/hydraulic **Dimensions** wheelbase: 4,820mm; overall length: 8,440mm; overall width: 3,226mm; height to top of cab: 3,250mm; gross weight: 51,800kg; load capacity: 31,800kg **Performance** maximum speed: 50km/hr

Maker: DJB Engineering Ltd, Peterlee, County Durham

Three models of DJB articulated 6-wheeled dump trucks are made, the 35-ton D350C, 40-ton D400 and 55-ton D550. As with other DJB trucks they make wide use of Caterpillar components, including engines, transmissions, axles, hydraulic steering gear, batteries, gauges and silencer. The D550 is powered by a 3408 V-8 engine, while the smaller models use the 3306 6-cylinder power unit. Low pressure wide-base tyres give good traction even on very muddy and steep surfaces. The D350C and D550 have 6 × 4 drive, (optional 6 × 6 on the 350C) while the D400 has permanent 6-wheel drive. While mainly aimed at the dump truck market, the DJBs can also be used as U frame trucks for skip haulage, water wagons and general carrying over rough ground, and as tractors for logging and pipe hauling. Approximately 90% of DJB's production goes for export.

Engine Caterpillar 3408 PCTA V-8 turbocharged diesel 17,996cc 450bhp (336kW) **Transmission** Clutch: torque converter; Gearbox: Caterpillar 988B 4F 4R; Rear Axles: Caterpillar 980B double reduction tandem **Frame** (front) internally braced deep box section with integral bumper (rear) enclosed full box section **Brakes** dual circuit air/hydraulic, with hydraulic retarder integral with torque converter **Dimensions** wheelbase: 6,755mm; overall length: 11,353mm; overall width: 3,658mm; height to top of cab: 3,860mm; gross weight: 87,800kg; load capacity: 50,000kg **Performance** maximum speed: 48km/hr (also theoretically obtainable in reverse)

Maker: Euclid Inc, Cleveland, Ohio

Euclid was the first company in the world to make purpose-built off-highway dump trucks, and have been active in this field since 1934. They have had a number of changes of ownership, being part of General Motors from 1953 to 1968, and of White from 1968 to 1977, since when they have been owned by Mercedes-Benz. Current production includes 4 × 2 dump trucks from 25 to 170 tons payload, articulated bottom-dump trucks from 30 to 110 tons payload, and articulated bottom-dump coal haulers from 120 to 150 tons payload. The R-25 illustrated is the smallest model, and is powered by either Detroit Diesel or Cummins engines of 228 or 240bhp. Transmission is by Allison planetary gearbox with full power assistance and automatic shifting from second to fifth speeds. In addition to their Cleveland headquarters, Euclid have factories in Belgium, Australia, South Africa and Canada.

Engine Detroit Diesel 6-71N 6-cylinder diesel 6,976cc 228bhp (170kW) *or* Cummins N-855-C 6-cylinder diesel 14,000cc 240bhp (179kW) **Transmission** Clutch: torque converter; Gearbox: Allison CLBT-750 5F 1R automatic; Rear Axle: Euclid double reduction **Frame** channel section ladder type **Brakes** dual circuit fully air-operated **Dimensions** wheelbase: 3,940mm; overall length: 7,800mm; overall width: 3,070mm; height to top of cab: 3,630mm; gross weight: 40,460kg; load capacity: 22,680kg **Performance** maximum speed: 44.9km/hr.

Maker: Euclid Inc, Cleveland, Ohio

This is one of the larger models of Euclid dump truck, which run from the 25-ton R-25 to the 170-ton R-170. Various sizes of Detroit Diesel or Cummins engines are used, of which the largest is the Cummins KTA-3067 V-16 developing 1,600bhp and with a capacity of over 50 litres. The smaller models use Allison planetary automatic transmissions while the R-120 and R-170 have electric drive with a General Electric alternator coupled directly to the engine, and General Electric motors in each rear wheel.

Engine Detroit Diesel 16V-92T V-16 turbocharged diesel 24,103cc 860bhp (641kW) *or* Cummins VTA-1710-C V-12 turbocharged diesel 28,000cc 800bhp (596kW) **Transmission** Clutch: torque converter; Gearbox: Allison DP-8961 6F 1R automatic; Rear Axle: Euclid double reduction **Frame** channel section ladder type **Brakes** dual circuit air/hydraulic **Dimensions** wheelbase: 4,420mm; overall length: 9,270mm; overall width: 4,880mm; height to top of cab: 4,450mm; gross weight: 128,300kg; load capacity: 77,100kg **Performance** maximum speed: 51.3 or 60.7km/hr, according to axle ratio

FAUN K.100   D

Maker: Faun Frisch Baumaschinen GmbH, Lauf a.d. Pegnitz

Faun built their first heavy dump trucks in the 1950s, and they are now an important part of the company's production, being made in six models with payloads from 23 to 100 tons. The smaller models are available with four wheel drive as an option. The 40.5 is offered with a choice of three engines, by Deutz, Cummins or Detroit Diesel, and has a 5-speed automatic Alison transmission. The largest Faun dump truck, the 100 ton Model K.100 uses a 1050bhp Cummins KTA 2300 engine, with two turbochargers and two aftercoolers. This is one of the biggest rear dump trucks constructed in series in Europe.

Engine Cummins KTA 2300-C1050 V-12 turbocharged and aftercooled diesel 37,800cc 1050bhp (783kW) **Transmission** Clutch: torque converter; Gearbox: Allison DP 8961 6F 1R automatic; Rear Axle: Faun double reduction **Frame** box section with tubular cross members **Brakes** dual circuit air/hydraulic + hydraulic retarder integrated in powershift transmission **Dimensions** wheelbase: 4,700mm; overall length: 10,262mm; overall width: 5,340mm; height to top of cab: 4,885mm; gross weight: 154,275kg; load capacity: 90,700kg **Performance** maximum speed: 59.1km/hr

Maker: M.A.N. Unternehmensbereich G.H.H. Sterkrade, Oberhausen

G.H.H. Gutehoffungshütte Sterkrade Aktien-gesellschaft, manufactures wheel-loaders up to 15 tons payload, dumpers, utility vehicles, personnel carriers and other special vehicles for underground mining. This activity started in 1964, but at that time the company had already existed as a shipyard for 135 years. Rear end dumpers are made for payloads of 3.5, 12, 25, 40, 43 and 50 tons. For instance the MK-V40.1, a rear end dumper which is powered by a Deutz water-cooled engine, like all the other dumpers of G.H.H.. Torque converter, power shift transmission and front driven axle are made by Clark. All the trackless vehicles of G.H.H. have articulated frames, some are flame-proofed, others have radio or cable remote control. Their headquarters are located in Oberhausen, West Germany, although they have a production facility in Riyadh Saudi Arabia as well. G.H.H. is wholly owned by M.A.N.

Engine Deutz BA12M816LLK-W 12-cylinder turbocharged after-cooled diesel 842bhp (620kW) **Transmission** Clutch: Clark CL16852 torque converter; Gearbox: Clark 4F 2R power shift; Transfer Box: none; Front Axle: planetary, driven; Rear Axle: G.H.H. non-driven **Frame** box section **Brakes** dual circuit hydro-pneumatic/hydraulic **Dimensions** wheelbase: 4,705mm; overall length: 9,315mm; overall width: 3,548mm; height to top of cab: 3,100mm; gross weight: 87,600kg; load capacity: 43,000kg

Maker: Gremo International I/S, Frederikshavn

The popularity of articulated dump trucks increased during the seventies. Both Scandinavian forestry and dump truck factories expanded their existing programs by adding a vehicle of this kind. Gremo in Denmark is one of them. The company already manufactured forestry vehicles like the forwarders, types TT8H, TT12C, 803 and 804, when they added the TP14 to their program. The TP14 is a 22-ton articulated dump truck, featuring a Caterpillar engine and driving axles, just like the British articulated dump trucks of D.J.B.

Engine Caterpillar 3304T turbocharged diesel 4,250cc 165bhp (122kW) **Transmission** Clutch: torque converter; Gearbox: 4F 1R, full power shift; Transfer Box: none; Front Axle: TAG, planetary; Rear Axle: Caterpillar 950, planetary **Frame** channel section ladder type, articulated **Brakes** three separate brake systems, air over hydraulic **Dimensions** wheelbase: 5,100mm; overall length: 8,300mm; overall width: 2,500mm; height to top of cab: 3,260mm; gross weight: 35,000kg; load capacity: 22,000kg **Performance** maximum speed: 30km/hr

Maker: Heathfield Engineering Ltd, Newton Abbot, Devon

Heathfield is a division of Centrax Ltd, makers of axles, gearboxes and gas turbine compressor blades. They built their first dump truck in 1966, and have since specialised in 4 × 2 off-highway trucks, at present made in two models for 20 and 33 tons payload. All are powered by Cummins 855 6-cylinder engines, normally-aspirated in the smaller model and turbocharged in the larger. They have rubber suspension units, independent at the front, and exhaust gases are routed through the body walls to warm sticky loads for easier discharge. Many Heathfields are exported, but among important home market customers are the National Coal Board and the British Steel Corporation.

Engine Cummins NTA-855-C-360 6-cylinder turbocharged diesel 14,000cc 235bhp (175kW) **Transmission** Clutch: torque converter; Gearbox: Allison CLBT-750 5F 1R automatic; Rear Axle: Heathfield/Kirkstall double reduction **Frame** box section with four cross members **Brakes** dual circuit air/hydraulic **Dimensions** wheelbase: 3,430mm; overall length: 7,135mm; overall width: 3,890mm; height to top of cab: 3,605mm; gross weight: 52,680kg; load capacity: 30,000kg **Performance** maximum speed: 50km/hr

Maker: Carl Kaelble GmbH, Backnang

Kaelble began production of dump trucks in 1952, and they have been an important aspect of the firm's activity ever since. Currently they make three types of dump truck, the conventional K 20-B and KVW 30, the larger KV33 with 390bhp V10 Mercedes-Benz OM423 engine and two models with articulated frames and 4 × 4 drive, the KK 35 and KK 50. the K 20B is powered by a Mercedes-Benz 6-cylinder engine, and unlike many larger dump trucks which use automatic transmission, it has a conventional 6-speed synchromesh gear-box. Suspension is also conventional, by semi-elliptic springs front and rear. The larger KVW 30 is of similar appearance, but uses a 355bhp Mercedes-Benz V-10 engine of 15,950cc capacity, and has a ZF automatic transmission. Payload of the KVW 30 is 30,000kg.

Engine Mercedes-Benz OM 355 6-cylinder diesel 11,575cc 265bhp (176kW) **Transmission** Clutch: Fichtel & Sachs single dry plate; Gearbox: ZF S 6-80 6F 1R all-synchromesh; Rear Axle: double reduction **Frame** channel section ladder type **Brakes** dual circuit fully air-operated **Dimensions** wheelbase: 3,700mm; overall length: 7,230mm; overall width: 2,750mm; height to top of cab: 3,040mm; gross weight: 35,400kg; load capacity: 20,000kg **Performance** maximum speed: 43km/hr.

Maker: Carl Kaelble GmbH, Backnang

This is one of two dump trucks with centre-articulated frames made by Kaelble. Powered by a 465bhp Mercedes-Benz V-12 engine, it is one of the largest dump trucks of this design made in the world, with a payload of 45,000kg. As with other articulated dump trucks, steering is hydrostatic by two hydraulic cylinders, and the front wheels do not turn at all in relation to the frame. Bodies are either a rock type as illustrated, or a coal dump body with rear discharge flap. In addition to the KK 50, Kaelble make the smaller KK 35 with 310bhp 6-cylinder M.A.N. engine and 31,500kg payload.

Engine Mercedes-Benz OM 404 V-12 diesel 20,910cc 465bhp (309kW) *or* Mercedes-Benz OM 404A V-12 turbocharged diesel 20,910cc 580bhp (386kW) **Transmission** Clutch: twin dry plate; Gearbox: Twin Disc TAC-51-2003 5F 1R; Transfer Box: Kaelble; Front Axle: Kaelble double reduction; Rear Axle: Kaelble double reduction **Frame** box section **Brakes** dual circuit air/hydraulic **Dimensions** wheelbase: 6,750mm; overall length: 11,100mm; overall width: 3,500mm; height to top of cab: 3,600mm; gross weight: 83,500kg; load capacity: 45,000kg **Performance** maximum speed: 43km/hr.

Maker: Komatsu Ltd, Tokyo

Komatsu is a large engineering concern producing crawler tractors, snow vehicles, excavators, bulldozers and dump trucks. The first of these appeared in 1951, and Komatsu now makes a wide range with payloads from 20 to 176 tons. Nearly all of them use Cummins engines, which are made under licence by Komatsu. The HD 180 is the smallest of the present range, and is powered by a 12.7-litre 6-cylinder engine. It is the only Komatsu dump truck to have a full-width two-man cab, and also the only one to have a conventional clutch and manual gearbox. Larger models have automatic transmissions, with electric drive on the heaviest trucks.

Engine Komatsu-Cummins NTO-6-B 6-cylinder turbocharged diesel 12,170cc 250bhp (184kW) **Transmission** Clutch: single dry plate; Gearbox: 7F 1R constant mesh; Rear Axle: double reduction **Frame** channel section ladder type **Brakes** dual circuit fully air-operated, with Jacobs retarders in rear wheels **Dimensions** wheelbase: 4,000mm; overall length: 7,295mm; overall width: 3,000mm; height to top of cab: 3,300mm; gross weight: 34,900kg; load capacity: 18,110kg **Performance** maximum speed: 56km/hr.

Maker: Komatsu Ltd, Tokyo

The HD 1200 is the second largest Komatsu dump truck, with a maximum payload of 132-tons (130,000kg), and is powered by a 37.7-litre Cummins V-12 engine developing 1,200bhp. It is made in two models, the 1200-1 with electric drive, and the 1200M-1 with Torq-flow torque converter and planetary automatic transmission. The electric drive system consists of engine, alternator, control cabinet which automatically matches generator output to engine speed, and electric motors in each rear wheel. The latter provide additional braking for when the brakes are applied the traction motors become generators, and the generated power is changed into heat by the brake resistor and dissipated into the air. Only when the brake pedal is depressed further do the mechanical brakes come into operation.

Engine Cummins KTA-2300 V-12 turbocharged diesel 37,700cc 1,200bhp (895kW) **Transmission** Clutch: none; Gearbox: electric drive, with alternator, control cabinet and series-wound DC motors in each rear wheel; Rear Axle: fully floating; planetary gear final drive from electric motors **Frame** box section ladder type **Brakes** dual circuit air/hydraulic, with electric braking in rear wheels **Dimensions** wheelbase: 5,400mm; overall length: 10,885mm; overall width: 6,550mm; height to top of cab: 5,170mm; gross weight: 205,855kg; load capacity: 130,000kg **Performance** maximum speed: 57.5km/hr

Maker: Kress Corporation, Brimfield, Illinois

Kress exceeded their competitors by introducing the CH160. Already for years, the tractor-trailer combinations of Euclid, Terex and Wabco had been operational in the mines, and all of them proved to be efficient, mainly due to their enormous payload capacities. To design something even more efficient than the vehicles generally accepted, is not easy. But Kress succeeded, and with the CH160 they introduced a wholly new concept. This 'single-unit' coal carrier has several advantages in comparison with the conventional tractor-trailer units. The wide-open top improves the loading time, the full-opening gates reduce the unloading time. The CH160 is easier to handle as the front wheels can turn 90° in both directions. The engine is located behind the rear axle and it is very accessible.

Engine Cummins KTA-1200C, V-12 turbocharged diesel 37,720cc 1,200bhp (895.2kW) **Transmission** Clutch: TC-890 torque converter; Gearbox: 6F 1R; Rear Axle: Cat 777 **Frame** box section **Brakes** hydraulic **Dimensions** wheelbase: 10,490mm; overall length: 17,120mm; overall width: 5,309mm; height to top of cab: 3,000mm; gross weight: 209,999kg; load capacity: 160,000kg **Performance** maximum speed: 46.5km/hr

Maker: Unit Rig & Equipment Co, Tulsa, Oklahoma

Unit Rig & Equipment was founded in 1935 to build oilfield equipment, and later developed off-highway military vehicles for the US and foreign governments. They began production of dump trucks in 1963, using the name Lectra Haul as they all incorporated electric final drive through motors in the rear wheels. The current range consists of four 4 × 2 trucks, with payloads from 85 to 200 tons and an articulated bottom dump coal hauler. The Mark 36 has a payload of 170 tons and is powered by either a Cummins or Detroit Diesel V-16 engine, both developing 1,600bhp. It and the 200-ton M-200 are the largest two-axle trucks in the world. Both use generators and wheel motors made by General Electric. Unit Rig has made more than 3,000 giant dump trucks since 1963, as well as aircraft tractors and 60-ton fork lift trucks. Most M-200s have been sold to Russia for hauling coal and phosphates in Siberia. Unit Rig's main plant is at Tulsa, but they have recently set up subsidiary plants at Conroe, Texas, Niagara Falls and Stevensville, Ontario.

Engine Cummins KTA-3067C V-16 turbocharged and aftercooled diesel 50,300cc 1,600bhp (1,193kW) *or* Detroit Diesel 16V-149TI V-16 turbocharged and intercooled diesel 39,200cc 1,600bhp (1,193kW) **Transmission** Clutch: none; Gearbox: electric drive, with alternator, control cabinet and GE776 series-wound DC motors in each rear wheel; Rear Axle: fully floating; planetary gear final drive from electric motors **Frame** double box section **Brakes** dual circuit air/hydraulic, with electric braking in rear wheels **Dimensions** wheelbase: 5,330mm; overall length: 11,810mm; overall width: 7,030mm; height to top of cab: 5,790mm; gross weight: 249,480kg; load capacity: 154,190kg **Performance** maximum speed: 55km/hr

Maker: Mogilyev Auto Works, Mogilyev, Byelorussia

Mogilyev works belongs to the BelavtoMAZ conglomerate and makes equipment for road construction work, for opencast pits and underground mines. This 4 × 4 tipper was put into production in 1979 as the MoAZ-522A, then called an 18-tonner. Current specs are somewhat modified, but the model 6507, as all the MoAZ machinery, is based heavily on parts of BelAZ and MAZ trucks. Special features are semi-automatic transmission, pneumohydraulic suspension and tyres in size 177 × 670–635 (26.5–25.00). A tractor MoAZ-7405 is also made; its semi-trailer has load capacity of 22,000kg.

Engine YaMZ-238N V-8 turbocharged diesel 14,860cc 300bhp (220kW) **Transmission** Clutch: torque converter; Gearbox: 6F 1R semi-automatic; Front Axle: double reduction; Rear Axle: double reduction **Frame** channel section ladder type **Brakes** dual circuit air-operated **Dimensions** wheelbase: 3,550mm; overall length: 7,540mm; overall width: 3,245mm; overall height: 3,350mm; gross weight: 39,000kg; load capacity: 20,000kgs **Performance** maximum speed: 50km/hr

Maker: Moxy A/S, Molde

Engine Scania DS8 A06 6-cylinder turbocharged diesel 7,790cc 205bhp (151kW) **Transmission** Clutch: torque converter; Gearbox: Clark 13.5HR 32 420.12 4F 4R automatic; Front Axle: double reduction; Rear Axle: double reduction **Frame** box section **Brakes** dual circuit fully air-operated **Dimensions** wheelbase: 5,692mm; overall length: 8,751mm; overall width: 2,490mm; height to top of cab: 3,130mm; gross weight: 36,050kg; load capacity: 22,000kg **Performance** maximum speed: 30km/hr

The Moxy (pronounced 'Moosie') centre-articulated dump truck was developed by a branch of a big industrial group, Glamin A/S. The branch was called Glamox, from which the name Moxy was coined. Proto-types were developed in 1974/5, and the 22-ton D16 was put into production in 1976. Three models are currently made, the 4 × 4 Model 3200 for 12 tonne payloads, powered by a Ford 7710 engine, 6 × 6 Model 5200 (22 tonnes) and the 6 × 6 Model 6200S (25 tonnes), both Scania powered. The two larger models are fitted with six wheel drive as standard, although on the 5200 the front axle can be disengaged in the higher ratios. In addition, the 6200S is fitted with a fully independent front suspension system to permit higher travel speeds with a full load. Although built in Norway, the larger Moxys are marketed worldwide from England by Yorkshire-based Brown Engineering Ltd, while the 3200 is made in Yorkshire. More than 1100 Moxys were operating by the summer of 1985, and there are dealerships throughout Europe, the Far East, Australia, Africa and Canada.

Maker: Nissan Diesel Motor Co. Ltd, Tokyo

This is the largest dump truck made by Nissan, and is the only one of typical half-cab off-highway type made by the company. It is powered by a 350bhp V-10 engine and like most dump trucks uses an automatic transmission. Although the cab is less than half the width of the truck, it can seat two men comfortably.

Engine Nissan RD10 V-10 diesel 350bhp (261.1kW) **Transmission** Clutch: Torque converter; Gearbox: Allison CLBT-750 5F 1R automatic; Rear Axle: double reduction **Frame** channel section ladder type **Brakes** dual circuit air/hydraulic **Dimensions** wheelbase: 3,900mm; overall length: 7,900mm; overall width: 3,480mm; height to top of cab: 3,560mm; gross weight: 43,500kg; load capacity: 23,000kg **Performance** maximum speed: 57km/hr

Maker: Nordstroms (Dumper Division), Enkoping

The Nordstrom 666B centre-articulated dump truck was introduced in 1975, and has proved very successful in a wide variety of jobs since then. In particular, they have been the predominant trucks in the Norway Road project above the Arctic Circle, and they have also been used in other road construction work and in iron ore mines in Sweden, and in dam construction in Holland and Wales. Powered by a Caterpillar 3208 diesel engine, the 666B drives through the front wheels and the leading axle of the rear frame. The final axle can be lifted when the truck is running unladen. It has air suspension for the front wheels, and rubber suspension on the bogie. Three different designs of dump body are available, as well as a chassis for carrying containers or for lime spreading and other agricultural work. In 1985 production of the 666B started at the D.J.B. factory at Peterlee, County Durham.

Engine Caterpillar 3208 6-cylinder diesel 10,414cc 210bhp (157kW) **Transmission** Clutch: torque converter; Gearbox: Allison MT-653 4 or 5F 1R; Front Axle: double reduction; Rear Axle: double reduction **Frame** box section **Brakes** dual circuit air/hydraulic **Dimensions** wheelbase: 5,710mm; overall length: 9,100mm; overall width: 2,500mm; height to top of cab: 3,140mm; gross weight: 39,550kg; load capacity: 25,000kg **Performance** maximum speed: 50km/hr.

Maker: Perlini International, Verona

Perlini is a specialist dump truck manufacturer, although they also make trailers, airfield fire tenders and third axle conversions for other makes of truck. Their first dump truck was made in 1962, and they have since delivered more than six thousand. The current range consists of four models, with payloads from 22 to 90.7 tonnes. Engines are Fiat, Detroit Diesel or Cummins in various sizes up to 37.7 litres. The smallest model, the DP 255 has a choice of manual or automatic gearbox, but all the others have Allison automatic transmissions. Suspensions are oleo-pneumatic at front and rear, with built-in shock absorbers.

Engine Detroit Diesel 8V-149 TIB V-8 turbocharged diesel 19,600cc 900bhp (671.1kW) *or* Cummins KTA 2300C V-12 turbocharged diesel 37,690cc 1,000bhp (746kW) **Transmission** Clutch: torque converter; Gearbox: Allison DP 8962 6F 1R automatic; Rear Axle: double reduction **Frame** box section side members with tubular cross members **Brakes** dual circuit fully air-operated, with retarder built into transmission **Dimensions** wheelbase: 4,830mm; overall length: 10,515mm; overall width: 5,150mm; height to top of cab: 4,860mm; gross weight: 154,000kg; load capacity: 90,700kg **Performance** maximum speed: 63.7km/hr.

Maker: Rimpull Corp, Olathe, Kansas

The Rimpull Corporation were suppliers of components to dump truck manufacturers for a number of years before they began to make complete trucks themselves in 1975. The name is derived from the special drive axle with double planetary reduction at the wheel rims which combined with double reduction in the differential gives a quadruple reduction with 40% extra torque. Another unique feature of Rimpull trucks is the mounting of the radiator behind the cab where it is away from dust and does not interfere with the driver's visibility. The current range includes six 4 × 2 dump trucks from 75 to 120 tons capacity, two 6 × 4s of 100 tons, four bottom dump coal haulers from 120 to 200 tons, and two 4 × 2 water trucks with 15,000 and 20,000 gallon tanks for spraying road surfaces in open cast mines, quarries and other sites where dump trucks operate. A choice of Cummins or Detroit Diesel engines is offered in all Rimpull trucks.

Engine Detroit Diesel 12V-149TI V-12 diesel 29,343cc 1,200bhp (895.2kW) *or* Cummins KTA 3067 C1350 V-16 diesel 50,221cc 1,350bhp (1,007kW) **Transmission** Clutch: torque converter; Gearbox: Allison CLBT 9680 6F 1R automatic; Rear Axle: Rimpull DA 304 quadruple reduction **Frame** channel section ladder type **Brakes** dual circuit air/hydraulic **Dimensions** wheelbase: 5,385mm; overall length: 11,379mm; overall width: 5,893mm; height to top of cab: 4,597mm; gross weight: 201,480kg; load capacity, 121,932kg **Performance** maximum speed: (Cummins engine) 32 to 49km/hr depending on final drive ratio).

Maker: Terberg Benschop BV, Benschop

In 1985 Terberg added to their already wide range of vehicles by entering the dump truck market. Comparatively small as dump trucks go, the TS 25 has a gross weight of 40,000kg and a load capacity of 25,000kg. It is powered by a Volvo TD70G engine and has a 5-speed Allison automatic transmission. The interior of the Hyva body is completely lined with rubber, which extends its working life and makes for quieter loading operations. Three TS25s have initially been built for the transport company Kole of Kloetinge, Netherlands.

Engine Volvo TD70G 6-cylinder turbocharged diesel 6,700cc 213bhp (157kW) **Transmission** Clutch: torque converter; Gearbox: Allison MT 653DR 5F 1R automatic; Rear Axle: Kessler double reduction **Frame** channel section ladder type **Brakes** dual circuit fully air-operated **Dimensions** wheelbase: 4,500mm; overall length: 7,800mm; height to top of cab: 3,410mm; gross weight: 40,000kg; load capacity: 25,000kg **Performance** maximum speed: 52km/hr

Maker: Terex Equipment Ltd, Motherwell, Scotland

Until 1980 Terex was a division of General Motors formed after GM had sold their Euclid dump truck operation to White. From 1980 it was part of the German IBH Group which collapsed in 1983. The Scottish operation was re-acquired from the receivers by General Motors and reformed as Terex Equipment Ltd. A wide range of earth-moving equipment is made at Motherwell, including four models of loader, three scrapers, two bulldozers and six dump trucks from 15.4 to 77 tonnes payload. They are powered by Detroit Diesel or Cummins engines, and all but the smallest have Allison automatic transmission. The American Terex Corporation with headquarters at Hudson, Ohio, is still operating under US bankruptcy laws, and has not been re-acquired by General Motors.

Engine Detroit Diesel 16V-71T V-16 turbocharged diesel 18,600cc 665bhp (496kW) *or* Cummins VTA28 V-12 turbocharged and aftercooled diesel 28,000cc 675bhp (504kW) **Transmission** Clutch: torque converter; Gearbox: Allison CLBT-6061 6F 1R automatic; Rear Axle: double reduction **Frame** full box section with integral front bumper and closed loop cross member **Brakes** dual circuit fully air-operated **Dimensions** wheelbase: 4,270mm; overall length: 9,960mm; overall width: 4,510mm; height to top of cab: 3,975mm; gross weight: 92,200kg; load capacity: 49,900kg **Performance** maximum speed: 68.3km/hr

Maker: Terex Equipment Ltd, Motherwell, Scotland

Introduced in 1984, the Terex 2366 is an addition to the growing number of articulated dumptrucks, and was designed and manufactured in Scotland. It has independent suspension and permanently-engaged drive to all wheels. Front suspension is by self-levelling air units and rear by rubber/metal laminated units between the axles and beam ends. The 2366 has full hydrostatic power steering. There are five different dump bodies, with varying sizes of tailgate and tail extension, and a sixth version is a rough terrain load carrier fitted with a self-load/unload system capable of handling ISO 20ft containers. Wide base tyres are available for swamp or desert conditions.

Engine Deutz BF 6L 413FR 6-cylinder air cooled turbocharged diesel 9,572cc 227bhp (169kW) **Transmission** Clutch: torque converter; Gearbox: ZF 6WG 180 6F 3R; Rear Axle: double reduction **Frame** box section, articulated **Brakes** dual circuit fully air-operated **Dimensions** wheelbase: 5,710mm; overall length: 9,360mm; overall width: 2,500mm; height to top of cab: 3,095mm; gross weight: 39,800kg; *or* 40,290kg according to body; load capacity: 23,000kg **Performance** maximum speed: 54km/hr

Maker: Volvo BM AB, Eskilstuna

Volvo BM is a special division of Volvo making rigid and articulated dump trucks. The latter are offered in two series, the 861 and the more powerful 5350. BM stands for Bolinder Munktells, an old-established firm making steam traction engines and petrol agricultural tractors, which merged with Volvo in 1950. Dump trucks were made from 1963, and three years later came the first of the 860 series of articulated dump trucks, from which today's models have been developed. The frame pivots both vertically and horizontally behind the front axle. Drive from the TD 60B engine is taken to the front axle and leading rear axle, and a 6 × 6 version is also made. Special models of the 861 include a high-altitude version and a low-emission version suitable for underground operation in mines. It is also offered as a long-wheelbase chassis on which can be mounted bodies for log or pipe carrying, concrete mixers or cable laying. More than 15,000 articulated dump trucks have been made up to 1985; export markets include Great Britain, France, Germany, Canada, Nigeria, Peru, Paraguay, Sri Lanka, Malaysia and Japan. The 5350 is generally similar, but is powered by the Volvo TD 70G 213bhp engine.

Engine Volvo TD 60B 6-cylinder turbocharged diesel 5,480cc 170bhp (125kW) **Transmission** Clutch: torque converter; Gearbox: Volvo BM 4F 4R synchromesh; Transfer Box: single speed; Front Axle: double reduction; Rear Axle: double reduction **Frame** (tractor unit) flat topped channel section, (trailer unit) welded box section **Brakes** dual circuit; air/hydraulic front brakes, fully air-operated rear brakes **Dimensions** wheelbase: 5,590mm; overall length: 9,400mm; overall width: 2,500mm; height to top of cab: 2,900mm; gross weight: 31,900kg; load capacity: 18,720kg **Performance** maximum speed: 30km/hr.

Maker: Volvo BMB, Eskiltuna

Since January 1983 the rigid dump trucks made by Kockum Landswerk have been sold under the Volvo BM name, as Kockum became a wholly-owned subsidiary of Volvo BM. Five models are currently made, with payloads ranging from 25 to 65 tons. The three smaller models (25, 35 and 40 tons) use Volvo 6-cylinder or Scania V-8 engines, while the 55-ton 555 illustrated is powered by a 617bhp Detroit Diesel 16V-71N, and the largest version, the 65 ton 565, uses a 674bhp Detroit Diesel 16V-71TV. Cummins and Detroit Diesels are available as options on the smaller models. A variant of the 540 known as the 540 RB has a rubber sheet instead of the steel skin of the standard body. This reduces the shocks to the body caused by heavy rock, reduces the noise level and also the risk of deforming the body. Kockum-type dump trucks are at work in more than fifty countries, in temperatures varying from –40°C near the Arctic Circle to +50°C at the Equator, and at altitudes between 4,000 metres above sea level in Peru to 600 metres below ground in Sweden.

Engine Detroit Diesel 16V-71TV V-16 turbocharged diesel engine 18,600cc 674bhp (496kW) *or* Cummins VTA 1710C V-12 turbocharged diesel 28,000cc 675bhp (497kW) **Transmission** Clutch: Allison TC680 torque converter; Gearbox: Allison CLBT 6061 6F 1R automatic; Rear Axle: double reduction **Frame** box section **Brakes** dual circuit air/hydraulic **Dimensions** wheelbase 4,300mm; overall length: 9,400mm; overall width: 4,180mm; height to top of cab: 4,030mm; gross weight: 87,000kg; load capacity: 50,000kg **Performance** maximum speed: 65km/hr

Maker: Wabco Construction & Mining Equipment Group, Peoria, Illinois

Wabco is an abbreviation of Westinghouse Air Brake Company who launched a line of dumptrucks under the name of Haulpak in 1957. They now make eleven models in the Haulpak series, from the 35D 35-tonner illustrated up to the 6 × 4 3200B which, with a capacity of 235 tons, is the largest truck currently made in the world. They also make articulated bottom dump coal haulers. The 35D, although it is the 'baby' of the Haulpak range, still has a V-12 engine of nearly 14 litres capacity developing 450bhp. Transmission on all the Haulpaks up to the 120 ton 120C is by torque converter and automatic gearbox; larger models have electric drive by separate motors in each rear wheel. As well as their plant at Peoria, Wabco have factories in Belgium (Gembloux), Brazil (Campinas) and Australia (Rydalmere, NSW). Two models of Wabco, the 35D and 75B, are made under licence in China.

Engine Detroit Diesel 12V-71N V-12 diesel 13,960cc 456bhp (340kW) *or* Cummins KT-1150-C 6-cylinder diesel 18,831cc 450bhp (336kW) **Transmission** Clutch: Allison TC690 torque converter; Gearbox: Allison CLBT-5861 6F 1R automatic; Rear Axle: double reduction **Frame** box section with integral front bumper and cross member **Brakes** dual circuit air/hydraulic, with dynamic retarder in transmission **Dimensions** wheelbase: 3,300mm; overall length: 8,010mm; overall width: 3,780mm; height to top of cab: 3,790mm; gross weight: 59,538kg; load capacity: 31,561kg **Performance** maximum speed: 66.77km/hr.

Maker: Wabco Construction & Mining Equipment Group, Peoria, Illinois

The prototype Wabco 3200 was built in September 1971, and following exhaustive tests, five further prototypes were completed which were tested in selected locations throughout the world. Lessons learnt were incorporated in the first production models which left the factory in 1974. By September 1985, 46 Model 3200s had been made, a remarkable figure for a truck which is the largest in the world apart from the 350-ton Terex Titan of which only one was made. The Wabco 3200 is powered by a General Motors Electro-Motive Division V-12 engine normally used in railway locomotives. With a capacity of nearly 127 litres it develops 2,475bhp at only 900rpm, ensuring very long engine life. Unlike the smaller Wabcos which have electric motors in each rear wheel, the 3200 has a single motor above each axle, driving through double planetary reduction. The final reduction can be tailored to meet any particular job. Tyre diameter is over 10 feet (3,048mm). The cost of a Wabco 3200B early in 1985 was $1,925,000.

Engine General Motors EMD 12-645-E4 V-12 diesel 126,900cc 2,475bhp (1,846.35kW) **Transmission** Clutch: none; Gearbox: electric drive, with EMD AR-5B alternator and two EMD D79 × 3A motors; Rear Axles: Wabco double reduction planetary drive **Frame** box section with integral front bumper and cross members **Brakes** dual circuit air/hydraulic, with electric dynamic retarder **Dimensions** wheelbase: 10,230mm; overall length: 16,540mm; overall width: 7,670mm; height to top of cab: 6,200mm; gross weight: 392,710kg; load capacity: 227,000kg **Performance** maximum speed: 40km/hr.

Maker: Machinefabriek Werklust BV, Apeldoorn

Werklust began truck production in 1974 with a front-wheel-drive 6-wheeler for skip transportation, powered by a Mercedes-Benz engine and with a Terberg front axle. This has now been superseded by the WD 3 6 × 6 centre-articulated dump truck powered by a Detroit Diesel 6-cylinder engine and using Allison automatic transmission. 6 × 2 drive can be selected for operation on good surfaces. The coupling between front and rear frames allows lateral oscillation of 90°, which eliminates the transfer of torsional stress from one frame to the other. In addition, the rear tandem axles can swing independently of the frame, and the truck can assume quite remarkable angles on rough ground. The transmission offers four speeds forward and reverse, and the Werklust has two tipping speeds for fast and slow discharge of material. With the fast speed (ie: higher angle of body) the load can be emptied in ten seconds.

Engine Detroit Diesel 6-71T-N75 6-cylinder diesel 6,990cc 273bhp (200kW) **Transmission** Clutch: torque converter; Gearbox: Allison TRT-4820-1 4F 4R automatic; Front Axle: double reduction; Rear Axles: double reduction **Frame** box section **Brakes** triple circuit air/hydraulic **Dimensions** wheelbase: 6,055mm; overall length: 9,525mm; overall width: 2,750mm; height to top of cab: 3,000mm; gross weight: 49,500kg; load capacity: 32,000kg **Performance** maximum speed: 45km/hr

Maker: Dart Truck Co, Kansas City, Missouri

The Dart 4000 series of articulated bottom-dump coal haulers has two models, with capacities of 120 and 160 tons, of which the truck illustrated is the largest. They are mainly used for carrying coal from open-cast mines to railheads or for onward distribution in smaller highway trucks. Even the 'baby' of the range, the Model 4120, uses Detroit Diesel or Cummins engines of 24 or 28 litres' capacity respectively, while the Model 4160 offers a choice of Detroit Diesel 1,050bhp 29 litres or Cummins 1,050bhp 37.7 litre power units. All models have an Ingersoll Rand air starting motor with 19 cubic foot air reservoir. These are all catalogued models, but Dart can build even larger trucks to special order, such as the 120 ton tractor coupled to three 140 ton trailers, two of which were built in 1969 for hauling salt from solar evaporation ponds in Baja California to the processing plant.

Engine Detroit Diesel 12V-149T V-12 turbocharged diesel 29,320cc 1,050bhp (783.3kW) *or* Cummins KTA2300-C1050 V-12 turbocharged diesel 37,690cc 1,050bhp (783.3kW) **Transmission** Clutch: torque converter; Gearbox: Allison DP8961 6F 1R automatic; Rear Axle: Dart DS720 double reduction differential and final planetary reduction in each wheel **Frame** box section side and integral cross members **Brakes** dual circuit air/hydraulic **Dimensions** wheelbase: 4,826mm; overall length: 8,230mm (tractor), 23,800mm (complete vehicle); overall width: 5,512mm; height to top of cab: 4,851mm; gross weight: 232,285kg; load capacity: 136,078kg **Performance** maximum speed: 50km/hr

Maker: Euclid Inc, Cleveland, Ohio

Like a number of American dump truck makers, Euclid builds a line of bottom-dump articulated trucks specifically designed for use in open-cast coal mining, as well as smaller bottom dump trucks for earth moving. The coal haulers come in two models, of 120 and 150 tons payload respectively. Detroit Diesel and Cummins are used, in sizes from 18.6 to 37.7 litres, and power outputs from 700 to 1,050bhp. They both have hydraulic doors in the trailer bottoms, controlled by two double-acting cylinders mounted transversely which allow for precisely controlled dumping of the load. There are four braking systems; air/hydraulic service brakes, two independent emergency circuits, parking brake operating on the transmission and a retarder integral with the transmission housing which provides constant speed control on downhill journeys.

Engine Detroit Diesel 12V-149-T V-12 turbocharged diesel 29,343cc 1,050bhp (783kW) *or* Cummins KTA-2300-C V-12 turbocharged diesel 37,661cc 1,050bhp (783kW) **Transmission** Clutch: torque converter; Gearbox: Allison DP-8961 6F 1R automatic; Rear Axle: Euclid double reduction **Frame** box section side members bridged by three cross members, front bumper and front suspension tube **Brakes** dual circuit air/hydraulic **Dimensions** wheelbase: 4,880mm; overall length: 9,337mm (tractor), 24,140mm (complete vehicle), overall width: 5,310mm; height to top of cab: 4,650mm; gross weight: 229,340kg; load capacity: 136,080kg **Performance** maximum speed: 59.4 to 74.7km/hr, according to axle ratio.

Maker: Wabco Construction & Mining Equipment Group, Peoria, Illinois

Wabco makes two models of articulated bottom-dump coal hauler, both using tractive units based on their dump trucks. The smaller is the 120CT based on the Haulpak 75C, and the larger (illustrated) is the 150CT derived from the Haulpak 85D. Both offer a choice of Cummins V-12 or Detroit Diesel V-12 power units, and use a similar automatic transmission, the Allison DP-8961. The bottom-dump trailer has power-operated doors opened and closed hydraulically. The braking systems are very comprehensive, consisting of air/hydraulic service brakes, two emergency systems that apply brakes automatically if there is a failure of the main service brake system, parking brake, wheel brake lock activating service brakes during loading and dumping, and a dynamic retarder in the transmission that reduces wear on the service brakes.

Engine Detroit Diesel 12V-149T V-12 diesel 29,300cc 1,050bhp (783kW) *or* Cummins KTA-2300C V-12 diesel 37,700cc 1,050bhp (783kW) **Transmission** Clutch: torque converter; Gearbox: Allison DP-8961 6F 1R automatic; Rear Axle: double reduction **Frame** box section with integral front bumper and horse-collar front cross member, tubular rear **Brakes** dual-dircuit air/hydraulic, with electric dynamic retarder **Dimensions** wheelbase: 4,700mm; overall length: 19,860mm (complete vehicle): overall width: 4,850mm; height to top of cab: 4,110mm; gross weight: 187,435kg; load capacity: 128,960kg **Performance** maximum speed: 69.5km/hr.

Road Tractors

The heavy road tractor pulling a drawbar trailer is in a sense the oldest form of commercial vehicle, as it is directly descended from the steam traction engine which first began to earn its living in road haulage in the late 1850s. Practically all heavy haulage was done by steam for seventy years. The first purpose-built tractor for ultra-heavy loads was the Scammell 100-tonner of 1929, although this falls outside the usual definition of road tractor as it used a semi-trailer. Specialised road tractors appeared in Germany in the 1930s where there had long been a tradition of using agricultural tractors, suitably equipped, for road haulage. Encouraged by orders from the German Railways, the Kaelble company built road tractors of increasing power, culminating in a remarkably modern 6 × 6 with centrally-mounted 200bhp diesel engine, made in 1938.

For several years after the Second World War most heavy haulage was performed by ex-army tractors which had been used as tank transporters, some of the most familiar being Diamond T and Pacific. Some of the latter were modified by the British hauliers, Wynns of Newport, and fitted with diesel engines continued to work well into the 1960s. When purpose-built tractors were made again it was Germany which led the way, with Faun, Kaelble and the newcomers, Titan, making machines with 8-wheel-drive and engines up to 900bhp. For really heavy loads two or three of these tractors can be used, and specialist trailer makers such as Nicolas in France or Scheuerle in Germany build units with up to 176 wheels. Journeys with loads of 600 tons or more have to be planned like a military operation, with surveys made months ahead of every bridge and corner. Quite a fleet of back-up vehicles is needed, including fuel tankers, for three 800hp tractors will consume about 750 litres per hour between them, and they can hardly bank on finding conveniently located garages en route!

Curiously, the two countries where one would imagine the heaviest loads needed moving, the United States and the Soviet Union, do not make purpose-built tractors. When a 1,200 ton nuclear reactor had to be transported from Memphis to Phipps Bend, Tennessee, the contractors used seven Michigan wheel-dozers and an International Payhauler dump truck with a concrete ballast block replacing the dump body. In the Soviet Union the heaviest haulage work is done by Scammell Contractor 6 × 4 tractors, or by 8 × 8 trucks of the MAZ 7310 family modified for tractor work. Some western contractors also use regular heavy trucks modified for tractor work; the Swiss Zuber company uses a Saurer D 330B 8 × 4 and a Volvo F89 6 × 4 coupled to an 8-axle Goldhofer trailer for loads up to 150 tons.

*Ancestor of the modern road tractor was this 200bhp
Kaelble with 6 × 6 drive, built for German State
Railways in 1938.*

Maker: Faun Werke, Lauf an der Pegnitz

Since the 1950s heavy road tractors for drawbar trailer work have formed an important part of the Faun range, and they are widely used for both commercial and military jobs. The present range covers two-, three- and four-axle tractors with engine outputs up to 986bhp and capable of pulling loads up to 300 tons. The model illustrated has 6 × 6 drive and is powered by a Deutz V-12 air-cooled engine, with options of Daimler Benz OM 404 or Cummins NTC-400 units. Even more powerful are the 8 × 8 tractors with Deutz, Cummins or Detroit Diesel V-16 engines up to 800bhp. The trailer payload depends entirely on the number of wheels; with a four-axle trailer the tractor illustrated can draw up to 81 tons, but with a sixteen-axle trailer this can be increased to 318 tons. For journeys of any length, two or more tractors would be used for loads of more than 200 tons. The tractors illustrated are at work in Czechoslovakia.

Engine Klockner-Humboldt-Deutz BF 12L 413F V-12 diesel 16,964cc 512bhp (335kW)
Transmission Clutch: torque converter Allison TC-570; Gearbox: Allison CLBT-5860 6F 1R automatic; Transfer Box: ZF GA-800/3D two speed; Front Axle: double reduction; Rear Axle: double reduction **Frame** channel section ladder type **Brakes** dual circuit fully air-operated **Dimensions** wheelbase: 5,750mm; overall length: 8,610mm; overall width: 2,750mm; height to top of cab: 3,320mm; gross weight: (tractor) 22,000kg; load capacity: see text **Performance** maximum speed: 63km/hr

Maker: Hendrickson Mobile Equipment, Lyons, Illinois

Hendrickson have earned a reputation for specialised vehicles custom-built to operators' requirements, and this enormous tractor is a good example. It is one of two built in 1970 to haul 250-ton transformers to the Churchill Falls hydroelectric project in Canada. After this work was completed the tractors were abandoned, only to have a second lease of life some twelve years later. They were acquired by Stearns-Roger, contractor to the builders of the Alaskan Pipeline, and returned to the Hendrickson factory for a complete overhaul. In the summer of 1983 they were delivered to Alaska, where they haul crude oil processing plants weighing 800 tons seventeen miles from the harbour to the installation site. Each Model 360 weighs nearly 50 tons, a weight which is doubled by the ballast bass that they carry. The enormous tyres, about seven feet in diameter, are filled with calcium chlorate liquid ballast. Top speed of a Model 360 on its own is 56km/hour, but when working with the 384-wheel Goldhofer trailers they are restricted to 5km/hour because of the delicacy of their cargo. The final drive ratio is 29.5 to one.

Engine Cummins VTA-1710C V-12 turbocharged and aftercooled diesel 28,000cc 700bhp (522kW) **Transmission** Clutch: Clark 16000 torque converter; Gearbox: Clark 16820 8F4R automatic; Front Axle: Clark FDS6 4001; Rear Axles: Clark RD 85001 **Frame** channel section, ladder type **Brakes** dual circuit fully air-operated **Dimensions** wheelbase: 6,370mm; overall length: 11,735mm; height to top of cab: 4,972mm; gross weight of tractor: 50,803kg; pulling capacity: 985,580kg **Performance** maximum speed: 56km/hr

Maker: Carl Kaelble GmbH, Backnang

Kaelble have a long tradition of making heavy road tractors, dating back to the early 1930s when they began supplying vehicles to German Railways. Their current range of tractors includes bonnetted and forward-control models with 6 × 6, 8 × 6 and 8 × 8 drive, and engines by Daimler Benz or MAN up to 800bhp. The tractor illustrated is powered by a Daimler Benz OM 424 V-12 engine developing 420bhp, or the same unit with turbocharger developing 525bhp, in which case the model designation is KDVW 24Z/S 520. They are available with three-seater standard cabs, six-seater crew cabs or two-bunk sleeper cabs. With a fourteen-axle platform trailer these tractors can pull 300 tons, giving a payload of 260 tons. Two or more tractors are often used in tandem for even heavier loads. They can also be used with semi-trailers for payloads up to 185 tons.

Engine Daimler-Benz OM 424 V-12 diesel 20,910cc 420bhp (309kW) **Transmission** Clutch: ZF WSK-400 torque converter; Gearbox: ZF 4S-150GP 8F 1R automatic; Transfer Box: ZF A600/3D; Front Axle: double reduction; Rear Axles: double reduction **Frame** channel section ladder type **Brakes** dual circuit fully air-operated **Dimensions** wheelbase: 4,950mm; overall length: 8,200mm; overall width: 2,500mm; height to top of cab: 3,050mm; gross weight: (tractor) 34,000kg; load capacity: see text **Performance** maximum speed: 85km/hr.

Maker: Carl Kaelble GmbH, Backnang

This is one of Kaelble's range of forward-control tractors which are made in three models, the 420 with 420bhp Daimler-Benz engine, the 520 with the same engine turbocharged giving 520bhp, and the 620 with MAN turbocharged and aftercooled cylinder engine giving 615bhp. On all but the latter, the Deutz V-12 air-cooled engine is offered as an alternative. Transmissions are automatic, by ZF or Allison. All models have 6 × 6 drive, and there are same larger Kaelbles with 8 × 6 or 8 × 8 drives. The tractor illustrated is one of a number supplied to German Federal Railways in 1981. The ballast box can be removed when the tractor is operated in conjunction with a swan-neck semi-trailer. With a single tractor and sixteen-axle trailer, total load can be as high as 400 tons, with a payload of 350 tons. With semi-trailer, payload would be about 170 tons.

Engine Daimler-Benz OM 424 V-12 diesel 20,910cc 420bhp (309kW) **Transmission** Clutch: ZF WSK-400 torque converter; Gearbox: ZF 4S-150GP 8F 1R automatic; Transfer Box: ZF A600/3D; Front Axle: double reduction; Rear Axle: double reduction **Frame** channel section ladder type **Brakes** dual circuit fully air-operated **Dimensions** wheelbase: 4,950mm; overall length: 8,050mm; overall width: 2,500mm; height to top of cab: 3,020mm; gross weight: (tractor) 34,000kg; load capacity: see text **Performance** maximum speed: 85km/hr.

Maker: Mol N.V., Hooglede

This is the most powerful of the Mol road tractors, and is in fact a French design, having been made originally by PRP-Willème, and then by the Creusot-Loire division of the Empain combine who are well-known manufacturers of armaments and armoured vehicles, and who acquired PRP in 1979. It is powered by a Cummins KT-450 450bhp 6-cylinder engine, although other units up to 650bhp can be fitted as well. This drives through a Clark torque converter and Clark Powershift automatic transmission with eight forward and four reverse speeds. The spacious cab provides seating accommodation for a crew of six, or seats for three and two bunks. GCW is 250,000kg, at which a speed of 20km/hr is possible.

Engine Cummins KT-450 6-cylinder diesel 14,000cc 450bhp (335kW) **Transmission** Clutch: Clark CL-8612 torque converter; Gearbox: Clark 8821 8F 4R; Front Axles: Kessler double reduction; Rear Axles: Kessler double reduction **Frame** channel section ladder type **Brakes** dual circuit fully air-operated **Dimensions** wheelbase: 6,000mm; overall length: 8,190mm; overall width: 3,000mm; height to top of cab: 3,190mm; gross weight: (tractor) 28,480kg; load capacity: 250,000kg **Performance** maximum speed: (empty) 60km/hr.

323

Maker: Titan GmbH, Appenweier

Titan had made mobile crane chassis and other specialist vehicles from 1970, and in 1977 they added a range of three- and four-axle tractors to their production as a result of a suggestion by Heinrich Schutz, a haulage contractor specialising in ultra-heavy loads. Titan tractors are derived from Mercedes-Benz vehicles, and use that company's sheet metal and most components. In fact Titan buys Mercedes-Benz tractors complete and then replaces the engines with more power-ful ones, also of M-B manufacture, while also strengthening the frame and axles. The full Mercedes-Benz warranty applies to all Titan tractors. At first the 420bhp OM 404 engine was used, but this has now been supplemented by the OM 404A which is the same unit with turbocharger, developing 525bhp. Titans are made in 6 × 6, 8 × 4, 8 × 6 and 8 × 8 forms. The photo shows two tractors operated by Schutz towing a 176-wheel Scheuerle trailer carrying a 550-ton steel ring for a nuclear power plant, with a third tractor pushing.

Engine Mercedes-Benz OM 404 V-12 diesel 20,910cc 420bhp (309kW) **Transmission** Clutch: ZF Transmatic torque converter; Gearbox: ZF 4S 150 GPA; Transfer Box: ZF 2-speed; Front Axles: ZF double reduction; Rear Axles: ZF double reduction **Frame** channel section ladder type **Brakes** dual circuit fully air-operated **Dimensions** wheelbase: 5,200mm; overall length: 7,580mm; overall width: 2,500mm; height to top of cab: 2,905mm; gross weight: (tractor) 21,000kg; load capacity: up to 200,000kg **Performance** maximum speed: (tractor only) 65km/hr

Index